THANKSGIVING ALL YEAR ROUND

A MEMOIR

JEWS OF RUSSIA AND EASTERN EUROPE AND THEIR LEGACY

SERIES EDITOR
Maxim D. Shrayer (Boston College)

EDITORIAL BOARD
ILYA ALTMAN (Russian Holocaust Center and Russian State University for the Humanities)
KAREL BERKHOFF (NIOD Institute for War, Holocaust and Genocide Studies)
JEREMY HICKS (Queen Mary University of London)
BRIAN HOROWITZ (Tulane University)
LUBA JURGENSON (Universite Paris IV—Sorbonne)
ROMAN KATSMAN (Bar-Ilan University)
DOV-BER KERLER (Indiana University)
VLADIMIR KHAZAN (Hebrew University of Jerusalem)
MIKHAIL KRUTIKOV (University of Michigan)
JOANNA BEATA MICHLIC (Bristol University)
ALICE NAKHIMOVSKY (Colgate University)
ANTONY POLONSKY (Brandeis University)
JONATHAN D. SARNA (Brandeis University)
DAVID SHNEER (University of Colorado at Boulder)
ANNA SHTERNSHIS (University of Toronto)
LEONA TOKER (Hebrew University of Jerusalem)
MARK TOLTS (Hebrew University of Jerusalem)

THANKSGIVING ALL YEAR ROUND

A MEMOIR

GAVRIEL SHAPIRO

Boston
2016

Library of Congress Cataloging-in-Publication Data: A catalog record for this book is available from the Library of Congress.

ISBN 978-1-61811-505-8 (hardback)
ISBN 978-1-61811-506-5 (electronic)
ISBN 978-1-61811-517-1 (paperback)

©Academic Studies Press, 2016

Cover design by Ivan Grave.

On the cover:
(top). The prison release paper. Moscow, June 30, 1972;
(left). In front of the Tower of David. Jerusalem, Israel, ca. 1980;
(right). After the doctoral graduation. University of Illinois, Urbana–Champaign, May 1984.

Book design by Kryon Publishing, www.kryonpublishing.com

Academic Studies Press
28 Montfern Avenue
Brighton, MA 02135, USA
press@academicstudiespress.com
www.academicstudiespress.com

To my visionary father, in blessed and loving memory

Enter into His gates with thanksgiving, and into His courts with praise: be thankful unto Him, and bless His name.

—Psalm 100:4

If you will it, it is no dream.

—Theodor Herzl

CONTENTS

Note on Transliteration	viii
List of Illustrations	ix
Acknowledgments	xi
Foreword	1
1. Ancestry	5
2. Immediate Family	50
3. Growing Up in Postwar Soviet Russia	70
4. Emergence of National Awareness and the Struggle for Immigration to Israel	119
5. Arrest, Imprisonment, Trial, and Aftermath	153
6. Life in Israel	194
7. Graduate Studies in the United States	220
8. Living, Teaching, and Writing in America	233
Afterword	272
Index	273

NOTE ON TRANSLITERATION

This book employs a somewhat simplified version of the Library of Congress system for transliterating the Russian alphabet. The only exceptions are Russian names whose spellings have become standard in English (e.g., Yuri, Tolstoy, Dostoevsky, Gorbanevskaya).

The book follows the *Encyclopedia Judaica* and YIVO systems for respective transliterations of Hebrew and Yiddish. The only exceptions are "ח," which is romanized as "ch," and Hebrew names whose spellings have become standard in English (e.g., Haifa, Hadassah, Itzchak, Tchernichovsky, Zion).

ILLUSTRATIONS

All photographs, unless stated otherwise, are from the family archives
Frontispiece: The author, aged twenty-seven, shortly after his arrival in Jerusalem.

1.	Berko Leizerovsky, maternal great-grandfather.	6
2.	Evgenia Leizerovsky (née Shafran), maternal great-grandmother.	7
3.	Sara Leizerovsky (née Zil´bershmidt), maternal grandmother.	11
4.	Gavriel Leizerovsky, maternal grandfather, in a group photo.	12
5.	Gavriel Leizerovsky's calling card.	13
6.	Yaakov Kontorer, maternal great-great-grandfather.	14
7.	Enta-Reiza Zil´bershmidt (née Kontorer), maternal great-grandmother.	15
8.	Gersh Zil´bershmidt, maternal great-grandfather.	15
9.	Barukh Shapiro, paternal great-grandfather.	18
10.	Chaia Ashbel (née Reines), paternal great-great-grandmother.	21
11.	Iosef Menachem Ashbel, paternal great-grandfather.	22
12.	Zisl Shapiro (née Ashbel), paternal grandmother.	26
13.	Zisl, Matl, and Eliyahu Shmuel.	27
14.	Hirsch and Zisl Shapiro.	28
15.	Father and Shura as first-grade classmates.	34
16.	Father's last drawing.	40
17.	Uncle Dov at his meteorological station.	41
18.	The Ashbel family.	49
19.	Father among pupils and teachers of the Soviet Trade Mission School in the company of Maxim Gorky.	54
20.	Father as a freshman at the Moscow Aviation Institute.	55
21.	Father meditating.	58
22.	Mother with her parents and maternal grandmother.	60
23.	Mother taking part in Professor Vinogradov's hospital round.	60

Illustrations

24. Mother with her students at the First Moscow Medical Institute.	62
25. Luba as a schoolgirl.	66
26. Luba with parents on the eve of her departure for Israel.	67
27. My birthplace.	71
28. With Grandma Sara at a dacha.	72
29. With parents at Clean Ponds.	73
30. With parents in Gudauta, Abkhazia.	80
31. As a first grader at school no. 312.	81
32. The "wee Geordie" of the class.	83
33. Called upon in English class.	89
34. "Starring" in the movie *The Grandmaster*.	104
35. A stamp commemorating the eighth Independence Day of the State of Israel.	120
36. With fellow refuseniks Nina and Moisei Bel´for, and Mark Nashpitz.	142
37. The prison release paper.	166
38. The court ruling on my appeal.	173
39. The exit visa.	177
40. With Luba upon my arrival in Israel.	195
41. Parents on the eve of their immigration to Israel.	201
42. Our family reunited.	201
43. Parents in front of the Old City of Jerusalem.	202
44. With Father in front of the Western Wall.	203
45. With parents and Luba in the company of Uncles Moshe, Dov, and Aminadav.	207
46. At a family picnic.	207
47. With parents and Luba at our double Hebrew University of Jerusalem commencement.	212
48. Serving in the IDF.	217
49. After the doctoral graduation.	229
50. Attending my first Cornell Slavic faculty picnic.	250
51. With Luba.	250
52. With Tzakhi and Dina.	251
53. Tatiela with Kari.	258
54. Visiting Dmitri Nabokov.	264
55. Taking part in the reception at the VIIIth World Congress of the International Council for Central and East European Studies.	271

ACKNOWLEDGMENTS

I thank Cornell Department of Comparative Literature for its munificent backing of this project. I am most grateful to the College of Arts and Sciences, and personally to Dean Scott C. MacDonald, for a generous and timely support.

My sincere thanks also go to various individuals and institutions that assisted me in the realization of this project: Patrick J. Stevens of Cornell University Library; Robert H. Davis, Jr., Columbia and Cornell Librarian for Russian, Eurasian and East European Studies; Dan Haruv, Vladimir Khazan, and Shaul Stampfer of the Hebrew University of Jerusalem; Timna Elper of the National Library of Israel; Yaacov Ro'i of Tel Aviv University; Dov-Ber Kerler of Indiana University; Rabbi Mendel Laine of Kehot Publication Society, Brooklyn, New York; Gunnar Berg of the YIVO Institute for Jewish Research, New York City; Jessica Calagione of The Wylie Agency LLC, New York City; Bette Graber and Emory Johnson of Penguin Random House, New York City; Ronald Hussey of Houghton Mifflin Harcourt, New York City; Tat´iana Kudriavtseva and Larisa Semenovna Eremina of the "Memorial" Society, Moscow, the Russian Federation.

All works of Vladimir Nabokov are cited by kind permission of The Wylie Agency LLC.

This book much benefited from the information and feedback provided by my kith and kin: Tzofnat Ashbel, Shaul and Shifra Katz, and Dina and Nati Layba (Jerusalem, Israel); Tzakhi Freedman and Sheana Shechterman (Tel Aviv, Israel); Yossi and Gina Ashbel (Holon, Israel); Yoav and Ron Me-Bar (Haifa, Israel); Il´ia Liak (St. Petersburg, the Russian Federation); Margarita Ashbel, Natal´ia Basharina, and Mikhail Moiseev (Novosibirsk, the Russian Federation); and Kimberly Sheintal (Sarasota, Florida).

Acknowledgments

I am greatly indebted to my partner, Tatiela Laake, for her invaluable assistance and loving support with this project in so many more ways than I can express or count. I also thank my editor, Steven Moore, for his solicitous and helpful comments.

I wish to express my sincere appreciation to Igor Nemirovsky, the director and publisher of Academic Studies Press, for his keen interest in this project, and to Maxim D. Shrayer, the editor of "Jews of Russia & Eastern Europe and Their Legacy," for finding my manuscript worthy of publication in this prestigious series. I further wish to extend my special thanks to Kira Nemirovsky for the accommodating schedule and for her expert editing of this book, and to Matthew Charlton for promptly addressing and rectifying various issues that arose in the process.

Above all, I am immensely grateful to my mother, Ella Leizerovsky, my sister, Luba Freedman, and especially to my father, Yaakov Shapiro, זכרונו לברכה, who inspired and encouraged me to write this book.

FOREWORD

Each November, friends, colleagues, students, neighbors, and even strangers ask me how I intend to celebrate Thanksgiving. In response, I tell them that although I observe this important American holiday year after year, I have reasons to express my gratitude to the Almighty every single day—hence the title of this book.

I wanted to write this memoir for a long time but kept putting it off. This is because until recently my university career took precedence. That meant conducting academic research and publishing scholarly monographs. When I considered broaching this project, I was perfectly aware of its unusual nature. I knew that it is one thing to explore a world of fiction while delving into various pertinent aspects of an author's biography but quite another to explore one's own life while delving into personal memory. Contemplating this task, I also thought that it would enable me to look at my life in retrospect, thereby allowing for its reexamination and reassessment. I also imagined—and my premonition proved accurate—that taking a trip down memory lane would be therapeutic, perhaps even cathartic, making closure of some chapters of my life possible.

As is frequently the case, there was also the question of "who needs it?" There were some "well-wishers" who suggested that I should stick to my scholarly pursuits and not add one more to the already existent countless autobiographies. Other "well-wishers" advised me not to become engrossed in the past but rather to focus on the future. Apparently they are unaware that time, a sheer human invention, does not in fact exist. The division between past, present, and future is merely a convenience and is tantamount to partitioning an open space into a suite of rooms. There were others, however, who encouraged me to get on with the task. When I finally decided to do so, I thought that my story might be of interest to readers. Each human life is unique, and my life experience in three different countries and on as many continents might be fascinating, possibly even enlightening to some.

In many ways, the history of my ancestors is a history of Jewry, albeit a selective and partial one. It contains expulsions and exile, residence restrictions to the Pale of Settlement, pillages and pogroms.[1] In more recent times, the persecution of Jews culminated in the most egregious attempt at the "Final Solution"—the Holocaust. In spite of all the vexations and vicissitudes of its two-millennium experience in Diaspora, all the calamities and upheavals, Jewry as a whole has succeeded in surviving, in preserving its own identity. It has done so by adhering to the faith of its forefathers, all the while entertaining the everlasting dream of returning to its historical homeland—the Land of Israel. In 1948, this dream, at long last, came to fruition with the revival of the sovereign Jewish State. It is my firm belief that every Jew, no matter the location and circumstances, is not only inextricably and forever linked to the collective destiny of the entire House of Israel but also as inextricably and forever linked to the destiny of the State of Israel.

My life thus far has been divided into three uneven chapters: twenty-seven years in Soviet Russia, six years in Israel, and thirty-seven years in the United States. During my formative years in the Soviet capital, I gradually came to the realization that I was deprived of elementary freedoms. This realization deepened and intensified when the Iron Curtain began to rust, crack, and crumble. These chinks in the regime's façade enabled me to listen to overseas radio stations whenever their programs were not jammed, to read Russian literature printed in *samizdat* and *tamizdat* as well as occasional books and newspapers in Hebrew and English, and to meet with foreigners.[2] As time went by, I became keenly aware that I had no future in the country of my birth. Ultimately, the conditions became so intolerable that I was overtaken with the physical sensation of airlessness, as if being placed under a gigantic glass bell.

My existence under the totalitarian Soviet regime was further exacerbated by widespread anti-Semitism. As a result, from early childhood on,

---

1 The Pale of Settlement is the name given in Imperial Russia to the region to which Jews were confined and beyond which their permanent residency was generally prohibited. Pogrom (from the Russian *gromit'*—"to wreak havoc") is a term used to describe an organized, often officially sanctioned massacre of Jews in the Russian Empire in the late nineteenth and early twentieth centuries.

2 Samizdat (literally, "self-publishing") was a system of clandestine publication and dissemination of government-banned materials within the Soviet Union; likewise, tamizdat (literally, "publishing over there") was a system of smuggling into the Soviet Union and distributing the outlawed literature published overseas.

I was made to feel unwelcome in Soviet Russia. This sentiment compelled me to question my identity and to look for an alternative. Under the influence of the Zionist ideology, which I imbibed from my father and his close friends, I came to the realization that Israel, the Jewish historical land and the realm of my primogenitors, was my home, the country where I aspired to live.

The Soviet regime, which denied its citizens most elementary rights, such as relocation to another country, put numerous obstacles in the way of my aspirations. It took me two years of intense combat with the Red Pharaoh, including job loss, harassment, arrests, imprisonment, and trial, to reach the coveted goal. Of course, I was not struggling in a vacuum or alone: the successful outcome of my fight for emigration would have been impossible had it not been for other Soviet Jews, my comrades-in-cause, the Jewish brethren on both sides of the Atlantic, international public opinion, the U.S. administration, the Israeli government, family and friends, and—first and foremost—the Almighty.

Although I resided in Israel for only six years, that period was of great importance to my life. While in Israel, I abandoned my previous field of chemistry. Having been in fact denied any freedom of choice, I reluctantly studied the subject at Moscow University. Instead, I obtained a B.A. in Russian studies at the Hebrew University of Jerusalem. This degree became a stepping-stone for my further education and development as a Slavist. After graduating from the university, I served in the Israel Defense Forces, and this military service played an essential role in forging my strong bond with the country.

When I went to the United States to pursue my advanced degrees, I entertained the idea of realizing myself professionally in Israel upon the completion of my studies. This aspiration was at the forefront of my mind. Regrettably, I failed to bring it to fulfillment despite my many attempts at trying. While living in the United States and enjoying a successful academic career at Cornell University, I have regularly returned to Israel, where I spend on average about two months a year. Aside from visiting my family and friends, I am frequently invited to my alma mater (the Hebrew University of Jerusalem) to give lectures, in which I share the results of my research with colleagues and peers. Their challenging questions have always been beneficial to my scholarship. These visits to Israel enable me to stay connected to the country. Besides, I closely follow the local news and maintain regular correspondence with my dear ones.

Even though I did not succeed in my attempts to find a teaching position in Israel, I am all the more immensely grateful to the United States, my home for over three and a half decades. The United States has most generously provided me with ample opportunities to lead an academic career and to implement my ambition of becoming a teacher and a literary scholar. I am particularly thankful to the University of Illinois at Urbana–Champaign for admitting me to its graduate program. The program afforded most favorable conditions for my studies, including bountiful financial support, a lively intellectual atmosphere, and a superb library. The challenges I experienced as a graduate student while studying for my M.A. and Ph.D. degrees taught me a great deal. Above all, I became aware of the dependent and therefore vulnerable status of students, undergraduate and graduate, vis-à-vis their teachers, especially their thesis advisors and mentors, and I have ever since been mindful not to overstep the bounds of my authority. Most important, I try to be as helpful as I possibly can to my students by making myself available to them for consultations and counsel at all times.

As I am writing these lines, I am looking out the window of my family apartment in the French Hill neighborhood of Jerusalem. My reminiscences take me from this northeastern quarter of the Israeli capital much farther northeastward to Russia, which for centuries had been the abode and habitat of my forefathers. Although a great deal of information about their lives has not survived, much of it has been preserved in ancestral chronicles and accounts, thereby making it possible to trace my lineage far back on both sides of the family. Last but not least, writing this autobiography allowed me to connect with my forebears by tapping into their collective memory. That memory, which had accumulated over many a year and passed from generation to generation, in turn, allowed me to comprehend better my own origins and my own destiny.

Jerusalem and Ithaca
January 2012–July 2015

CHAPTER 1

ANCESTRY

> Jews are rootless cosmopolitans,
> individuals devoid of nation or tribe.
> —Soviet newspapers

I consider myself very fortunate to be able to trace my roots as far back as nine generations and to have ample data at my disposal about both sides of my family. This information, which I shall share in the present chapter, gives me a gratifying sense of continuity. It further provides me with an opportunity to honor my ancestors when calling them by name and to narrate their life stories, thereby bringing them out of obscurity and oblivion. It also enables me to ponder my own place on the branching family tree.

And so I begin with my maternal side. My mother's father, Gavriel Leizerovsky (1888–1943), was born in Dvinsk (present-day Daugavpils, Latvia). His father, Berko (1862–1913), co-owned two tobacco factories in the city. Leizerovsky, though, was not Berko's real surname. When Berko was about to be drafted into the tsarist army, his family found the Leizerovskys, a childless Jewish couple who formally adopted him. Needless to say, they were handsomely compensated. In this way, Berko, as the only son, became exempt from the military service. His actual last name was Tur. Legend has it that the Turs trace their ancestry back three thousand years to the sixth son of King David—Ithream. Some rabbinical commentators suggest that Ithream's mother, Egla ("heifer" in Hebrew), who died giving birth to him, was the sobriquet of Michal, the daughter of King Saul.[3] According to the familial history, after the Jews were

---
3 http://halakhah.com/pdf/nezikin/Sanhedrin.pdf, 76.

Berko Leizerovsky, maternal great-grandfather.

expelled from the Land of Israel, some of Ithream's descendants settled in Spain, moved with the onset of the Inquisition from the Iberian Peninsula to the city of Amsterdam, and then to Mainz. Following the waves of persecution, plunder, and pillage, they migrated from this German town via Poland to Courland, which became part of Latvia and, in turn, of the Russian Empire. A 1799 silver ruble from the rein of Paul I has been kept in the Tur-Leizerovsky family. The coin passed from father to son and eventually ended up in the possession of Il´ia Grigor´evich Liak, my mother's paternal cousin. Il´ia once explained that 1799 marked the year when the Turs became Russian subjects.

    I guess it was Berko's maternal grandparents who paid the Leizerovskys to adopt him and thus to obtain the exemption from military service. Berko's father, Abram Tur, forsook him and his wife, Matil´da (née Levit), and left for the United States. Many years later, when Berko became a successful businessman, Abram tried to reconnect with his son.

Evgenia Leizerovsky (née Shafran), maternal great-grandmother.

Deeply hurt by Abram's desertion, Berko chose to ignore his father's missives. After several such attempts, Abram wrote to a Dvinsk rabbi lamenting his son's disrespectful behavior. The rabbi summoned Berko, and after he presented his side of the story, the rabbi ruled in his favor and reproved Abram for abandoning the family.

Berko married Evgenia (aka Zhenia, née Shafran, 1868–1932), who hailed from the Belarusian town of Grodno. Berko and Zhenia had four children: my grandfather Gavriel, Eliyahu (Il´ia), Maria (Mashutka), and Tat´iana (Tania). Il´ia, a bright and handsome young man, committed suicide, reportedly as a result of unrequited love. Mashutka, a gorgeous redhead, was given as a wife to the good-for-nothing Aizik Viaz´mensky, whom Grandma Sara dubbed in her colorful Yiddish *gurnisht mit nisht*—literally, "absolute nothing with nothing."[4] (Incidentally, I recall Grandma Sara's numerous Yiddish

---

4   Here and henceforth all translations, unless otherwise indicated, are mine.

expressions; one of them comes to mind now when I am myself a senior citizen—*ungeshtupt mit yurn*. Although the expression literally means "stuffed with years," Grandma Sara translated it for me as *utykannyi godami*, that is, "stuck in with years." That latter phrase vividly describes a person, advanced in age, being like a pin cushion spiked with scores of pins and needles.) Aizik had no interest in any work, let alone learning. He carried this shortcoming as a badge of honor and loved to present himself as the one who "read five books less [than others]" (*prochel na piat' knig men'she*).

One day, when Mashutka was ice-skating, she slipped, fell, and injured the back of her head. (Another version of this family story has it that Mashutka was unhappy in her marriage and took poison.) Whatever the cause, she started losing her sight and soon went completely blind. Aizik and Mashutka had a son, Boris (Bobka), born in 1913. After having been unsuccessfully treated by Russian ophthalmologists, Mashutka, accompanied by my grandmother and little Bobka, went in the early 1920s to consult doctors in Berlin. Mashutka did not receive the desirable cure in the German capital either and returned with Grandma Sara to Russia. Mashutka and Aizik resided in Petrograd-turned-Leningrad. In 1935, soon after Sergei Kirov's assassination—on Stalin's orders, as it became later known—Mashutka and Aizik, like many others, were banished from the former imperial capital. Mother told me that Grandma Sara and Aizik's sister-in-law, Etta, the wife of Aizik's brother Abram, had been sending parcels of food and warm clothing to Viatka, where Mashutka and Aizik had been forced to resettle. Ironically, Viatka was the capital of the province in which the slain Kirov, a prominent Soviet leader, whom Stalin viewed as one of his chief political rivals, grew up, and it was soon named after him.

And what about Bobka? Before Mashutka left Russia for the eye treatment in Germany, she and Aizik had decided that Bobka should stay in Berlin with his uncle and Aizik's other brother, Matvei (Motia). Bobka first lived in Germany, then relocated in the mid-1930s to the Netherlands, and before the outbreak of World War II providentially moved to Cuba, where he became a rather prosperous businessman. In 1959, with Fidel

Castro's rise to power, Bobka lost everything—lock, stock, and barrel—and absconded to Florida. In the late 1960s, Bobka visited Moscow to see my mother, his maternal cousin, and his paternal uncle Abram's family. Regrettably, I was out of town and did not have an opportunity to meet the man. I vividly remember a sepia photograph of Bobka that hung on the wall in our downtown Moscow residence. This high-quality englassed picture, apparently taken in the late 1920s in Berlin, portrayed a good-looking lad in his mid-teens and smartly dressed, standing with his arms crossed.

After Berko Leizerovsky died in Dvinsk, the widowed Zhenia moved to Petrograd to live with her youngest daughter, Tania, who resided there after marrying Grigory (Grisha) Liak.[5] Every so often Zhenia visited her firstborn and my grandpa in Moscow. Mother remembers her as a handsome old woman who, although small in stature, carried herself with great dignity.

Tania and Grisha had two sons: the above-mentioned Il´ia (1921–2013), whom they named after her prematurely deceased brother, and Leonid (1929–87). Leonid, whom I met only once or twice, was a gifted painter and art restorer. I knew Il´ia a great deal better. A native and lifelong denizen of Russia's former imperial capital, Il´ia was stricken in his boyhood with the then incurable osteomyelitis (bone infection) that affected his right knee. As a result, he had a bad limp all his adult life. During World War II, Il´ia was not drafted into the army because of this impairment, remained in his native city, and survived its horrific nearly two-and-a-half-year blockade by the Nazis. Il´ia was a talented shipbuilding engineer and always stayed with us on his business trips to Moscow. Il´ia was fascinated by the family history. Every time he came for a visit, I heard him and my mother reminiscing about the family and took great pleasure in listening to his spellbinding stories about relatives close and distant. The last time I saw Il´ia and had a very informative conversation

---

5 During World War I (1914–18), in which Germany was Russia's principal adversary, the Germanic sounding name of the imperial capital, St. Petersburg, was replaced by Petrograd, its Slavic equivalent. In 1924, after Vladimir Lenin had died, the city was renamed after him, only to regain its original appellation in 1991.

with him was several years ago in Jerusalem, where he and his wife, Bella, visited their daughter, Alla, and her family. I am greatly indebted to Il′ia for the bulk of the information about my mother's paternal side of the family.

Grandpa Gavriel received a fine education. Initially he studied at the Dvinsk Second Gymnasium. As schooling steadily deteriorated throughout the world, these imperial gymnasia remained unrivalled in terms of their depth and breadth of education. Thus, Mother told me that Grandpa Gavriel—who studied math in the classical gymnasium, where it was, understandably, not a main subject—easily helped her to solve high school algebra and trigonometry problems thirty years after his graduation. Upon finishing the gymnasium, Grandpa Gavriel earned a law degree from the Novorossiisk University in Odessa. Obviously, it would have been much closer to home and more convenient for him to study in St. Petersburg. But as a Jew with no special privileges, grandfather was not permitted to live in the imperial capital and therefore had to travel to the far south to obtain a higher education. However, his coming to Odessa was clearly meant to be, for there he met his future wife and my grandmother, Sara. Grandma was visiting her sister Sofia, who was married to a local well-to-do tobacco industrialist named Chaim (Efim) Dukel′sky-Dikler.[6] While taking university courses, Grandpa Gavriel supported himself by giving lessons. In particular, he tutored Sofia and Efim's school-age son, Boris (1903–42). (Boris graduated from the Odessa Medical School in 1925, became a military surgeon, and was appointed head of the army surgical service in the Battle of Moscow, in which he lost his life.) It is small wonder that Grandpa Gavriel fell head over heels in love with Grandma Sara. In one photograph of that period, she appears as a stylishly dressed young woman with a nice figure, lustrous dark hair, and magnetic brown eyes.

---

6   In all probability, Efim was related to Benedikt Dukel′sky-Dikler, a poet who immigrated to Paris in the early 1920s and whose verse collection, *Sonnets* (1926), Vladimir Nabokov subjected to a scathing criticism.

Sara Leizerovsky (née Zil´bershmidt), maternal grandmother, in her youth. Kherson, 1915.

My grandparents were married in 1915 and went to live in Petrograd, where Grandpa Gavriel worked as a legal consultant for the British company "Laola." In late 1916, the company opened a branch in Moscow, to which Grandpa was transferred. He appears in a rare group photograph with his co-workers, bald-domed and impeccably dressed. Grandpa liked his job, which also paid well. This enabled him and Grandma Sara to live comfortably. They acquired a spacious apartment and regularly traveled abroad.

Gavriel Leizerovsky, maternal grandfather (second row, on the bench, third from the right) in a group photo of the Laola company. Moscow, late 1916.

The Bolshevik coup d'état shattered all that almost overnight. Being a man of law and a proponent of liberalism, Grandpa could not appreciate the dictatorial nature of the new regime. To say that he was a staunch opponent of the Communist rule would be a gross understatement. Shortly after the Bolshevik takeover, when the Baltic States became independent, Grandpa Gavriel strongly considered leaving Soviet Russia for his native Dvinsk, which became part of sovereign and democratic Latvia. Although in no way a supporter of the new regime either, Grandma Sara objected to the move because her siblings, to whom she was very close, at the time all resided in Moscow. Grandma's stance saved my grandparents and my mother from perishing in the Holocaust. Had they moved to and stayed in Latvia until the outbreak of World War II, and had not relocated to the United States, they would have suffered the tragic fate of Grandpa's extended kin, many of whom lost their lives in the nefarious Daugavpils and Rumbula massacres.

Aside from law, Grandpa Gavriel was interested and well versed in history. Already in the early 1930s, he remarked on the affinities between Bolshevism and Nazism. When his gymnasium classmate contacted him at that time and offered him a cultural attaché position at the Soviet embassy in Tokyo, Grandpa Gavriel turned it down, even though Grandma Sara, who now wished to live abroad, urged him to accept it. He maintained, and perceptively so, that it would be best to keep a low profile under the totalitarian regime. To follow this prescript of his, Grandpa worked as a rank-and-file official in the Ministry of Transportation. Although he succumbed to stress and malnutrition in wartime Moscow at the age of fifty-five, he at least died in his own bed—not a small accomplishment in the epoch of raging terror and mass executions in Soviet Russia.

In our downtown Moscow residence, which Grandpa Gavriel acquired shortly before the Bolshevik takeover, there was an antique pearwood desk with a tripartite trumeau mirror. Its two flanking sections could rotate to allow for various angles of vision. The desk's central drawer contained some objects that belonged to my late grandfather. I was fascinated by his gold-chained vest-pocket watch, several pince-nez eyeglasses, and his calling cards. On these, his given name, patronymic, and surname, noticeably Russified, as it was common in those times of encouraged assimilation—Gavriil Borisovich Leizerovsky—were printed in pre-Revolutionary orthography. (The phrase "*Okonch. Iurid. fak.*" at the bottom right-hand side of the card signifies in abbreviated form that Grandpa Gavriel was a law school graduate.) Upon immigrating to Israel, my sister, Luba, took with her one small side drawer of that desk as a memento. The drawer is a precious relic from our childhood and youth, and we recently gazed at it together with great nostalgia.

Гавріилъ Борисовичъ
Лейзеровскій

Оконч. Юрид. фак.

Gavriel Leizerovsky's calling card.

Yaakov Kontorer, maternal great-great-grandfather. Berislav, 1885.

My maternal grandmother, Sara, née Zil'bershmidt (1890–1955), was born in Berislav, southern Ukraine, located about fifty miles from the better known city of Kherson. Her mother, Enta-Reiza (1858–1934), was a daughter of Yaakov Kontorer, attorney-at-law. Yaakov Kontorer was known as *talmid chakham*, an honorific title accorded to distinguished Torah scholars, and was highly respected in the local Jewish community. Our family archive contains an 1885 photograph that, judging by its verso Hebrew inscription, Yaakov intended as a present for his daughter and son-in-law, perhaps for their tenth wedding anniversary. In this picture, Yaakov appears as a handsome, kind-eyed middle-aged man. His face exudes high intelligence, even wisdom, and a deep sense of noble spirit.

Yaakov had eight children, of which Enta-Reiza was the first. I have little information about Enta-Reiza's siblings, but I do know that one of her brothers, Anisim, followed in his father's footsteps. He too became an attorney

Gersh Zil′bershmidt, maternal great-grandfather.

Enta-Reiza Zil′bershmidt (née Kontorer), maternal great-grandmother. Kherson, 1880s.

after studying at the Novorossiisk University Law School a quarter of a century prior to his nephew by marriage, Grandpa Gavriel. In 1910, Anisim Yakovlevich Kontorer was listed as a member of the Odessa Council of Attorneys, founded in 1904. Her other brother, Iosif (1867–1941), immigrated to the United States in 1890 and settled in Chicago. Once there, Joseph Contorer, as he became known, owned a shoe store and an umbrella store.

Sara's father and my great-grandfather, Gersh Zil′bershmidt, was a well-to-do grain merchant. Gersh and Enta-Reiza, who was sixteen and a half at the time of their marriage, had four children: three daughters, Dina (1878–1965), Sofia (1880–1969), my grandmother Sara, and one son, Izrail′ (1887–1974), Grandma being the youngest of the siblings. Having grown up in southern Ukraine, Grandma had a corresponding personality, sunny and gregarious. Her food tastes likewise reflected the place of her birth. She introduced me to olives and feta cheese, both of which I have enjoyed all my life, and to pickled watermelon rinds, which I never learned to appreciate. Grandma Sara had a sweet tooth that led to a funny episode. An acquaintance of hers once visited us and was treated to tea with pastry and chocolate candy. When Grandma, who already had eaten a couple of sweets, went for more, Mother out of concern for her health asked her to refrain. This was because Grandma had a severe case of diabetes that, coupled with a heart condition, eventually caused her to die at the age of sixty-five. The astounded acquaintance, not knowing the true reason for Mother's plea, gossiped about Grandma's "pitiable" position in the household: "Can you imagine? Her own daughter keeps tabs on the amount of food this poor woman consumes and has no qualms about embarrassing her in front of company!" I inherited a sweet tooth from Grandma Sara but prefer dark chocolate over the milk variety. At one point in my boyhood, I gobbled up so much chocolate that Mother, out of concern for *my* health, had to lock it away from me.

Grandma Sara was a decent cook but no match for her two older sisters, each of whom made a superb gefilte fish from carp or pike, the best I have ever had, and mouthwatering apple strudel, interlaid with cinnamon, raisins, and walnuts. Mother said that their cooking skills, however, had paled in comparison to those of Enta-Reiza. After Gersh had died in 1925 from diabetes complications, Enta-Reiza came to Moscow to live with Grandma Sara and her family. Mother said that Great-Grandma Enta-Reiza and Grandpa Gavriel had habitually spoken Yiddish to each other and had had an uncommonly harmonious relationship for a mother-in-law and son-in-law.

All four Zil'bershmidt siblings received a gymnasium education in nearby Kherson. Dina, Sofia, and Grandma Sara finished the First Gymnasium for Girls, the oldest secondary educational institution in the city. Izrail' graduated from the First Gymnasium for Boys, which reportedly numbered among its students the epidemiologist Vladimir Khavkin, the historian Evgeny Tarle, and the second prime minister of Israel, Moshe Sharet. Upon finishing the gymnasium, Izrail'—who wished to study mining engineering but as a Jew was precluded from enrolling in the St. Petersburg Mining Institute—was sent to acquire a higher education at the University of Liège, in Belgium. In 1915, the same year as my grandparents, Izrail' married a notable soprano, Zinaida Lisichkina, who shared the stage with Fedor Shaliapin before and after World War I. In 1924, accompanied by his wife, Izrail´ went on a business trip to Western Europe, never to return to Soviet Russia. They first resided in Germany, where Izrail´ worked as a mining engineer and Zinaida sang in the Bremen Opera. In the late 1930s—most timely indeed—they crossed the Atlantic and settled in New York City. Izrail´ continued to work as an engineer, and Zinaida performed at New York's Carnegie Hall and at Boston Symphony Hall and taught at Julliard School and the Columbia Opera Workshop.

Upon moving to the United States, Izrail´ sent Grandma Sara an Underwood Cyrillic typewriter. The typewriter turned out to become a valuable and vitally important present. After Grandpa Gavriel had died and times became tough, my widowed Grandma, who was skilled at typing and occasionally worked at it to make some extra money in the previous decade, had to turn to this livelihood in earnest. She thus was able to provide a supplementary and by no means paltry income to my parents' rather modest start-up salaries. I vividly remember how Grandma Sara would feed several white sheets, interlaid with black carbon paper, into her Underwood. The paper-feeding was invariably accompanied with that characteristic knob-turning crackling sound. Then Grandma would click-clack away on this highly attractive compact machine that emitted an unforgettable melodious ring at the end of each line.

✵ ✵ ✵

Unlike the ancestors on my mother's side, who came from the opposite ends of the Pale of Settlement—Latvia and southern Ukraine—the ancestors on my father's side all hailed from present-day Belarus. My paternal great-grandfather, Barukh Shapiro, was born in Mstislavl´. Father once shared with me what Barukh told him, based on his own father's account, about the so-called Mstislavl´ Riot. In 1844, the Jews of Mstislavl´ were falsely accused of attacking Russian soldiers stationed in town. The authorities arrested leaders of the Jewish community and imposed a harsh penal conscription on its population—one additional military recruit for every ten men. The local Jews then turned for help to Itzchak Zelikin (also known as Itzchak Monastyrshchiner), a wealthy merchant and an influential, compassionate man who interceded with the tsarist administration on their behalf. His feat was nothing short of a miracle because Tsar Nicholas I

Barukh Shapiro, paternal great-grandfather.

revoked the punitive measures: the arrested leaders were set free and the penal conscripts were sent home. The Mstislavl′ Jews offered many thanksgiving prayers to the Almighty and created numerous legends about this event, which in their eyes epitomized the triumph of divine justice.[7]

Barukh Shapiro was a pious Jew. He owned a small leather workshop in his native town that manufactured phylacteries (*tefillin*) and prayer-book covers. Barukh married Chaia (née Dubnov), who was related to Shimon Dubnov, the eminent Jewish historian. Chaia died in 1876 after giving birth to their only child, Hirsch, who was to become my grandfather. Barukh soon remarried and had three additional children. The stepsiblings were fond of Hirsch, but Barukh's second wife treated him like a proverbial stepmother would. Meanwhile, the Dubnovs, Hirsch's maternal grandparents, immigrated to the United States and settled in Nebraska. When Hirsch turned nineteen, they invited him to come to live with them and to acquire a good education. Hirsch studied business and accounting and became

---

[7] For more information about the incident, see Shimon Dubnov (S. M. Dubnow), *History of the Jews in Russia and Poland, from the Earliest Times until the Present Day*, 3 vols., trans. I. Friedlaender (Philadelphia: Jewish Publication Society of America, 1916–20), 2:84–87.

proficient in English. In 1900, Barukh received a letter from his uncle in Riga, who asked him to come and assist him in running his leather factory. Barukh could not neglect his own modest leather workshop (he worked there with only one assistant) because the livelihood of his family depended on it. So he summoned Hirsch back to Russia to help out his great-uncle. Hirsch did not dare to disobey his father and left for Riga at once. Although Barukh had three children by his second wife, who also died rather young, he lived in his old age with the family of Hirsch, his firstborn. As a child, my father remembered his grandfather putting on phylacteries each morning, except of course on Shabbat and High Holidays. Father kept his grandfather's phylacteries over a long period of time and once even showed me how to lay them. It occurred to me that perhaps Barukh made these phylacteries in his workshop, with his very own hands.

Upon the Bolshevik seizure of power in November 1917, the newly established regime took advantage of Hirsch's expertise in business bookkeeping and sent him to the Soviet Trade Mission in Berlin, where he worked as an accountant between 1925 and 1932. Hirsch was not permitted to bring with him all members of his family; his father, Barukh, and his eldest son, Dov-Ber, were in effect held hostage in Moscow. Evidently the Soviet regime was concerned that otherwise the family might not return to Russia and would remain in the West. Apparently, Hirsch knew too much about the Trade Mission dealings. Father and Aunt Niuta strongly suspected that his tragic death—he was thrown off a Moscow streetcar in 1933—was not an accident but rather a deliberate, cold-blooded murder.

My other paternal great-grandfather, Iosef Menachem Ashbel, was born in 1857 into a distinguished rabbinical family. He came into the world in Beshenkovichi, about thirty miles west of Vitebsk, in the home of his maternal grandparents, but grew up in Lubavitchi, the well-known Chasidic center. Iosef Menachem's great-great-grandfather was Rabbi Issakhar Ber. Originally from Kobyl´nik, a town in the Minsk Province, Rabbi Issakhar Ber came to Lubavitchi as the son-in-law of Rabbi Iosef, the town *maggid*, on the recommendation of Baal Shem Tov, and in time succeeded his father-in-law at that post.[8] In 1755, Rabbi Issakhar Ber studied with Baal Shem Tov and became a

---

8   See Rabbi Joseph I. Schneersohn, *Lubavitcher Rabbi's Memoirs,* 2 vols., trans. Nissan Mindel (Brooklyn, NY: Kehot Publication Society, 1960), 1:33–34. *Maggid* is a traditional Eastern European Jewish religious

great devotee of Chasidism.⁹ Rabbi Issakhar Ber had the privilege and the distinction of being the first teacher of Schneur Zalman (1745–1812), who later became known as the Rabbi of Liady.¹⁰ Rabbi Schneur Zalman loved and honored his teacher and spoke of him as "the treasure of my heart and soul; a friend and brother he is to me."¹¹ Rabbi Schneur Zalman was affectionately nicknamed "Der Alter Rebbe" and was also known as the Baal *HaTanya* (literally, Master of *The Tanya*) after his most recognized work.¹²

Rabbi Issakhar Ber was also an in-law of Rabbi Menachem Mendel of Vitebsk (1730–88), an early leader of Chasidic Judaism, who was instrumental in spreading its teachings throughout the Pale of Settlement. In 1777, Rabbi Menachem Mendel, along with his three hundred disciples, immigrated to the Land of Israel and settled in Safed. In 1783, after having been expelled from Safed by the Ottoman authorities, Rabbi Menachem Mendel and his flock moved to Tiberias, where in 1786 they built a synagogue. Destroyed in the 1837 Galilee earthquake, the synagogue was rebuilt in the second half of the nineteenth century and exists to this very day.

In 1804, when Jews were ordered to assume last names, Rabbi Issakhar Ber opened the Hebrew Bible and chose "Ashbel," the name of the third son of Benjamin. His firstborn, Rabbi Iosef Ashbel, was the son-in-law of Rabbi Noach Altschuler, a descendant of Rabbi David ben Aryeh Loeb, who together with his son, Rabbi Yechiel Hillel ben David, was known for the books, *The Fortress of David* and *The Fortress of Zion*. They in turn were descendants of the illustrious Rabbi Shlomo Itzchaki, better known as Rashi (1040–1105), the author of the comprehensive commentary on Tanakh and Talmud.¹³ Rabbi Noach Altschuler was also the grandfather of Menachem Mendel Schneerson (1789–1866), nicknamed "Tzemach Tzedek" ("Righteous Scion"), the founder of the famous Lubavitcher dynasty.

---

preacher, skilled as a narrator of Torah and religious stories. Rabbi Israel ben Eliezer (1698–1760), better known as Baal Shem Tov (acronymed as Besht), is considered to be the founder of Chasidic Judaism.
9   Ibid., 1:37–38.
10 Ibid., 1:44.
11 As cited in Nissan Mindel, *Rabbi Schneur Zalman of Liadi: A Biography* (Brooklyn, NY: Kehot Publication Society, 1969), 242n17.
12 "Der Alter Rebbe," one of Schneur Zalman's nicknames, means "the Old Rabbi" in Yiddish. *The Tanya* is an early work of Chasidic philosophy and the main work of the Chabad approach to Chasidic mysticism.
13 Curiously, the Rashi lineage may be also traced on the Shapiro side of the family. See "Shapira" in http://www.davidicdynasty.org/descendant-family-trees/.

Chaia Ashbel (née Reines), paternal great-great-grandmother.

Rabbi Issakhar Ber's two grandsons—one his exact namesake and the other Noach Mendel—were both learned rabbis and successful businessmen. The son of the former, Moshe, did not inherit his father's and uncle's business acumen. Although his father had bequeathed him a substantial sum of money, Moshe squandered it on futile commercial undertakings and became quite impoverished. Moshe Ashbel (1830–99) was married to Chaia Reines (1841–1913). Chaia, in all likelihood, was related to Rabbi Itzchak Yaakov Reines (1839–1915), the founder of the Mizrachi Religious Zionist Movement and the author of *A New Light on Zion* (*Or chadash al tzion*). In this treatise, he refuted the assertions made by those rabbinical colleagues of his who opposed political Zionism.

Moshe and Chaia had six children, all boys. Two of them immigrated to the United States and pursued successful business careers. Two others moved to Western Europe, first to Switzerland and then to Germany,

Iosef Menachem Ashbel, paternal great-grandfather.

where they became opera singers. Moshe and Chaia had yet another son, who went deaf as a little child from the complications of meningitis. As a result, he developed a serious speech impediment, was sent to a trade school, and became a blacksmith. Of the six children, only Iosef Menachem, the firstborn, remained in the bosom of the traditional rabbinical education. In the beginning, he was schooled in Lubavitchi and thereafter attended the famous Volozhin yeshiva, where he quickly earned for himself the reputation of a prodigy of learning (*ilui*).[14] In his poem "A Picture of Life in the Preceding Generation" ("*Tmunat chaei hador she*

---

14 Yeshiva is a Jewish educational institution that focuses on the study of traditional religious texts, mainly Tanakh (the Hebrew Bible) and Talmud.

lifnei"), Iosef Menachem reminisces about the yeshiva's rigorous daily regimen and points out the total unpreparedness of its students for life in the outside world. After the family relocated to Vitebsk, Iosef Menachem continued his studies at the local yeshiva.

Ber Beirakh (d. 1906), a wealthy financier and *talmid chakham* from Vitebsk, and his wife, Chava (d. 1909), lived in a spacious two-story stone house on the city's central thoroughfare, Palace Street (*Dvortsovaia ulitsa*). The street was so named because of the location of the governor's mansion. Ber and Chava shared the house with Ber's older bachelor brother, Yaakov, who was a pharmacist by profession. They had only one child, daughter Malka (1861–1913). When Malka was six years old, a great misfortune befell her and the family: the little girl was stricken with polio, for which there was no cure. The disease affected Malka's legs. She could hardly walk and for the most part was confined to an armchair. (Grandma Zisl remembered her mother sitting in an armchair near a hearth, her legs always covered with a plaid lap robe.) Ber and Chava loved Malka dearly, felt protective of her awful handicap, and kept her from socializing with anyone outside the family circle. Malka was entrusted into the care of Golda, a maidservant who attended to all her immediate needs. Malka, a strawberry blonde with large blue eyes and refined features, would have been regarded as a raving beauty had it not been for her severe impediment. Even though Malka did not receive a systematic education, she had a bright mind, excellent memory, and was fairly conversant with Torah. At the time, women were not allowed to participate in rabbinical studies, but Ber did not want to deprive his beloved daughter of the sought-after knowledge. He would leave the door ajar so that Malka could listen to debates of the scholarly circle that met in the house. (In later years, Malka was present at her children's private lessons and struck everyone by her ability to remember and grasp the material.)

When Malka turned fifteen, Ber began seeking a husband for her. For this matrimonial pursuit, he hired a matchmaker and instructed him to go to the local yeshiva and to speak with its head about a suitable young man. This young man ought to be a proficient rabbinical scholar and from a family with good lineage. The yeshiva rabbi warmly recommended Iosef Menachem, who easily met these criteria. Although Iosef Menachem and his parents seemed to be aware of Malka's impairment, nevertheless they decided to go through with the marriage. Matrimony in those days was a contract, first and foremost. In return for marrying Malka, Iosef Menachem would be guaranteed financial security so that he could fully devote himself to the study of sacred texts. In addition, marriage would exempt him from compulsory service in the tsarist army.

Malka, who had never seen any man outside the household, fell in love at first sight with the red-haired and blue-eyed Iosef Menachem, bright and good-looking. Iosef Menachem and Malka were married in 1876. They had three children: my grandmother Zisl (1879–1972), Eliyahu Shmuel (1882–1966), and Matl (1884–1953). Although Malka loved her husband dearly, Iosef Menachem, who was pushed into this marriage by his parents, did not reciprocate her feelings. After dwelling in the Beirakh house for well over a decade and spending most of his time studying Tanakh and Talmud with his father-in-law and his circle, Iosef Menachem started feeling constrained and unfulfilled and began seeking a job, mainly in teaching. After he could not find anything suitable in Vitebsk, he decided to look for positions elsewhere. In the interim, Iosef Menachem went to visit his parents, who by then had moved to Odessa, and stayed with them for six months.

Upon returning to the Beirakh home, Iosef Menachem recognized how oppressive and depressing its atmosphere was and realized that he was unable to remain there under any circumstance. He told Ber Beirakh that he could not continue to stay married to Malka and asked his father-in-law's consent for a divorce, but his request was denied. The situation was complex and tragic. On the one hand, Ber Beirakh thought that children needed their father. My grandmother and Eliyahu Shmuel were eight and five, respectively, and Matl was even younger. On the other hand, Iosef Menachem felt that he could no longer live such a restrictive life with a wife he did not love.

Distressed by this denial, Iosef Menachem decided to go back to Odessa. On his way there, he stopped in Ekaterinoslav (presently Dnepropetrovsk), where he met a local rabbi, Ber Vul´f, and stayed in his house for about a year, serving as the rabbi's son's teacher and as a local community *kashrut* supervisor.[15] Ber Vul´f recommended Iosef Menachem

---

15 *Kashrut* is the set of Jewish dietary laws.

for a teaching position in a settlement near Kherson, but things did not work out. Iosef Menachem then continued on to Odessa, where he once again lived with his parents, this time for about two years. At that period, Iosef Menachem supported himself by giving Tanakh and Talmud lessons. While staying in Odessa and reflecting upon his life, he decided to go to the Land of Israel. For this purpose, he obtained the necessary papers from the Russian imperial authorities and the Turkish consulate. From Odessa he proceeded to Constantinople, where he received additional required documents at the Russian consulate. In 1890, Iosef Menachem immigrated to the Land of Israel and never returned to Russia. All through the years, he was heartbroken over his forsaken children. On his deathbed, Iosef Menachem made his children by the second marriage in the Land of Israel swear that they would provide all necessary help to his offspring and their descendants who remained in Russia. As he rightly portended, some of those left behind in Russia would eventually come to the Jewish historical homeland. True to their pledge, Iosef Menachem's children by his second marriage helped the Russian branch of the family leave Soviet Russia and settle in Israel.

My grandmother Zisl, Iosef Menachem and Malka's eldest child, was educated at the Vitebsk Mariinsky Gymnasium for Girls. There she befriended Chana Rosenfeld, the elder sister of Marc Chagall's future wife, Bella.[16] Grandma Zisl told me that the entire Vitebsk Jewish community was abuzz when Chagall became engaged to Bella in 1909 and when he married her in 1915. (Although by then Grandma had already relocated first to Riga and then to Moscow, she kept in touch with her Vitebsk relatives and friends.) As Grandma remarked, there was an obvious misalliance: Bella's father was a wealthy jeweler, whereas Marc's father was a herring factory employee and his mother sold groceries from their home. According to Grandma, Chagall, as an artist, did not enjoy a high reputation at the time and was perceived by many in the city as a good-for-nothing dauber.

---

16 Incidentally, recent research has established that Bella was born in 1889, and not in 1895, as was previously believed. See Liudmila Khmel'nitskaia, "New Data to Bella Rosenfeld's Biography of the Vitebsk Period," http://chagal-vitebsk.com/node/173.

Zisl Shapiro (née Ashbel), paternal grandmother.

(From left): Zisl, Matl, and Eliyahu Shmuel in the beginning of their life paths. Vitebsk, ca.1903. Courtesy of Mikhail Moiseev.

After finishing the gymnasium, Zisl chose to study midwifery. Like her younger brother (of whom I shall speak shortly), Zisl also became involved in revolutionary activities. (Over time, Grandma Zisl's political beliefs underwent a noticeable change as she grew rather skeptical of the Soviet regime. I remember, for example, that in the late 1950s she argued with my cousin Gera against the expediency of collective farms.) When the tsarist secret police were looking for her, Ber Beirakh quickly found her a match in Hirsch Shapiro. As we recall, Hirsch was residing in Riga, where he was helping his great-uncle conduct business at the leather factory. In 1904, Hirsch and Zisl were married and made their home in the Latvian capital.

Hirsch and Zisl Shapiro. Riga, ca. 1910.

There they had the two of their three children: the aforementioned Dov-Ber (aka Boris, nicknamed Bebka, 1906–41) and Chaia Chava (aka Anna, nicknamed Niuta, 1909–96). Bebka was named after his maternal grandfather, whereas Niuta was named after both her paternal and maternal grandmothers. Bebka became a transportation engineer, and after Hirsch's tragic death it fell upon him to be the main breadwinner of the family. Being about ten years Bebka's junior, my father looked up to him. Father spoke of Bebka often and always with admiration and warmth. I remember Father telling me that when he was a boy, Bebka built a radio set for him—quite a novelty in Soviet Russia in those days. As a transportation engineer, Bebka was drafted immediately after the Nazi invasion of the Soviet Union in the summer of 1941 and was killed in the first weeks of the war. After Bebka's death, my father supported Bebka's wife, Batsheva (aka Virsavia, or Seva), and their son, German (aka Gera, b. 1935), for many years. Niuta worked as an editor and proofreader for several newspapers and publishing houses. For the rest of her life, she kept the last name of her first husband, Grigory Lubinsky, who had fallen in World War II.

Unlike Bebka and Niuta, Father was born in Moscow at the end of 1915, in the midst of World War I. He was named Yaakov after his maternal great-uncle. In August 1915, with the advance of the German army and the Battle of the Gulf of Riga, the family was forced to flee eastward and settled in Moscow. Consequently, Father's most formative years occurred during the terrible deprivation caused by the wars and revolutions. This arduous period in Russian history is reflected (albeit in a Petrograd setting) in Evgeny Zamiatin's story "The Cave." It is also graphically described by Meriel Buchanan, the daughter of Sir George Buchanan, British ambassador to Imperial Russia.[17]

Grandma Zisl's younger brother, Eliyahu Shmuel (aka Il´ia), was a gifted mathematician. He finished gymnasium with distinction and was preparing to enter university. His life, however, took a very different and unexpected turn. Il´ia had a pal who preached revolution to him and Zisl. Both fell under the pal's influence, joined the revolutionary circles, and were disseminating the newspaper *Spark* (*Iskra*), the official organ of the Russian Social Democratic Labor Party. At the time (1902–3), *Spark* was published in London and was edited by Vladimir Lenin. *Spark* was printed on a superfine paper so that it could be easily smuggled into Russia and

---

17 Meriel Buchanan, *Petrograd, the City of Trouble, 1914–1918* (London: W. Collins, 1918).

distributed around the country. In the end, the secret police caught up with Il′ia. He was arrested and exiled to Arkhangel′sk, the White Sea port in Russia's far north. Among the exiled revolutionaries there was a girl, named Frieda Rozenberg. Il′ia and Frieda became enamored of each other and were wed in 1904. He earned a living by giving math lessons, she became skilled at sewing and found work as a seamstress. The bitterly cold weather, most of all in winter, was detrimental to Frieda's health. She fell ill with acute pneumonia and died after eighteen months of their marriage. The bereaving Il′ia remained alone. His only contact with the outside world was the correspondence he conducted with his sisters: Zisl, who resided in Riga, and Matl, who studied in Dvinsk and St. Petersburg. While in exile, Il′ia found out that his maternal grandparents and his mother had died.

After serving the first ten years of his sentence in the far north, Il′ia was transferred to the Siberian city of Tomsk, where the tsarist government had gathered many revolutionaries. Aside from them, there dwelled on the outskirts of the city a Gypsy tribe that had also been exiled to Siberia. The tribe chieftain, Glebko, an educated man, had five daughters. The eldest among them, Maritsa, was sixteen years old and wished to receive schooling, and so Glebko commissioned Il′ia to teach her. Maritsa came daily from the Gypsy settlement to Il′ia's house to study and returned home before dark. As time passed, Il′ia and Maritsa fell in love and were soon married. Il′ia loved Maritsa dearly in spite of her poor housekeeping skills. She knew neither how to cook nor how to rear children but possessed an exceptional *joie de vivre*. They lived happily until one day Maritsa's sister showed up with terrible news: an epidemic of cholera had broken out in the Gypsy settlement, and their parents and siblings fell severely ill. Maritsa dashed to the settlement to care for her dear ones but was unable to save them. As Maritsa was tending to them, she herself contracted the disease and died. The grief-stricken Il′ia was left with three little boys, aged seven years to six months: Boris (1915–83), Gleb (1916–99), and Gennady (1921–93).

Feeling completely lost, Il′ia visited Maritsa's close friend, Alexandra (Shurochka) Kuznetsova (1900–1964), the descendant of a Russian serf who rebelled against his landlord and was likewise exiled to Siberia. Shurochka and her widowed mother, Matrena Ivanovna, invited Il´ia and his children to live with them. Before long Il´ia married Shurochka and had three additional children with her: Yuri (1923–42), Margarita (b. 1925), and Valentin (b. 1928). The family soon moved from Tomsk to Novosibirsk, known informally as the capital of Siberia. Il´ia worked as printing-plant manager of the newspaper *Red Siberia* (*Krasnaia Sibir´*) and later as CEO of the publishing house Poligrafizdat. (Grandma Zisl told me that for the duration of World War II, as part of the civilian evacuation, she and Niuta came to Novosibirsk, where they lived with Il´ia's family.) Among Il´ia's six children, all except Yuri, who was killed in World War II at the age of nineteen, acquired professions and most of them earned university degrees. In time, Boris became chief engineer and production manager of a large industrial plant, Gleb was a geodesist by occupation, and Gennady worked as an engineer and later became director of a factory. All through World War II, the young Margarita operated as a controller of rifle scopes at a military plant. After the war, she studied accounting and served as a bookkeeper until her retirement. Valentin worked as a construction electrician. Among all the surviving siblings, I remember meeting Boris and Margarita. Every now and then Boris would come to see us while on business trips to Moscow, whereas Margarita (nicknamed Maga) visited Aunt Niuta and Grandma Zisl in Moscow in the mid-1960s. In 1994, Maga moved to Israel to care for Niuta and stayed in Jerusalem long after her cousin's death. In 2005, Maga returned to Novosibirsk because it became increasingly difficult for her to live alone at her advanced age.

The youngest of the three siblings from Iosef Menachem's marriage to Malka, Matl, strawberry-blonde and blue-eyed, with fine, delicate features, much resembled her mother. One day, a worrisome thing happened. Matl was outdoors in the care of a nanny who became engrossed in a neighborly conversation and absolutely forgot about the little girl. Matl wandered off and got lost. When a peasant woman saw the strawberry-blonde, blue-eyed little girl crying, she imagined that the child perhaps came from a nearby village. The peasant woman was childless and decided to keep the little girl until her family was found. When the nanny returned without her charge, the Beirakh family was devastated. The search after the missing Matl lasted several weeks but brought no resolution. The grieving family already thought her forever lost when Lady Luck intervened. There was a woman who delivered milk and other dairy products to the Beirakh household. One day, as she was visiting her sister in the countryside, she spotted a pretty little girl playing in the yard next door. The milkwoman recognized the child and approached her sister's neighbor. She told her that the child belonged to a wealthy Jewish family, and that if the girl is brought back, a munificent reward would be offered. The peasant lady heeded the milkwoman's advice. She returned Matl to her parents to the great delight of the entire family and was generously recompensed for it.

Like her older sister, Matl graduated from the Vitebsk Mariinsky Gymnasium for Girls. In 1906, she decided to leave home. As did many young women her age, Matl wished to acquire a profession and to become independent. Accordingly, she moved from Vitebsk to Dvinsk, where she enrolled in a pharmacy course. In this she evidently followed in the footsteps of her great-uncle Yaakov. While in Dvinsk, she joined a circle of Jewish youngsters who were meeting in the house of the Poliakov family. The family was well known in the city for its hospitality and cultural interests. The Poliakov family had three siblings: two girls, Mania and Mina, and a young man, named Chaim (Efim). (Mania soon married a man from the local Dvinsk family, whose last name was Tur. Tur, as we remember, was the original surname of my maternal grandfather's family, which hailed from that same city. It is possible therefore that the two branches of my family got related through this marriage.) Soon Matl became the circle's center of attraction, and to no surprise: she was bright, well educated, and beautiful. It was not long before Matl and Efim fell in love. After two years of study, Matl earned her degree in pharmacy but could not find a job. Subsequently, she moved to St. Petersburg, where she began to study biology. To support herself, she worked as a secretary to none other than Alexander Kerensky, one of the leaders of the populist socialist party called the Toilers (*Trudoviki*). (In time, in the summer of 1917, Kerensky became prime minister of the short-lived Russian Provisional

Government.) Matl revered her boss, joined the Toilers Party, and, in all likelihood, named her future daughter after him—Alexandra. Matl and Efim conducted an intense correspondence and were married in 1914 after finishing their respective studies. Efim, who was trained in business, earned his living by managing family country estates. The newlyweds settled in the eastern Crimean city of Feodosia, where Alexandra, or Shura (1915–99), as she was called in our family, was born. More than half a century later, in the summer of 1969, I visited this charmingly bright and sunny town, with white-stone little houses, the birthplace of the famous Russian seascape painter of the Armenian descent, Ivan Aivazovsky.

With the onset of World War I, Efim was exempted from military service as the only son, and Matl worked for the Russian army as a pharmacist. In late 1917, Efim received a letter from his sister Mania, informing him that her husband had died, and asked Efim to take over the management of an estate near the Ukrainian town of Belaia Tserkov´. Efim and his family moved to the suburbs of the town, where they were joined by the younger Mina, who was still single. They all enjoyed the quiet rural surroundings and lived in a spacious wooden house, in which the redheaded Shura was the only child. This pastoral atmosphere did not last long. With the Bolshevik takeover in Petrograd and Moscow, the civil war between the Whites and the Reds broke out all across the country. In addition, the Ukrainian nationalist forces were taking advantage of this confrontation in an attempt to win their country's independence. This internecine strife among various military forces occurred in an atmosphere of complete lawlessness and was frequently accompanied by pogroms. In 1921, Efim was murdered in one of the waves of such pogroms perpetrated by the bands of Simon Petliura. Devastated by this terrible loss, the widowed Matl and little Shura came to Moscow, where by then the family of her elder sister, Zisl, had established itself. Shura and my father were almost exact coevals: she was born on December 12, 1915, his senior by less than two weeks. When time had come for Father and Shura to go to school, they were enrolled in the same first grade and were deskmates.

In the fall of 1923, Matl, an erstwhile Kerensky associate, became acutely aware that her prospects in Soviet Russia were grim and wrote to

Father (front row, far left) and Shura (front row, far right) as first-grade classmates. Moscow, 1923.

Iosef Menachem. She asked her father to obtain an immigration certificate from the British authorities for her and the eight-year-old Shura, which he duly arranged. So in the spring of 1924, Matl and little Shura moved to the Land of Israel, where Iosef Menachem was living with his second wife and their five children. Upon her arrival in Jaffa, Matl found a job in a local pharmacy, where she worked for a while until relocating to Hadera. She resided there from that time onward and worked as a pharmacist for the regional community. Matl died suddenly at the age of sixty-nine, days before the bar mitzvah of her grandson Yoav.

Meanwhile, after finishing the Tel Aviv Hertzliya Gymnasium, Shura (in the Land of Israel she was called Alex) continued her studies in the teachers seminary. In 1939, she married Israel Mayber (1905–84), a native of the Ukrainian town of Yarmolintsy, who had immigrated to the

Land of Israel around 1920 along with his older sister. When I met Israel, he looked like a smaller version of the actor John Wayne. Despite his meager formal education, Israel was well read, mainly in Hebrew. In the Land of Israel, he at first was engaged in road and building construction but soon joined the Haganah.[18] Since the Haganah was outlawed by the British Mandate authorities, Israel worked as a carpenter and manufactured dolls as a cover for his Haganah activities. Throughout World War II he was in charge of the Dead Sea Industries security and served as an instructor at the Haganah courses for senior officers. In the War of Independence, Israel was appointed as the commander of a sniper school in Jerusalem. Just as the war ended, Israel joined the police force. He quickly rose through the ranks and ultimately became chief of the municipal district of Jerusalem (*nefet habirah*). It was a challenging job that Israel Mayber took most seriously. He was fighting Arab infiltrators (*mistonenim*) by night and Jewish criminals by day. Being a fair-minded individual, sensitive to the human plight, Israel also did his best to alleviate the suffering of tens of thousands of new immigrants who had to live in tents under primitive conditions. In the final years of his career, Israel focused his attention on rehabilitating juvenile delinquents. In 1940, Alex and Israel's son, Yoav, was born. (In due time, Yoav developed into an accomplished physicist and an aficionado and connoisseur of the ancient Mayan civilization. Most recently, Yoav, together with his wife, Ron, has also become involved in the project of saving numerous olden-days Hebrew songs from extinction by transcribing their lyrics and recording them on disc.) That same year, Alex earned an M.Sc. in botany from the Hebrew University of Jerusalem. Her advanced studies were interrupted twice: first, during World War II, when Alex served in the A.T.S.[19] Then again, with the outbreak of the War of Independence in 1948, when she enlisted in the Israel Defense Forces, eventually reaching the rank of major. After the conclusion of the war, Alex resumed her graduate studies, earning a Ph.D. in 1953. Upon graduation, she continued working at her alma mater, specializing in seed germination. Alex co-authored a textbook on the

---

18 Haganah ("Defense" in Hebrew) were paramilitary units that were organized to combat terrorism against Jews in the Land of Israel between 1920 and 1948.
19 The Auxiliary Territorial Service was the women's branch of the British army during World War II.

subject, which originally appeared in 1963 and went through four editions, the last coming out in 1989.

When I contacted Alex in 1970, she held a professorship in botany at the Hebrew University of Jerusalem. Alex was a woman of strong character and possessed a great sense of duty. She dedicated the majority of her time to the Hebrew University of Jerusalem and did much for the advancement of science in the country. Alex was a person of few words but many deeds and of numerous accomplishments. I always knew that she would do her absolute utmost to render the necessary help. I personally owe Alex a great deal. She sent me the required invitation to come to Israel, arranged for my Israeli citizenship in absentia, and worked assiduously toward my release from totalitarian Soviet Russia, which she and her mother had successfully fled almost half a century earlier. I shall discuss later (in Chapters 4 and 5) her tireless work for my emigration. Suffice it to say here that aside from contacting numerous Israeli government officials, Alex wrote to the UN Secretary-General Kurt Waldheim and conveyed my letter addressed to Tamar Eshel, the Israeli representative to the UN Commission on Human Rights.

After this account of the lives of Iosef Menachem, Malka, and their children in Imperial Russia and beyond, the time has come to return to the second chapter of his life in the Land of Israel. In his memoir, Iosef Menachem recalls that he arrived in the country on a Friday, spent Shabbat in the house of his paternal aunt Perl in Jaffa, and afterward went to Jerusalem. Incidentally, eighty-odd years later, I too arrived in the country on a Friday, spent Shabbat with my paternal great-uncle, Iosef Menachem's youngest son, Moshe, and his family, and afterward went to Jerusalem. Upon my arrival, Iosef Menachem's children, all in their late sixties and seventies, exclaimed in astonishment: "Father has come!" (*Abba ba!*). They told me that I greatly resembled Iosef Menachem in physical appearance, personality, and mannerisms, including my Hebrew, which they labeled "Shabbat Hebrew" (*ivrit shel shabat*). If this was not enough, both he and I were born in the same month of Elul: Iosef Menachem two days and

I two weeks before Rosh Hashanah, the Jewish New Year. To complete the comparison, it so happened that I too became a teacher. Like Iosef Menachem, I taught Hebrew while in Russia, albeit briefly and surreptitiously, but later taught Russian language and specialized in Russian literature.

Upon coming to Jerusalem, Iosef Menachem was admitted to the famous Etz Chaim Yeshiva, at the time the largest in the Land of Israel and adjacent to the spectacular Churva Synagogue in the Old City. Soon he met Ruchama Ram (1865–1949), his future second wife. Ruchama also hailed from Vitebsk, the city in which Iosef Menachem had lived with his first wife, Malka, and their three children prior to his departure. When Ruchama landed in Jaffa in 1892, she was met there by her brother Nachman, one of the founding fathers of the town of Hadera. Shortly after arriving in the Land of Israel, Ruchama fell ill with malaria, and it was decided that only Jerusalem's dry climate could help her recover. And so instead of staying with her brother, Ruchama went to Jerusalem to live with her maternal great-uncle Moshe Wittenberg (1825–99).

Moshe Wittenberg and his wife, Chesia, immigrated to the Land of Israel around 1882. The couple had no children of their own and accepted Ruchama as their granddaughter. Both well educated and proficient in Russian, Ruchama handled her great-uncle's business correspondence. Wittenberg, a wealthy entrepreneur and renowned philanthropist, built housing for the poor to the west of the Meah Shaarim Quarter, and the neighborhood, in which these almshouses stood, still bears Wittenberg's given name, Batei Moshe. In 1884, Wittenberg purchased a building on Haguy Street in the Old City, which has been unofficially known by his surname to this very day (the Wittenberg House).

The building has a fascinating history. Recent research has revealed that in the mid-nineteenth century it was the site of the Mediterranean Hotel. In 1867, Mark Twain briefly stayed in the hotel, from which he wrote one of the fifty letters that served as the basis for *The Innocents Abroad*. About the same time, Sir Charles Warren, a renowned British archeologist, who conducted the first major excavations of Jerusalem's Temple Mount, lodged there. In the early 1880s, the building belonged to Emmanuel Kalis, a Christian Arab, who sold it to the Latin

Patriarchate of Jerusalem at the height of his negotiations with Moshe Wittenberg. Wittenberg, who had his eye on the house, did not despair and offered an exorbitant sum to the new owner. Helping with his negotiations was Eliezer Ben Yehuda, the future creator of the first Modern Hebrew dictionary. Ben Yehuda studied at the Sorbonne, where he became proficient in French, and upon settling in Jerusalem in 1881, taught at the Alliance Israélite Universelle school. Ben Yehuda was acquainted with some officials in the Latin Patriarchate and helped Wittenberg mediate the house acquisition. When Ben Yehuda refused to take any fee for his assistance, Wittenberg remunerated him by subscribing to his Hebrew-language newspaper, *Hatzvi*, albeit secretly. This is because like most Orthodox Jews at the time, Wittenberg vehemently objected to the use of the holy language (in Yiddish *loshn koydesh*) for mundane purposes. In 1987, the Wittenberg House made the headlines when Ariel Sharon purchased one of its apartments, where he resided with his wife, Lily, several days a week. Sharon in the end sold this apartment to the Ateret Cohanim seminary.[20]

In the spring of 1894, Iosef Menachem sent his first wife, Malka, a divorce certificate (*get*) by special messenger. At first, Malka was exceedingly happy, thinking it was a letter from her husband, whom she still dearly loved. When the messenger handed her the envelope, and Malka realized her unfortunate mistake, she fainted. About six months later, Iosef Menachem married Ruchama, with whom he had five surviving children, born between 1895 and 1907: Dov (1895–1989), Aminadav (1897–1975), Rivka (1902–94), Tzivia (1905–88), and Moshe (1907–92). (Shlomo, born 1899, died of malaria when he was ten months old.)

Ruchama, an astute businesswoman, at one point owned a haberdashery store. Occasionally, she would ask Iosef Menachem to mind it for her. A "practical" man, Iosef Menachem would sit and read the Holy Scriptures. Whenever a customer entered the store and asked him a question about such mundane things as fabric or buttons, he would shout in exasperation:

---

20 See Shimon Gibson, Yona Shapira, and Rupert L. Chapman III, *Tourists, Travellers and Hotels in Nineteenth-Century Jerusalem* (London: Maney, 2013), 160, 168, 172n48; http://he.wikipedia.org/wiki/%D7%91%D7%99%D7%AA_%D7%95%D7%99%D7%98%D7%A0%D7%91%D7%A8%D7%92.

"Scram! You disturb me in my studies!" Iosef Menachem's vocation, in which he had a long and distinguished career, was Hebrew language instruction. In the words of Iosef Ioel Rivlin—a prominent scholar of Islam, Koranic translator and commentator, and the father of the current Israeli president, Reuven Rivlin—Iosef Menachem was "one of the first Hebrew teachers" who "belongs to the earliest period of the Hebrew education in the Land of Israel."[21]

In their old age, Iosef Menachem and Ruchama lived in downtown Tel Aviv with their daughter Tzivia. One day, Iosef Menachem was taking his usual stroll. As he passed by a school, a group of kids, happy about their early dismissal, stampeded out of the schoolyard onto the sidewalk and knocked him down. As a result, his right hip was badly broken. Iosef Menachem never recovered from this fall and died soon afterward at the age of eighty-one.

Dov, Iosef Menachem and Ruchama's firstborn, devoted his entire professional life to studying the weather and climate of the Land of Israel. In 1925, he went to Berlin to continue his education at the Frederick William University (since 1949 known as Humboldt University). He defended and published his doctoral thesis in 1930 under the title "The Rainfall Conditions in Southern Lebanon, Palestine, and Northern Sinai" ("*Die Niederschlagsverhältnisse im Südlichen Libanon, in Palästina und im Nördlichen Sinai*").

Father told me that when he lived in Berlin as a child in the mid- to the late 1920s, he would occasionally see Uncle Dov. Father also recalled that while in Berlin, Zisl conducted correspondence with Iosef Menachem in the Land of Israel. Once my father enclosed in her letter his juvenile poem in Hebrew and a drawing of a lion, the symbol of Judah, and soon received from his grandfather, whom he never met, a reply, also with a Hebrew poem enclosed. There is an intriguing sequel to this story. My niece, Dina, has recently told me that when she was a little girl, Father drew animals for her, usually horses. One day, however, shortly before his untimely death, when Dina was eight and a half years old, Father sketched a lion, apparently similar to the one he drew in his childhood. Hence the

---
21 Iosef Ioel Rivlin, *Rav Iosef Menachem Ashbel z"l* (Jerusalem, 1938), 1.

Father's last drawing. Courtesy of Dina Layba.

circle, which spanned more than sixty years and five generations, became complete. The drawing had an important significance: as I mentioned earlier, there has been a traditional belief in the family, of which my father was evidently aware, that both the Ashbels, via Rabbi Iosef's marriage into the Altschuler family, and the Shapiros descend from the Davidic dynasty, with a lion being the well-known symbol of the tribe of Judah, to which King David belonged.

Upon his return from Berlin to the Land of Israel, Dov Ashbel established meteorological stations all over the country and in due course became professor at the Hebrew University of Jerusalem. Uncle Dov was affectionately called by his fellow countrymen "the one who makes the weather in Israel" (*mi she ose mezeg haavir baaretz*). When I met Uncle Dov, he was a slender man of small stature in his late seventies. Uncle Dov was born in Jerusalem, lived there most of his life, and knew it like the back of his hand. It was a special treat to walk with him around the city. But even though he was intimately familiar with his birthplace, Uncle Dov told me that whenever he would move about Jerusalem he would discover something new, something previously overlooked.

Although by then long retired from the university, Uncle Dov still pursued scholarship. He conducted research at his private lab, to which he went twice a day, each a round trip of about a mile. I visited Uncle Dov many a time in his lab on Washington Street. He had an office on the ground floor and meteorological instruments on the top of the penthouse balcony. There was no elevator in the building, and Uncle Dov would spryly climb several flights up and down the stairs in spite of his rather advanced age. As an expert meteorologist, Uncle Dov was a trifle skeptical of weather forecasting in general and wittily remarked that there was always a good chance that it might be correct on any given day.

Uncle Dov at his meteorological station.

Aside from his main career in meteorology and climatology, Uncle Dov was interested in linguistics. He was fluent in a dozen languages: in addition to many European tongues, Uncle Dov knew Arabic and Ottoman Turkish, the latter from serving as an officer in the Turkish army during World War I. Uncle Dov compiled a dictionary, with which he attempted to demonstrate that Hebrew was the progenitor of modern European languages.

When asked whether he would like to drink coffee or tea, Uncle Dov would answer, "cotea," facetiously jumbling the names of the two popular beverages. He drank neither, preferring instead hot water with a splash of milk. Uncle Dov was frugal, did not care much about his physical appearance, and always wore the same darkish suit. Yet he spent a great deal of money on books and scholarly periodicals and was most generous in matters pertaining to education.

Uncle Dov was married to Chana (née Lev, 1896–1992) who had immigrated to the Land of Israel in 1921. Chana was originally from Sejny, a town on the border between Lithuania and Poland. A part of the Russian Empire for more than a century, Sejny came under Polish control in 1919, in the aftermath of World War I. Dov met Chana when she was a member of the Work Battalion *(Gdud Haavoda),* paving the road from Tiberias to the country's northernmost region. At the time, Dov held a teaching position at Kfar Gil'adi, a newly founded (1916) kibbutz in the Upper Galilee. Dov and Chana had three daughters: Eliah (1923–2000), who was born in the kibbutz, Tzfona (1926–48), and Dafna (1933–2003). Both Eliah and Dafna lived rather long and productive lives, were married, and raised children. Eliah became an accomplished potter and ceramics expert and authored books on the subject. Dafna graduated from the teachers seminary, and for a long time, like her grandfather Iosef Menachem, worked as a Hebrew teacher. In later years, Dafna completed a Ph.D. in clinical psychology and specialized in working with bereaving families, especially with those who lost their dear ones in wars and terrorist attacks.

Sadly, a long, productive life was not the fate of Tzfona, who showed great promise in her girlhood and youth. She was born in Poland when Chana was visiting her parents, hence the given name.[22] Tzfona grew up in Jerusalem after Chana brought her to the Land of Israel when she was eighteen months old. Upon finishing high school, Tzfona studied nursing, became a registered nurse, and continued working at the Hadassah Hospital on Mount Scopus. She nurtured numerous patients back to life with great devotion. Upon their recovery, many of them would stop by at Dov and

---

22 "Tzafon" in Hebrew means "north."

Chana's home to express their deep gratitude for Tzfona's remarkable care. Tzfona loved music and was an accomplished pianist. She planned to go to Italy to study medicine to become a doctor. Alas, her plans never came to fruition. During the War of Independence, on April 13, 1948, when Tzfona just turned twenty-two, Arab forces attacked a convoy with patients, doctors, and nurses heading for the Hadassah Hospital and set it on fire. Tzfona was among the seventy-nine who lost their lives in this abhorrent and cowardly assault, known as the Hadassah Medical Convoy Massacre. The untimely passing of this gifted virtuous young woman has been a shocking unforgettable tragedy for the family and a grievous loss to the country and to humanity at large. May Tzfona's memory be for a blessing!

It was hard to find two more dissimilar individuals than Dov and his brother Aminadav, even though they were born only sixteen months apart. Dov was slim and wiry, whereas Aminadav was a bit taller and more solidly built. Dov was studious and impractical like his father, but Aminadav, an astute businessman, presumably inherited the pragmatic streak from his mother. Aminadav was born in Gedera but lived most of his formative years in Petach Tikva. He graduated from the agricultural high school that was founded in the community. At the outbreak of World War I, Aminadav was called up to the Ottoman army as the result of a clerical error: the conscription records listed him two years older than his actual age. To evade the draft, Aminadav boarded an American ship and fled, first to the city of Alexandria in Egypt and then to Cyprus. In Cyprus, he taught Hebrew to a local Jewish family; he later went back to Egypt and worked there at a biscuit factory. Dov was drafted into the Ottoman army and was sent to an officers school; Aminadav, after returning to the Land of Israel, volunteered for the Jewish Legion under the auspices of the British army. As in the memorable poem "Between the Straits" ("*Bein hametzarim*") by Shaul Tchernichovsky, the brothers were serving on the opposite sides. Fortunately, unlike in Tchernichovsky's dramatic poem, Dov and Aminadav did not literally face each other and both survived the war. In its aftermath, Aminadav worked for a while in agriculture. In 1922, he joined the Israel Land Development Company (*Chevrat Hakhsharat Hayishuv*), gradually rose through its ranks, and eventually became chairman of its board of directors (1964). Aminadav Ashbel perfectly understood the paramount importance of acquiring and developing land in the country, and the company prospered under his able leadership. Numerous differences in appearance and personality notwithstanding, what united Dov and Aminadav was a great devotion to Israel, which each of them served through his own arena of activity. They both were avid readers and possessed superb Hebrew, rich in vocabulary and magnificent in pronunciation, not to a small degree because their father was an outstanding teacher of the language. Luckily, I had many an opportunity to listen to them and to savor their splendid power of expression in the revived ancient tongue.

It so happened that I resided with Uncle Aminadav for several months. When I arrived in Israel, he had been a widower for nine years after the death of his wife, Sara (née Halpern). Upon my coming to live in Jerusalem, I was initially sent to Ulpan Etzion in the Baka neighborhood located in the south of the city.[23] But since I was reasonably proficient in Hebrew and did not need to take an intensive language course, the relatives asked me to move in with Uncle Aminadav, who lived alone and was seventy-five years old at the time. His only child, Rachel (or Rocha as she was affectionately called, 1926–2010), lived with her family in Rechovot. She and her husband, Chanokh Bielorai, worked in the nearby Volcani Center for Agricultural Research. Once in two or three weeks, Uncle Aminadav would go to Rechovot to visit Rocha and her family.

Even at his rather advanced age, Uncle Aminadav rode to his office at 14 Hillel Street every day. (Uncle Aminadav had an attached chauffeur, Itzchak, a tall good-natured Iraqi-born man in his mid-forties.) At home, Uncle Aminadav maintained a quiet, sedentary lifestyle. He read a great deal, listened to classical music, occasionally attended theatrical productions and museum exhibits, but was mainly working on a book, *The Israel Land Development Company: Affairs and Enterprises in the Israeli Cities* (*Hakhsharat hayishuv: parashiiot umif'alim baarei haaretz*), the sequel to his *Sixty Years of the Israel Land Development Company* (*Shishim shenot hakhsharat hayishuv*, 1969). Regrettably, he did not live to see the publication of the sequel, which came out posthumously in 1976.

---

23   *Ulpan* is a school for adult immigrants, in which they learn the basics of Hebrew.

Uncle Aminadav, who was probably five feet six, upon looking at my tallish and slender figure, called me "*goy gadol*." As I saw it, the phrase was charged with double entendre. On the one hand, it directly referred to the Almighty's promise to Abraham and his descendants to be a "great nation," which in this context implied that I was a "big-sized Jew"; on the other hand, the locution *goy*, aside from a "Gentile," denoted an "ignorant Jew" and *goy gadol* a "greatly ignorant Jew." I presume Uncle Aminadav teasingly implied that I was ethnically Jewish but ignorant of Judaism and Jewish heritage.

During my first months in Israel, I faced a few challenges and would occasionally sigh in exasperation. Upon hearing my sighing, Uncle Aminadav would ask, with concern in his voice, and usually in Yiddish: "What are you groaning about?" (*Wos krekhtstu?*), frequently repeating the same question in Hebrew, "*Al ma ata neenach?*" Like most Israelis of his generation, whose youth and considerable part of adulthood coincided with the thirty-year British Mandate, Uncle Aminadav was quite reserved. After all, one of the advocated traits in the country at the time was "to show restraint" (*lehavlig*). I remember the moment when I received a phone call from my parents and learned that they obtained an exit visa and would be coming to Israel soon. Upon hearing this news, I was so overtaken with immense joy that I fell down on the carpet in the living room and began rolling back and forth and crying with tears of happiness. Stunned by my manifestation of what he perceived as excessive emotion, Uncle Aminadav advised me: "Stop going berserk!" (*Tafsik lehishtolel!*). I enjoyed staying with Uncle Aminadav and learned a great deal from him, but nonetheless I was elated when my parents finally arrived and all four of us were reunited under one roof.

Aunt Rivka, who like Aminadav was born in Gedera and grew up in Petach Tikva, took a great interest in nature already at an early age. As a child, she became fascinated with flowers, watching narcissi, tulips, and poppies year after year. While studying at the Tel Aviv Hertzliya Gymnasium, she founded a nature lover's group that planted a "scientific" botanical garden of wild flowers. Upon finishing high school, Rivka went on to study the natural sciences in Italy, first in Naples and then at the University of Rome, from which she received her Ph.D. After graduation, Rivka did not return home straight away but worked at the Aquarium of the Zoological Station in

Naples, the first international institute that specialized in marine animals, where she conducted research on the metabolism of fertilized and unfertilized sea urchin eggs. In 1930, Rivka joined the Department of Parasitology at the Hebrew University of Jerusalem, where she carried out a pioneering research on the cure of malaria. In 1939, Rivka went to Cambridge University, where she took a course in biochemistry, after which she returned to Jerusalem and worked on spontaneous tumors in hamsters. In 1947, she presented a seminal scientific paper on cancer research at an international conference in St. Louis. This paper had been so well received that Rivka was invited as a research fellow to Harvard, where she spent four years. In 1951, she returned to Israel and joined the newly established Hadassah Medical School at the Hebrew University of Jerusalem.[24]

When I arrived in Israel, Aunt Rivka was seventy years old. She was limping and walked with a cane that suggested some serious hip problem, but her eyes and her optimistic, good-natured personality exuded an abundance of energy. Unlike her oldest brother, Dov, who by her own admission exerted the greatest influence on her, Rivka was both scholarly and gregarious. She had a great zest for life and was epicurean by nature. Although Aunt Rivka received no artistic training whatsoever, she discovered the joy of painting in her late forties. Painting became her favorite pastime, and she acquired a special penchant for depicting bright flowers.[25]

Aunt Rivka was not without idiosyncrasies. Once she chanced upon a clothing store, where she found a blouse much to her liking. The store, however, did not have her size. "I'll get it for you tomorrow," promised the shop owner. "That's no good," rejoined Rivka, "Cause I don't know if I'll want it tomorrow." Aunt Rivka was very sociable. She knew virtually everybody in Israel, which was much more compact back then. She had one problem though: she could not keep a secret. If one wished to disseminate some information, all one had to do was to disclose it to Aunt Rivka and to ask her not to share it with anyone. This request was a guarantee that the information would be spread widely. For this reason, she was known in the family as RBC, or the Rivka Broadcasting Corporation.

---

24 See Rivka Ashbel, *As Much as We Could Do: The Contributions Made by the Hebrew University and Jewish Doctors and Scientists from Palestine during and after the Second World War* (Jerusalem: Magnes, 1989), 297–300.
25 Ibid., 300.

I loved Aunt Rivka dearly and was immensely grateful to her for all her benevolent help during my initial steps in Israel. After I arrived in the country, I found out that she had made a valuable contribution to the struggle for my release from Soviet Russia. She wrote a letter to Emilio Sereni (1907–77), a leading member of the Italian Communist Party, whom she asked to intercede with the Soviet authorities on my behalf. Aunt Rivka became well acquainted with the Sereni family during her studies in Italy. She was above all good friends with Emilio's elder brothers, Enrico (1900–1931), a physiologist and director of the Naples Aquarium, and Enzo (1905–44), an Italian Zionist who immigrated to the Land of Israel in 1927 and who was among the founders of Kibbutz Giv'at Brenner. During World War II, Enzo Sereni was parachuted into northern Italy behind the enemy lines as part of a British special operation. But he was captured by SS forces and later perished in Dachau.

Over the years, Aunt Rivka interviewed numerous personalities who contributed to the advancement of Israeli science. She had accumulated an enormous amount of tapes and decided to transcribe them, which she did with the assistance of a bright youngster, Eldad Idan. I remember how shocked I was when Eldad, a teenager, habitually addressed Aunt Rivka, approximately four times his senior, merely by her first name. I came to realize that it was common in Israel at the time and probably even more so nowadays. Eventually, Aunt Rivka published two seminal volumes of memoirs, the aforementioned *As Much as We Could Do (Kol asher iakholnu)* and *From Zion Goeth Forth Torah (Ki mitzion tetze torah)*. The books were originally written and came out in Hebrew and were subsequently translated into English.

I knew Aunt Tzivia and her husband, Menachem Katz (1902–93), much less than the rest of the senior siblings: Dov, Amindav, and Rivka lived in Jerusalem, where I also lived. Uncle Moshe and his wife, Shula (about whom I shall speak shortly), often invited me and Luba to their Gat Rimon residence. Tzivia and Menachem Katz lived on Shalom Aleichem Street, in downtown Tel Aviv. I visited them a couple of times, and they were most genial and hospitable. Both Tzivia and Menachem, who worked in construction, were among the country's pioneers. They represented an important chapter of modern Israeli history, having literally built the country with their own hands. They spoke with great pride about their having been, like Dov's wife, Chana, part of the Work Battalion, in which capacity they paved countless roads and erected numerous buildings around the country. One such building is the Rockefeller Museum in East Jerusalem, which houses artifacts unearthed at archaeological excavations in the Land of Israel. I was fascinated by their stories about this glorious period in the country's history. I have stayed in touch, albeit intermittently, with their Jerusalem-based son, Shaul, and his wife, Shifra, to this very day. Shifra is a retired biology teacher. I vividly recall that shortly after my arrival in Israel, Shifra invited me to speak to her class about the plight of Soviet Jewry. Shaul has been a research fellow at the Jerusalem Van Leer Institute and the Harman Institute for Contemporary Jewry. His professional expertise is the history of science in Israel, from the Ottoman Empire and British Mandate periods to the present, specifically the history of the Hebrew University of Jerusalem. The latter was the subject of the book that Shaul co-authored.

Uncle Moshe, the youngest of Iosef Menachem and Ruchama's five siblings, graduated from the Mikveh Israel Agricultural School and worked for the Tnuva Export and the Jewish Agency. He was an experienced farmer and specialized in growing oranges and pecans. Once he took me around his orange grove and showed me how to pluck citrus gently, without damaging either the fruit or the branch. He also taught me the most spectacular way of peeling an orange: he first sliced off the top and then pared the rind into eight petals, thereby magically transforming the orange into a lotus. Whenever my sister, Luba, and I visited him and Shula in Gat Rimon, they would receive us with great kindliness and hospitality. Before going to bed, both Luba and I would always find a glass of warm milk mixed with fragrant honey on our nightstands. Ahead of our return to Jerusalem, Uncle Moshe would every so often give us a bag of oranges, reminiscent of the ones I ate many years earlier in Moscow, and a bag of pecans. Large, elongated, and thin-shelled, these nuts have a remarkably dense texture, are rather sweet, and make a delicious snack.

Shula (née Kavitsky, 1912–96) was born in the northern Ukrainian town of Konotop and immigrated with her family as a young girl to the Land of Israel in 1924. She attended the Geula High School in Tel Aviv and then specialized in testing schoolchildren's hearing. Regrettably,

Shula had a great deal of personal experience in the field—her own daughter, Sara (or Sarele, as she was lovingly called in the Ashbel family), had a major hearing impairment. Sarele was a gifted and dedicated research biologist. One of her main hobbies was traveling overseas. Sarele would customarily bring home from her journeys numerous souvenirs that invariably demonstrated her exquisitely refined taste.

The Ashbel family. Petach Tikva, the Land of Israel, ca. 1928. (Front row): Aminadav with Rocha on his lap, Ruchama, Eliah, Iosef Menachem, Matl, Menachem Katz;(back row): Moshe holding Tzfona, Chana, Tzivia, and Alex. Courtesy of Shaul Katz and Tzofnat Ashbel.

Ever since Iosef Menachem's arrival in 1890, the Ashbel family has remained deeply rooted in the Land of Israel. Its presence spans 125 years and counting. Its accomplishments and contributions to the country's advancement have been prominent and plentiful in fields ranging from road-building to meteorology, from agriculture to the history of science, from pottery to engineering, from botany to the history of art. May the Almighty continue to grant everlasting success to the future generations of the Ashbel family in serving the State of Israel!

CHAPTER 2

IMMEDIATE FAMILY

> Hear, my son, your father's instruction, and forsake not your mother's teaching, for they are a graceful garland for your head and pendants for your neck.
> —Proverbs 1:8–9

My father, Yaakov Shapiro, was born on December 24, 1915. As I mentioned before, in the course of World War I, when Grandma Zisl was pregnant with him, the family had to flee Riga eastward. The family settled in downtown Moscow, at number 10 on the street called Earth Rampart (*Zemlianoi val*), not far from the Kursky Railway Station. In the Soviet era it was renamed Chkalov Street after Valery Chkalov, an aircraft test pilot. In that same house, the legendary Israeli song composer Alexander Abramovich, better known as Sasha Argov, was born and grew up. Only a year younger, my father remembered playing with him as a child and remaining good buddies all through adolescence and early youth. Argov left Moscow in 1932 via Poland and arrived in the Land of Israel in 1934, at the age of twenty. This departure left an indelible mark on my father. He witnessed a real person, his childhood friend, immigrating to the Jewish homeland. Shortly before Sasha's departure, my father asked him about his life plans. When Argov, whose mother was a pianist, answered that he wished to become a composer, Father facetiously and rather thoughtlessly countered: "What can you do with the seven notes of music?" Upon Father's immigration to Israel more than forty years later, Argov reminded him of his juvenile quip. Indeed, Argov convincingly demonstrated what one can do, given the talent, with "the seven notes of music." Although Argov was a famed Israeli song composer, his music did not provide him with a steady and sufficient income. To support himself and his family—a wife and two children—Argov was obliged to work as a bank clerk. In later years, he co-owned the Russian bookstore Boleslavsky on Allenby Street in Tel Aviv. I remember visiting the store with my father and being introduced to this remarkable and most unpretentious man. Father and Argov occasionally met and reminisced about their younger years in Moscow.

As a boy, Father studied Hebrew with Iosef Leib Tzfasman (who alternately spelled his surname as Tzfatman). Tzfasman was born around 1890. He studied in a yeshiva, at the teachers seminary in Ekaterinoslav, and subsequently received an advanced technological training. In the 1920s, Tzfasman lived in Moscow, where he taught Hebrew and wrote poetry.[26] Tzfasman was one of the initiators of and contributors to the Hebrew collection *In the Beginning* (*Breishit*), published in 1926. Even though the joint place of its publication is listed as Moscow/Leningrad, the book was actually printed in Berlin. Almost the entire run of the collection was confiscated at the border and destroyed by the Soviets, which explains the book's extreme rarity.

That same year, Father and Aunt Niuta, who lived with their parents in Berlin because Grandpa Hirsch worked as an accountant at the Soviet Trade Mission there, were summering on the outskirts of Moscow. Bebka had just completed his military service, and Grandma Zisl went back to Russia with the two younger children to spend time with him. That summer in Moscow was exceptionally hot, and Grandma Zisl wanted to rent a summer cottage (*dacha*) for the children. When Tzfasman heard that Grandma was seeking a summer retreat for the youngsters, he invited the kids to stay in the agricultural commune "Zangen" ("Ears of Grain" in Yiddish). Grandma Zisl went to the place, checked it out, found it much

---

26   See Yehoshua A. Gilboa, *A Language Silenced: The Suppression of Hebrew Literature and Culture in the Soviet Union* (Rutherford, NJ: Fairleigh Dickinson University Press, 1982), 193.

to her liking, and sent my father and Niuta there for the summer. Tzfasman regularly visited the commune from Moscow to tutor Father in Hebrew and to organize literary gatherings, at which he and others read their compositions written in that language.

The commune was founded in a hamlet called Lytkino, about ten miles from the railroad station and the village of Kriukovo, in the vicinity of Moscow (now within the city limits). Its dwellings were situated in a picturesque location in the woods near the lake. This officially sanctioned commune bore the Yiddish appellation, but participants and visitors alike habitually referred to it by the corresponding Hebrew name—*Shibolim*. At the time, Yiddish was formally recognized and tolerated by the Soviet government as the language of East European Jewry, whereas Hebrew was frowned upon by the deeply antireligious regime as the language of the Old Testament. Years later, Hebrew became completely forbidden and outlawed—its practitioners were brutally persecuted, often incarcerated, or even murdered—because the Soviet authorities also viewed the language as the main vehicle for Zionist propaganda.

Judaism and Hebrew were among the Soviet government's principal targets. To complete the picture, it must be said that the regime, belligerently godless in general, also ill-treated members of the Russian Orthodox Church and even more so numerous members of various virtually underground Christian denominations, such as Old Believers, Baptists, and Pentecostals.[27] Mother told me that as a first grader in the late 1920s, she and her classmates were forced to harass parishioners of the nearby church of Archangel Gabriel on Easter. The schoolchildren were instructed to confront the worshippers, who brought Easter cakes and other food items for sanctification, and berate them for their "retrograde" views. While recounting these events of ages past Mother was visibly discomfited. Yet the true ignominy and full responsibility lay not with the indoctrinated little children but squarely with the Soviet system. My own brief experience with persecuted Christians occurred in the post-Stalin era, in the late 1950s. By then, as I shall relate in more detail in the following chapter,

---

[27] Between 1922 and 1941, the Soviet regime published a monthly called *Bezbozhnik* (*The Godless*), the mouthpiece of the League of Militant Atheists.

Grandma Sara died and nanny Polia started her own family. Mother and Father, who worked extremely hard and for extended hours, needed a caregiver for my baby sister. It was a revolving door for a long while until Mother found a nice woman, a bus driver by occupation, who reportedly lost her job for having been involved in a road accident. Later, when we earned her trust, the woman told us that there was no road accident but rather that she was fired for being a Baptist. She worked for us for quite some time and proved to be a most honest, decent, and dependable person.

To return to the "Zangen" story. As Father and Aunt Niuta recalled, about two dozen youngsters were part of this kibbutz-like commune and used the most innovative methods of agriculture in their training for immigration to the Land of Israel. They learned carpentry and built cottages with their own hands. They were growing cereal plants and vegetables and raising horses, cows, and chickens. With hard labor, they garnered impressive yields of crops, milk, and eggs. The success of "Zangen" aroused deep envy in the local peasants. Time after time, they raided vegetable gardens, stole produce, trampled down crops, and attempted to vandalize the commune's property. Because of these attacks, Zangeners needed to guard their premises day and night. These skills stood them in good stead in the Land of Israel when they had to participate in protecting Jewish settlements from Arab attackers. The "Zangen" farmers were selling their goods to the local residents and vacationers and vending leftovers at a Moscow farmers market. In the evenings, they regularly danced the Hora, sang songs, and recited poetry in Hebrew. The commune saved enough money to send a handful of its members to the Land of Israel.[28] "Zangen," which began around 1925, lasted for only three or four years until it and similar Jewish agricultural communes in Ukraine and Crimea were disbanded by the Soviet regime.

I vividly remember that Grandma Zisl had in her possession a collection of Chaim Nachman Bialik's poetry, with "I. Tzfasman" inscribed in Hebrew on its title page, presumably a gift to my father from his teacher. Father was certain that Tzfasman perished in the late 1930s in a labor

---

28 Anna Liubinskaia and Yakov Shapiro, "'Zangen'—kibuts pod Moskvoi" ["'Zangen'—a Kibbutz near Moscow"], *Krug* 425 (August 1985): 32.

camp. While conducting research for this book, I found out that Tzfasman, in fact, had survived the Gulag ordeal. An ailing man, he returned to Moscow from his exile during the so-called Thaw but did not abandon his love for Zion. Tzfasman wrote a note that was smuggled to his close friend in Israel, Mordekhai Guber, in which he remarked that if he only could, he would have crawled to the country on all fours. He died in Moscow in the early 1960s.[29] Had Father known that Tzfasman survived the Gulag, he would have done his utmost to brighten the remaining years of his erstwhile Hebrew teacher's life.

Apart from Hebrew, Father studied German, in which he became fairly proficient. (German was the preferred foreign language in pre–World War II Soviet Russia, but English supplanted it in the postwar period.) As a little boy in Moscow, he had a private tutor, an ethnic German. Father once told me, with a chuckle, that after the lessons his

Father (standing front row, first boy from the left in the V-neck shirt) among pupils and teachers of the Soviet Trade Mission School in the company of Maxim Gorky (center). Berlin, 1928.

---

29 Gilboa, *A Language Silenced*, 193.

grandfather Barukh would every now and then talk to the tutor. Grandpa Barukh spoke Yiddish, thinking that he was actually speaking German, and the tutor would cringe and yet would conduct the conversation out of politeness. Father's German improved, of course, by leaps and bounds all through his stay in Berlin. At that time, he attended a special school for children of the Trade Mission employees, and there is a 1928 photograph in which the school's pupils, my father included, appear in the company of the writer Maxim Gorky.

Upon finishing high school, my father was not allowed to continue his education right away. Being of a distinctly nonproletarian origin, he was advised first "to stew in a workers cauldron" (*povarit'sia v rabochem kotle*). After locksmithing for two years, Father was finally permitted to pursue his advance studies. He applied and matriculated at the Moscow Aviation Institute. Father told me that he had many remarkable teachers there, some of whom were quite unconventional. For example, the thermodynamics professor told dumbfounded students in the beginning of the course: "Only God knows the subject for an A, I know it for a B, and all you can hope for is a C, provided you work hard." Nevertheless, Father received an A for the course. He graduated from the institute with distinction in 1939, specializing in the design of aircraft engines.

Shortly after the Nazi invasion of Soviet Russia in June 1941, Father was sent to Kuibyshev (originally and now known as Samara), the city that served as the wartime Soviet capital, where he took part in the production of military aircraft. He returned to Moscow

Father as a freshman at the Moscow Aviation Institute. 1934.

in the summer of 1943 and worked for the next twenty years at the industrial plant that produced MIG engines. In 1948, Father defended his Ph.D. dissertation, written under the tutelage of Boris Sergeevich Stechkin, a renowned scientist, engineer, and inventor, whom he held in the highest esteem both as a human being and as an authority in the discipline. In 1963, with the escalation of anti-Semitism at his workplace, Father quit his job. He joined instead the Institute of Physics of the Earth and worked there for ten years as a senior research fellow until he immigrated to Israel. In retrospect, it was a providential move: after ten years, the Soviet regime could no longer claim that Father was familiar with any relevant military secrets. During his tenure at the institute, Father repeatedly led a group that conducted seismological research in Borovoe (northern Kazakhstan). Before he went there for the first time, an experienced colleague recommended he take along as much ethyl alcohol as he possibly could. "Despite being a liquid, this is the best and the hardest currency you can have there when hiring local workers," the colleague said. It proved to be a sound advice, for which my father was most grateful.

Like his grandfather Iosef Menachem, Father was terribly impractical. A few tales from the family collection will well illustrate this point. Shopping and other chores were not his forte. When asked where this or that staple food could be found, Father's regular response was "in the refrigerator." He therefore was vested with the responsibility of buying only salt and matches. Father's additional domestic contributions were ironing and carrying out various technical repairs. Although usually not showing any interest in cooking, he surprisingly demonstrated some unique culinary skills. Thus, he excelled at making the most deliciously tender matzo balls (or *kneydlekh*, as he called them in Yiddish) for Passover chicken soup and a pretty mean, silky-smooth cream of wheat porridge that he habitually sprinkled with sugar and cocoa powder. The porridge was much favored by my sister, Luba. Once Father's cooking landed him in trouble. One summer, the fourteen-year-old Luba was vacationing in the Moscow countryside with a sister of my mother's schoolmate and the schoolmate's eight-year-old son. Both Luba and the little boy loved to have cream of wheat porridge for breakfast, and the child's aunt was happy to oblige. When my parents came for a weekend visit, Luba asked Father to make them the porridge. After eating it, the boy concluded that Father's porridge was deliciously creamy and smooth, whereas his aunt's came out watery and lumpy. The boy's aunt, who had a petulant personality and a rather poor sense of humor, took it as a personal affront and was sulky around my father for quite some time. Father explained to us the simple secret of his porridge-making success: not to be stingy with milk and butter and to stir repeatedly while cooking.

Upon Father's arrival in Israel, some crook tried to sell him "a pound of pure gold." It appears that Father believed the swindler, and only Mother's intervention put a stop to that business transaction. For a while, members of the family got some mileage from this "pound of pure gold," which suggested gullibility on his part. Father was a highly intelligent man, but as a decent and trusting person, he could not imagine that anyone, most of all a fellow Jew, and especially in Israel, would be dishonest. He would frequently learn the bitter truth the hard way, but he never lost faith in the basic goodness of his fellow man.

While in Israel, Father studied for five months at the reputable Ulpan Beit HaAm in downtown Jerusalem. After finishing the course, he started looking for a job. At his very first interview, he fell victim to intellectual property theft. As though checking his credentials, the interviewer asked my father to solve an engineering problem, which he did quickly, successfully, and with great ease, and for which he was highly praised. Father was glad the interview went so well and looked forward to working at the company. Yet he was not hired. It turned out that the company engineers had been trying for months to get to the bottom of this conundrum, but to no avail. My father resolved the problem in twenty minutes! I remember how distressed and hurt he was upon learning about this trickery. It was most disheartening for me to see that my father encountered such contemptible behavior from fellow Jews in Israel, the country of his dreams. As disconcerting as this incident was, I knew that Father, a talented and experienced engineer, would find a job. Indeed, several weeks later he was hired by Beit Shemesh Engines. The work he did there was far beneath his level of expertise. Furthermore, it took him an hour each way to commute. For fifteen years, morning in and morning out (except, of course, Saturdays), he would get up as early as 6 a.m., and after a shower and breakfast would drive to the gathering point, from which he would ride the company bus to work. He would come back home in the same manner as late as 7 p.m. Despite the extended hours and unchallenging work, I never heard a word of complaint from him. Being an ingenious engineer, Father developed an invention, which he patented in Israel, the United States, the United Kingdom, and Belgium. It was designed to make an engine more compact and fuel-efficient and was intended for a variety of vehicles, including tanks and helicopters. In the last years of his life, Father tried, alas unsuccessfully, to overcome the red tape and to produce the engine in Israel.

Father meditating. Jerusalem, 1985.

In late June 1989, I phoned my parents ahead of my upcoming visit and had a very nice talk with my father. We kidded around and planned to do things together. Little did I know that it was to be our last conversation while he was alive. On Thursday night, July 6, I received a call from my mother. She was sobbing, and I immediately understood that something terrible happened. I heard her cry only once before when Grandma

Sara had died. She told me through the sobs that Father had been killed in a terrorist attack. As I found out later, he was riding a 405 bus back to Jerusalem from Tel Aviv, where he had discussed the production of his patented engine. Near Kir'yat Yaarim, as the bus was approaching Jerusalem, an Arab terrorist overpowered the driver and sent the vehicle into an abyss. This was a premeditated mass murder. The terrorist was identified by eyewitnesses as having been on this route before, evidently hammering out the details of his despicable action. The survivors reported that the terrorist sinisterly helped several elderly women to board the bus and was all smiles to his unsuspecting victims. Many passengers, including my father, were instantaneously killed, others were gravely injured.

I was shocked to the core upon hearing the news and made all the necessary arrangements to leave Ithaca, New York, for Jerusalem right away. The funeral was scheduled for Sunday, and the first flight I could get was leaving on Friday night. Although I customarily do not observe Shabbat, I prefer not to fly on that day. Needless to say, there was no choice this time. At one point, it was rather unclear whether I would be able to make it to the funeral at all. The plane was forced to land in Newfoundland because of a radar glitch. All I could do was to pray and hope for the best. Thank heaven, my prayers were answered—the radar system was repaired within a few hours, and the plane resumed its flight and reached Israel on Saturday night. Relatives met me at the airport and took me to Jerusalem. My sister had arrived earlier that evening from Italy, where she had been conducting research. The next morning, Father was laid to rest at the Har HaMenuchot cemetery. Many relatives, friends, and co-workers gathered to pay their last respects to my dear beloved father, a man of unassailable integrity, a gifted engineer, gentle soul, and a great patriot of Israel. This was the first time that I attended a funeral and, as the son, read the Mourner's Kaddish Prayer.

The Israeli government erected an obelisk near the site of the tragedy, and it became customary to gather there on July 6 to commemorate the victims and to lay wreaths of flowers. Most of all, I wish to thank Dan Kaner, the renowned Israeli radio journalist and presenter, for selflessly giving of his time, year in and year out, to conduct the memorial ceremony in his characteristically dignified manner.

Father's sudden and tragic death was the most excruciating experience of my life and left a great void in my soul. Twenty-six years later, this wound is not as severe, has healed somewhat, but the painful awareness of this untimely loss is forever instilled in my heart. At the same time, I am convinced that Father's immortal soul is omnipresent. I talk to him often, always try to imagine what he would do in this or that situation, and consult him on many issues large and small. I continuously feel his celestial protection over me and his untiring help with my projects—above all with this one, which I dedicate to his blessed and loving memory.

※ ※ ※

Mother with her parents and maternal grandmother. Moscow, 1934.

Four years younger than my father, Mother was born in Moscow on January 9, 1920. Grandpa Gavriel wished to name her after his deceased brother, Eliyahu, and so the Moscow Chief Rabbi, Yaakov Maze (1860–1924), named her Ioella, which was shortened to Ella. She was an only child, and regardless of many hardships endured by the family, received much more attention from her parents and better nourishment than did her future husband.

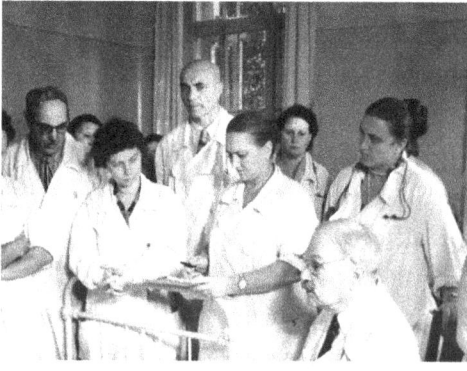

Mother (front row, third from the right), taking part in Professor Vinogradov's hospital round. Moscow, 1963.

Mother appeared to have blissful school years. She kept close and lifelong friendships with several of her classmates, such as Irina Balandina and Eida Lein, and still remains in touch with their children. Irina's son lives in Moscow, whereas Eida's two sons immigrated to the United States and reside near Boston.

As I said earlier, German was the primary foreign language in Soviet Russia of the 1920s and 1930s. Like my father, Mother studied German privately, in her case with a governess, or *bonna*, as she called her, Anna Karlovna. Mother always spoke fondly of Anna Karlovna. She also told me, with great sorrow, that Anna Karlovna and her sister, two old spinsters, were deported at the outbreak of World War II to Siberia to certain death for merely being ethnic Germans.

No wonder that German and Yiddish were my parents' private languages. When I would hear my father telling my mother, "*Schick das Kind zu schlafen!*" or "*Shik dem yingl shlofn!*," I knew that Mother would attempt to send me to bed.

Upon finishing high school in 1937, Mother and two of her classmates, following the fashion, applied to Moscow Institute of Transport Engineers (*Moskovsky Institut Inzhenerov Transporta*, or MIIT for short)—the same institute from which Father's older brother, Bebka, had graduated about a decade before—but fortunately she flunked the math entrance exam. (I say "fortunately" because I cannot envision my mother as an engineer. Upon her failing the exam, Grandpa Gavriel pithily averred that Mother should send a bouquet of roses to the examiner.) Providentially, even though the first two Moscow Medical Schools by then had already completed their admission procedures, the Third Medical School, founded only two years earlier (1935), just started them. Mother quickly applied to the school and was accepted, graduating four years later, in 1941, on the very eve of the war with Nazi Germany. Upon her graduation, Mother worked for two years as a general practitioner at a regional clinic in downtown Moscow. In 1943, she joined the Department of Internal Medicine at the First Medical School, where she had a long and distinguished career until immigrating to Israel in 1973. During that time, Mother defended her Ph.D. dissertation in 1951, and in addition to becoming an excellent internist, she developed into a prominent pulmonologist, an expert on lung diseases, above all on such respiratory disorders as bronchiectasis, emphysema, and asthma. Mother was much loved and deeply respected by her patients and colleagues as well as by many generations of students, whom she taught intricacies of the medical profession.

Mother with her students at the First Medical Institute. Moscow, 1964.

Although my parents both grew up in downtown Moscow within a mile of each other, they were not acquainted until they were introduced by a mutual friend. It so happened that Roza Markovna Sorkina, Mother's quondam colleague from the regional clinic, also knew my father and his family. Herself unmarried, she nonetheless served as an ideal matchmaker. Roza Markovna invited my future parents to a theatrical production and introduced them to each other. Mother used to say that at first she found Father unattractive and did not want to go out with him: Father had a handsome, gentle face and was nicely built (except for the slightly bowed legs resulting from rickets), but he was small in stature, poorly dressed, and awkwardly shy. Nevertheless, he eventually succeeded in winning Mother's heart. They were married for forty-five years up until my father's tragic passing.

Mother imbibed liberal democratic values from her parents, most of all from her father. She despised the Soviet regime and considered it a moral fall, let alone folly, to become a member of the Communist Party. (Neither of my parents joined it.) When asked to apply for membership, Mother would always counter, with a touch of sarcasm, that she did not see herself worthy of the honor. When Czechoslovakia sought autonomy from the Soviet Union in 1968, Mother and the rest of us hoped that the country's efforts to break away from the Big Brother would pan out, and we viewed the crushing of the Prague Spring as a personal setback. When a colleague of hers accused Czechs and Slovaks of being "ungrateful pigs" after "we liberated them from the Nazis," Mother spoke her mind, even though it was not only politically incorrect but also plain dangerous. She had no qualms about breaking off her relationship with this co-worker whom she regarded as a friend prior to the incident. Though not a member of the human rights movement, Mother, at great risk, harbored dissident materials in our apartment until my activities in the Jewish movement made it impossible.

After coming to Israel and upon studying in Ulpan Beit HaAm together with my father, she began looking for a job. I remember accompanying her to an interview with Moshe Rosenberg, director of the Rokach Pulmonary Center for the prevention and treatment of lung diseases. My presence was no more than a safety net. Mother conducted the interview with Dr. Rosenberg in Hebrew after being in the country for less than five months, and I came to her aid merely once or twice. Although Dr. Rosenberg was born in Germany and Mother spoke German rather well, he did not want to speak the language. This language ban was not uncommon among the Jews born in that country who had fled Nazi Germany and lost their dear ones in the Holocaust. Most important, Dr. Rosenberg wished to assess Mother's proficiency in Hebrew, since that was the language she ought to use with her prospective patients. Shortly after the interview, in September 1973, Mother joined the Center and worked there for more than twenty years, until the age of seventy-four. The Center administration very much wanted her to stay on, but the Health Ministry decided otherwise. Mother took this decision in stride: she did not grow despondent but rather found ways to occupy herself. She has done so by keeping up with her medical discipline through specialized periodicals, by reading fiction in Russian, listening to the radio in Hebrew, and watching TV and reading newspapers in both languages. Apart from all these pastimes, Mother ran the household and served as its "treasury secretary" (ever since Father's death, she has resided with my divorced sister). In recent years, as Mother has grown older, my sister has gradually taken over these functions.

Mother, who has never been seriously ill, has always impressed me with her boundless energy. In addition to treating patients and teaching students, she kept our family going, always being its center pillar and the mainstay. Until she slowed down a bit in her early eighties, I could hardly keep up with her step. Now, ninety-five and physically frail, she provides an instructive lesson of exemplary self-conduct in old age. She always listens to her body and acts accordingly. If she feels like resting at an "inopportune hour," in late morning or in early afternoon, she takes a nap; she eats when and what and as much as she deems fit. Of course, being a physician helps her to exercise good judgment and to act wisely. Although nowadays Mother bemoans her faulty memory, which naturally is not as sharp as before, she frequently has a surprise in store for both my sister and me. When the name of a certain Russian actor slipped my sister's mind, Mother provided it at once. When I forgot the Russian word for a "heeltap" (*naboika*), she immediately furnished it. Being in Mother's company is such a fabulous and rare treat! Regrettably, a rare treat because I usually come to Jerusalem only twice a year, each stay for about a month. On these visits, I spend as much time with Mother as I possibly can.

✼ ✼ ✼

My life has been blessed with a fabulous sibling. My sister, Luba, eight years my junior, was born on October 8, 1953. I vividly remember the feeling of tense anticipation in the air as Grandma Sara, nanny Polia, and I were waiting for Father's call from the Grauerman maternity hospital, where both my mother and I had been born. Precisely at 10 p.m., as our antiquated clock, which originally belonged to Great-Grandmother Enta-Reisa, began striking, Father phoned to let us know that a baby girl was born. Mother decided to name her Liubov´, which in Russian means "love," with "Luba" being a diminutive and affectionate form.

Luba was born with a hearing impairment. As a result of being hard of hearing, she also developed a speech impediment. Mother and Father spared no expense in their efforts to obtain the best available hearing aids, which, however, were impracticably cumbersome, and to improve her enunciation. They hired an experienced speech therapist, who significantly enhanced Luba's verbal communication skills and taught her to read lips.

Luba's scholarly nature became apparent when she was still a baby. We bought our first refrigerator in the fall of 1954 when Luba was barely one year old. Until then, all year round, easily spoiled provisions were stored in an icebox, and in winter some highly perishable groceries, well packed and hitched, were placed in a freezer of sorts outside our second-floor windows. Once, Luba was left alone for a moment. When Grandma Sara and I returned, we witnessed the following scene: Luba was standing in front of the open fridge, taking eggs out of the egg keeper, and squeezing them one by one. Apparently, she was perplexed by their being initially solid but turning into soft mush when squashed. She found this abrupt change of state and change of color—from white to yellow and transparent—rather gripping (pun unintended) and kept repeating the experiment time and again. When we came back, she was almost at the end of her test as nearly the entire egg keeper's contents were all over her hands and dress. Luba was immediately whisked away for a solid scrubbing, and I was as immediately dispatched to the store to buy more eggs. Luba's experiment brings to mind "A Little Girl Tugs at the Tablecloth" by the famed Polish poet Wisława Szymborska. In this charming poem, a fascinated child explores and examines the world around her by pulling the tablecloth and watching the motion of place settings and of various other objects situated on the table.[30]

From the age of eleven or twelve, Luba entertained the thought of becoming an Italian Renaissance art historian. She spent her spare time at the library of the Pushkin Museum of Fine Arts, where she had access to books on art history. Most memorable and pivotal to her decision were the Hermitage exhibit at the Pushkin Museum in the fall of 1963 and her first visit to the Hermitage in the winter of 1966. At school, she was perceived as an oddball by students and teachers alike. When the class was assigned to write a composition about revolution, most students wrote about "the Great October Socialist Revolution" and the glorious life it brought about for the Soviet people. Luba, on the other hand, wrote a paper about Van Gogh and his revolutionizing the fine arts, for which she

---

30 See Wisława Szymborska, *Monologue of a Dog: New Poems*, trans. Clare Cavanagh and Stanisław Barańczak (Orlando, FL: Harcourt, 2006), 39, 41.

received a big fat F. On one occasion, she was nearly expelled from school for stealthily reading in class a pre-Revolutionary translation of Émile Gebhart's booklet on Botticelli.

Luba as a schoolgirl.
Moscow, 1970.

Luba told me about her classmate Sasha Sipachev, whom she befriended and who likewise was regarded as a total misfit. One day, a teacher noticed that Sipachev was not doing his classwork and was engaged instead in something completely "irrelevant." The teacher came up to his desk and asked him what he was doing. Sipachev answered: "You see, Faina Borisovna, I have a beetle here that I am trying to train. The left portion of the desk is 'capitalism' and the right portion of the desk is 'socialism.' I attempt to teach the beetle to move from the regressive capitalism to the progressive socialism, but it refuses. I find it quite puzzling and highly unsettling." Another time, the class was asked to envision life after the triumph of the communist society. Each student raved about the anticipated splendid existence under the wise leadership of the Communist Party and described, sparing no bright colors, the happiness that awaits the Soviet people. When Sipachev's turn came, he summarized the future in just three words: "By ration cards."[31] When asked how he envisioned the system that would succeed communism, Sipachev answered: "Capitalism." When asked about the difference between the two, he responded: "Capitalism is the exploitation of man by man, and communism is the other way around."

---

31 Sipachev's dictum was not so far-fetched. Before the holidays, the Soviet regime customarily rationed flour and many other staple foods, and there was a constant shortage of numerous items that produced long lines.

As a Jewess and with hearing deficiency, Luba stood no chance of studying art history in the Land of the Soviets, and her prospects under that regime were utterly bleak. Luckily, while I was struggling to immigrate to Israel, Luba turned eighteen and soon thereafter submitted her emigration papers. Initially, her application was rejected on the grounds of her being "Gavriel Shapiro's sister." Nonetheless, in late May 1972, as I was hiding from the Soviet authorities during President Nixon's visit and afterward, she received an exit visa and left for Israel. This sudden change in Luba's life was far from easy. An inexperienced teenager, she was separating from her parents, to whom she was deeply attached. She was also leaving me, her brother, behind, with all signs pointing toward my imminent arrest and incarceration, without having the slightest idea when (or even if) she would ever see us again. To top it off, Luba was venturing into the unknown. She was going to distant relatives whom she had never met, with very poor knowledge of the essential languages (Hebrew and English), and with only a hundred dollars in her pocket. Indeed, she was facing a tough row to hoe.

Luba with parents on the eve of her departure for Israel.
Moscow, early June 1972.

Upon her arrival, Luba was met at the airport by Uncle Moshe—who at the time worked for the Jewish Agency and who sent her a formal invitation—and by Israel, Alex's husband. (Alex, who had prior engagements at the university, could not come to the airport that morning.) The ninety-three-year-old Grandma Zisl could not conceal her great disappointment upon seeing Luba and not her son, our father.

After a few days, Alex, Israel, and the rest of the family inquired after Luba's plans for the future. "I wish to become an Italian Renaissance art historian," she announced, and this declaration of hers left the relatives completely bewildered. They asked whether Luba had ever visited Italy, was proficient in Italian and English (they were well aware that her Hebrew was rudimentary at best), and her negative replies to all of these questions stupefied them. Furthermore, the Department of Art History at the Hebrew University of Jerusalem was relatively new and—except for Moshe Barasch, one of whose specialties was the Italian Renaissance—there was practically no one who possessed expertise or interest in that period. (Moshe Barasch [1920–2004], a preeminent scholar, in time became Luba's mentor and dissertation advisor.) To our down-to-earth kinfolk, who had been through it all, including numerous wars, this teenager's daydreaming drivel was tantamount to wishing to become prime minister of Israel (even though the Kiev-born Golda Meir had accomplished just that). Moreover, Luba's high school record was mediocre: the vast majority of her grades were Cs, with only a handful of Bs. Nevertheless, the family council decided that there was no harm in trying and that Luba should be given a chance, no matter how slim this chance might be.

Luba enrolled in the four-year B.A. program, the first year of which was supposed to prepare her for the studies proper, first and foremost by learning Hebrew and English. Forty-odd years later, there is not the slightest shred of doubt that Luba succeeded with flying colors. She quickly earned her B.A. degree and expeditiously wrote and defended her M.A. and Ph.D. theses with distinction, all the while being married and raising two children. As I write this account,

Luba, the author of five books and numerous articles, is the Jack Cotton Professor of Architecture and the Fine Arts at the Hebrew University of Jerusalem. She teaches in Hebrew, writes in English, and is proficient in Italian. This resounding success is a testimony to her incredible talent and to her firm resolve to answer her calling against all odds. In that, she had our parents as great role models and teachers by example: never give up your dream, always follow your heart.

CHAPTER 3

GROWING UP IN POSTWAR SOVIET RUSSIA

> An out-of-town Jew finds himself in Red Square. He approaches a police officer and asks him why such a high wall is needed around the Kremlin. The officer responds: "This is to prevent villainous criminals from crossing over." The Jew: "You mean from here to there, or from there to here?"
> —Soviet anecdote

> Something called the police state, or communism, is trying to turn the globe into five million square miles of terror, stupidity, and barbed wire.
> —Vladimir Nabokov, *Lectures on Literature*

I was born in Moscow, the capital of the Soviet Union, in the victorious year of 1945, three or so months after the end of World War II in Europe, late on Friday afternoon, August 24. When Father inquired of a nurse at the Grauerman maternity hospital whether his firstborn was a boy or a girl (at the time, of course, there existed no ultrasound technology for gender testing in babies), the nurse responded: "We don't know yet, but we do know it's a redhead." According to my mother, as a child I looked like a cherub: big blue eyes, red cheeks, and golden curly hair. I started talking at a very early age (and as my mother put it, "have never stopped since"), long before I learned to walk, and many a passerby was astounded to hear a baby speak so well from his perambulator.

My birthplace.

Mother decided to name me Gavriel after her father, who died two years before my birth. People at the hospital registrar's office found this idea hilariously absurd and tried to talk her out of it. There was a good reason for their discouragement. In Russia, the name is rare, usually carries an archaic overtone, and the homonym of its diminutive form (*gavrik*) connotes a range of meanings in different dialects, all inauspicious, from "simpleton" to "slyboots." Furthermore, the plural form (*gavriki*) is a rather unfavorable reference to a certain group of individuals. However, Mother was adamant, and so I received the name that indeed met with much ridicule while I lived in Russia. It is possible that Mother knew in her heart of hearts that I would be living most of my adult life in Israel and the United States, where the biblical name of God's messenger is respected and even revered. This was in stark contrast to Soviet Russia, with its totalitarian, antireligious regime that harassed and persecuted people of different faiths and denominations.

When I was a baby, my family found me a live-in nanny. Pelageia (Polia) Korniushina was a seventeen-year-old peasant girl from the village of Morozovy Borki in the Riazan´ Province, approximately 200 miles southeast of Moscow. She was recommended to us by our neighbor Pelageia Petrovna, her namesake, distant relative, and godmother. Polia was a cheerful and hardworking young woman who took very good care of me. A God-fearing soul, Polia would visit the nearby church of Archangel Gabriel, occasionally taking me, a little boy, along. A few flickering candles and the smothering smell of incense were my first experiences with religion.

With Grandma Sara at a dacha, summer 1948. Polia, wearing a white kerchief, stands in the back.

Polia spoke a brand of Russian that was considered inferior in Moscow. I remember learning a new expression from her—*suliai siuda* ("shov'it here"). I proudly demonstrated it to my mother while opening wide a pocket of my short pants. Mother was visibly upset by my display, asked me not to use that verb anymore, and explained how to say it properly. Curiously, Vladimir Dal'''s dictionary (the Russian equivalent of Noah Webster's) does include this uncommon, seemingly subpar verb, and notes that aside from "shove," it can also signify "push" and "jostle."

When I was nine or so and my baby sister, Luba, about one, Polia married a nice, hardworking man, named Fedor, a carpenter by trade. She went to live with him in the Moscow suburb of Tushino, now the northwestern part of the city. The couple had a son, Kolia (diminutive of Nikolai). My parents stayed in touch with Polia and her family throughout the years. I recall visiting them sometime in the early 1960s and being impressed by the atmosphere of benevolence and concord that reigned in their home.

I grew up in a Moscow communal apartment that was typical of postwar Soviet Russia. How did it happen that my family had such atrocious living conditions, absolutely unimaginable in most parts of the West? In 1915, as I previously pointed out, Grandpa Gavriel and Grandma Sara resided in Petrograd, where he served as a legal consultant to the British company. (In pre-Revolutionary Russia, Jews with a university degree were permitted to live in the imperial capital and other big cities, including Moscow.) In late 1916, Grandpa was transferred from Petrograd, where the company had its headquarters, to a newly opened branch in Moscow. Upon moving to the old capital, Grandpa acquired a spacious apartment on the second floor of a three-story stone house. The house stood in the heart of the city in Crooked-Knee Lane (*Krivokolennyi pereulok*), so named because of its uniquely bent shape. The lane is located not far from the Clean Ponds (*Chistye Prudy*) recreational area.

Clean Ponds! Most of my childhood and adolescence revolved around it. I was carried and driven there in my baby carriage and was taken there for strolls as a little child. As a schoolboy, I would go there in winter, alone or with friends, to skate at the

With parents at Clean Ponds. Moscow, March 13, 1946.

skating rink, into which a significant portion of Clean Ponds was seasonally converted. In summer, I would go there to sit on the bank or on a nearby bench and to watch waterfowl. The most striking of the birds were black swans with scarlet beaks, imported, as I was told, from faraway Australia. Last but not least, I frequented the next-door movie theater Coliseum (*Kolizei*). The building served in that capacity from the dawn of cinematography in pre-Revolutionary years. (Since 1974, it has been the site of the Sovremennik Theater.) In those olden days, one could watch documentaries in its foyer before the matinees, or listen to an orchestra and singers prior to the evening shows.

Not far from Clean Ponds, on Miasnitskaia Street, there stands the main post office, with its stately round clock on the façade of the building. Being a hyperactive child, I would get restless. Upon discerning this, Mother would suggest, as Grandpa Gavriel used to urge her, that I go and see if the clock was still in its place. I am sure Mother welcomed whatever rest from me she could get. The writer Yuri Nagibin, my mother's exact coeval, who also grew up in the neighborhood, movingly limned this part of downtown Moscow. I had goose bumps when I recently reread his collection of short stories entitled *Clean Ponds*.

After the Bolshevik takeover, the family apartment was "nationalized," and my grandparents and mother had to share it with five additional families. In the contemporary Soviet lingo it was euphemistically called "to consolidate" or "to compress" (*uplotnit'*). The regime "humanely" allowed our family to retain the two largest rooms, twenty and thirty square meters, respectively. The latter was indeed so big that Father and I played Ping-Pong there on our expandable dining table. For a long time, ours was the only family that had a telephone, whose down-and-up magic alphanumeric combination (K5–04–23) is forever chiseled into my memory.

Aside from our family of five, there were as many as twenty other occupants. Moreover, for a long while the apartment had no bathroom. The windowless space with paint-peeling walls that served as a bathroom in the olden days was occupied by newlyweds. After having a baby, the couple received a room in another public housing unit. Until they moved out, we washed ourselves the old-fashioned way: the water was boiled in large cauldron-like pots, was mixed with cold water to make the temperature comfortable, and then was poured into the back tank of the washing booth that we kept in the smaller room. I remember standing in a basin, with soap in my face, as the water would come streaming down from the spigot and bring relief to my burning eyes. When the young couple with the baby moved out and the windowless space was reconverted into a bathroom, each of the six families received its designated bathing day (Sunday was the day open to all). Early morning hours were the only exception, when all and sundry washed before going to work on a first-come, first-served basis. The bathroom morning traffic caused a great deal of friction, but somehow we all managed to wash up. Down the corridor, there was also a single toilet in a poorly lit cubicle. One toilet for twenty-five people was a serious problem and so was the one kitchen with merely an eight-burner stove. Cooking and cleaning were rather complicated affairs and caused much squabbling among the residents. Thus, one neighbor threatened to lodge a complaint with the police and with the Moscow Criminal Investigation Bureau (MUR) because his wiping rags had been reportedly disappearing.

What kind of people were our neighbors? The room next door was occupied by a family of five: a widowed woman of Polish descent, Yadviga Frantsevna Milevsky, her son, Anton, his Jewish wife, Revekka (aka Rivka), and their two children, a boy, named Zhenia (diminutive of Evgeny), and a girl, named Ira (diminutive of Irina). Zhenia was three years my senior and Ira was a year Luba's junior. There was a lot of noise coming from their room. Anton and Rivka constantly quarreled and yelled at each other, were mutually unfaithful, and eventually got divorced. Additional screaming came when Anton would take a belt to Zhenia for the slightest disobedience. I found it odd because Father never laid a finger on me, and Mother only once slapped me on the face when as a seven-year-old boy I unwittingly brought home a dirty word.

The room across the hallway from us was inhabited by an older childless couple. Valentina Yur´evna Berzon, reportedly a secret police agent, a toad-like woman of Latvian descent, who spoke Russian with a noticeable hissing accent, and her Russian husband, whom I remember merely by his funny last name, Korovkin (*korovka* means a "little cow" in Russian).

Korovkin was a waiter at a first-rate restaurant and no doubt was informing the authorities on the comings and goings of his patrons. Both Berzon and Korovkin were viciously anti-Semitic. For example, they claimed in all seriousness that my mother had bought her medical school diploma.

Next door to the Berzon-Korovkin duo there lived the Sazovs. Especially notorious were Nadezhda, an anti-Semitic hag, and her scumbag son, Vasily, both alcoholics and chain smokers. I do not remember what Vasily did for a living, but his mother's occasional source of income, in addition to a minuscule widow's pension, was to throw herself, with pinpoint accuracy, under a bus or a trolley car and to collect the insurance that she primarily squandered on booze. The drunken debauchery would routinely end up with the mother and the son beating the tar out of Vasily's wife, Sofia, and their daughter, Inna. A serious young woman who never touched alcohol or lit a cigarette, Inna eventually was able to move out and went on to study accounting.

Next door to the Sazovs resided a good-natured Jewish bachelor by the name of Alexander Anisimovich Rabinkov, a grocery store manager, who was the first in the apartment to acquire a television set, a KVN-49. This black-and-white model had such a small screen that it was sold in conjunction with a special magnifying lens filled with distilled water or glycerin. The model, whose name was an acronym of its creators' surnames (Kenigson, Varshavsky, Nikolaevsky), was out of whack so often that this abbreviation was facetiously interpreted as *Kupil—Vkliuchil—Ne rabotaet* ("bought, turned on, not working"). Nevertheless, even such a television set as this, with its tiny screen and abysmal performance, was quite a novelty in the early 1950s.

Across from Rabinkov dwelt a quiet old woman of peasant stock, the aforementioned Pelageia Petrovna. After she had died, a Jewish family, the Ginzburgs, moved in: Mikhail Zinov′evich, his wife, Dora Samoilovna, and their daughter, Ania. Mikhail Zinov′evich was a vulgar crook. When receiving a phone call (an additional phone line was installed in the hallway in the mid-1950s) and being addressed as Uncle Misha, he would counter the greeting with his distinctively crass sense of humor: "And why am I an uncle and not an auntie?" (*A pochemu ia diadia, a ne tetia?*). Ginzburg was the one who threatened to call the police about the disappearing rags. When going out, he would routinely bring along a cane to imply some sort of disability that would entitle him to preferential seating on public transportation. On the way back home, Mikhail Zinov′evich used the cane as a lever to carry heavy shopping bags filled with groceries and other merchandise.

There was also a small room adjacent to the kitchen, originally intended for a maidservant. For many years, it was the abode of a certain Surkov, a beggar. Nobody ever saw him washing up, and he was always dressed in tatters. It turned out that Surkov was a pathological miser: after he had passed away, they found an enormous amount of cash hidden under his mattress. Upon Surkov's death, this cubbyhole was occupied by the nutty Vera Vasil´evna Romanovsky. Vera Vasil´evna was born into a family of gentry long before the Bolshevik usurpation of power and was schooled at the Institute for Noble Girls. Being around the bend and apparently mistaking Grandma Sara for a member of the imperial family, Vera Vasil´evna would curtsy to her while wishing her good morning.

Finally, in the room across from the apartment entrance door, there lived the Rovinsky family: mother Ol´ga Nikolaevna, a cleanliness addict, her drunkard son, Viktor, who hanged himself on the toilet pull chain, Viktor's wife, Tat´iana, and their daughter, Lena, a doll-faced blonde with big gray eyes.

These living conditions—sharing the apartment and its utilities with twenty strangers—were absolutely intolerable. For many years, Father tirelessly worked on their improvement. Since my parents did not have the exorbitant amount of money needed to buy a cooperative apartment, an exchange was their only option. Almost every Sunday in the mid- to late 1950s, Father diligently went to the Housing Market Exchange, where people gathered and traded information about dwelling space, or *zhilploshchad´*, as it was called in the Soviet lingo. (Obviously, it would have saved everybody a lot of time had such information been available through classified ads, except Soviet newspapers did not run any in those days.) Sometimes Father took me along, and on occasion when it was cold, and at other times just for fun, he and I would stomp our feet and shout: "Seeking a separate apartment! Seeking a separate apartment!" (*Ishchu otdel´nuiu kvartiru! Ishchu otdel´nuiu kvartiru!*). Finally, after several years of concerted effort, in December 1959, Father succeeded in exchanging our two spacious rooms in the communal apartment at Crooked-Knee Lane along with his darkish, high-rise-obstructed bachelor room in another communal apartment in downtown Moscow, and an extensive monetary compensation, for a two-room apartment of our own, each room about twenty square meters. The apartment was located in the southwestern part of the city, not far from the then newly built Moscow University campus.

"A two-room apartment of our own"? This description may sound rather odd to a Western, particularly American ear. After all, in the United States people generally have private apartments in big cities or their own houses in suburbia, small towns, or the countryside. Americans normally describe their dwellings by the number of bedrooms plus a living room, dining room, and other amenities. On the other hand, to people who grew up in the Soviet Union, where housing conditions were horrendous, this Western description would appear incomprehensible and downright confusing. By night, my parents slept in one room while my sister and I shared the other. By day, the parents' room functioned as a living room, and the other room served as a study, in which my sister and I did our homework. We typically ate in the kitchen. On festive occasions, the parents' room was converted into a dining room to accommodate numerous guests. The apartment also had a sizable balcony, on which, weather permitting, we ate and took turns sleeping.

The building, 18 Lomonosov Prospect, in which our apartment, 271, was located, looked like a public housing project: a U-shaped, nine-story structure with twenty entrances that was home to more than nine thousand people. There were two elevators at each entrance, but whenever they both malfunctioned, which happened often, we had to climb the stairs to our fifth floor. Most windows in the house faced a large interior yard with sparse greenery. The yard, a kind of acoustic pit, was invariably the source of much tumult. It was loudest on warm weekend afternoons when a bunch of rowdy men gathered to play dominoes, with characteristic tile-shuffling clatter. It would become more deafening as each player knocked a tile down on the table with a bang and would emit a triumphant cry. Yet, all in all, we were deemed lucky because our living conditions were perceived by many as most enviable.

In 1967, with a great sacrifice and a substantial loan from Mother's cousin, Yaakov Potak (nicknamed Kuba, 1917–76), my parents bought a car, a Moskvitch-412, a Fiat look-alike. (Incidentally, five years later when

Kuba, a prominent metallurgy expert, heard about my parents' intention to immigrate to Israel, he exclaimed to my mother, with whom he grew up and whom he loved dearly: "What are you doing? Here, you at least earned enough for a roll and a bottle of milk!" Ironically, had my mother stayed, that would have been just about all she could have afforded for the daily ration on her pension. In Israel, after working for twenty years, she leads a dignified comfortable life as an elderly retiree.)

Although the car made our lives more exciting and diverse, its ownership was not without challenges. In time, Father joined a parking garage co-op. Until then, parking the car on the street usually resulted in some of its parts being pinched. Father considered himself fortunate if and when these stolen parts were sold back to him because they were extremely difficult to come by. I recall how very happy and grateful Father was when the guy who stole the wiper blades off our car sold them back to him for five rubles. After Father joined the parking garage co-op, which was located four or five streetcar stops away, it made the logistics of using the car rather complicated. Be that as it may, we much enjoyed having a car. Although Father encouraged me to learn how to drive, I never did while in Russia. (I learned when it became a necessity, about twenty years later in the United States, at the age of forty.) The car provided us with the freedom of mobility as we traveled all over the European part of the Soviet Union. Of course, this freedom was illusory—we were confined by the Iron Curtain.

Even though as a little child I was in the care of Grandma Sara and nanny Polia, it was decided that I should be enrolled in kindergarten to help me develop social skills. Its staff left much to be desired. My kindergarten teacher, Klavdia Ivanovna, was a tall, stout woman with bottle-blonde hair, the type that was known in Soviet Russia as an "officer's wife" (*ofitserskaia zhena*). Klavdia Ivanovna's personality and demeanor were hardly suitable for a pedagogue: she was not above stealing from the parcels that parents sent to their children in the kindergarten's summer camp. The postwar years were lean, money was tight, and my parents' salaries were pretty modest. Mother and Grandma Sara were buying strawberries and raspberries for me at great sacrifice, only to find out later that the good ones were consumed by my corrupt educators, while I received the bruised and partially putrid

With parents.
Gudauta, Abkhazia,
summer 1951.

ones. In retrospect, it represents the quintessence of the entire Soviet system, corrupt and rotten to the core.

I learned how to read at the age of six when I vacationed with my parents in Gudauta, an Abkhazian Black Sea resort. Mother would first read aloud several pages from the Russian translation of Wilhelm Hauff's *The Dwarf Nose* (known in Russian as *Karlik Nos*), and when I got completely hooked on the tale, she would ask me to take over. I very much wanted to know what happened next to the bewitched boy and begged my mother to continue, but she was adamant and would resume her reading only after I did my bit. How grateful I am that she did not yield to my petulant pleas! When I returned to my kindergarten that fall, Klavdia Ivanovna took advantage of my reading skills. She asked me to take over whenever she wished to have a tea break, appointing me her de facto teaching assistant. Many years later, when looking for an academic position in Israel and the

United States, I totally forgot to include this teaching experience in my résumé.

In 1952, when I was seven, my life underwent a drastic change as I moved from kindergarten to elementary school. School no. 312, where I spent most of my formative years, was located at 7 Minor John Chrysostom Lane (*Malyi Zlatoustinsky pereulok*), so named after the John Chrysostom Monastery that stood at the intersection of Armenian Lane. In the early 1930s, the regime demolished the monastery and, quite fittingly, built in its stead housing for the families of secret police operatives. Accordingly, the regime changed the lane's name to Minor Komsomol (*Malyi Komsomol'sky*).[32] Kindergarten had been coed, but in grade school boys and girls studied separately, as in the days of Imperial Russia. In the fall of 1954, when I began the third grade, schools were reformed into the coed system that had existed in the 1920s and 1930s, in the time of my parents.

The main and most beneficial difference was my elementary school teacher, Anna Ivanovna Drozhzhina, a portly, middle-aged lady with a kind

As a first grader (left side, third row, aisle) at school no. 312, with Anna Ivanovna Drozhzhina. Moscow, fall 1952.

---

32 "Komsomol" is an abbreviation for the Young Communist League. After the collapse of the Soviet regime, the lane regained its original name. As I recently learned, school no. 312 was closed down in 2007. Since then, the building has housed the so-called Finance University.

and handsome face. Unlike Klavdia, Anna Ivanovna was an outstanding educator who taught us not only reading, writing, and arithmetic but also by the example of her own fair-minded personality. Anna Ivanovna lived about an hour outside of Moscow and had to travel to the city by suburban train. One day, when Anna Ivanovna got sick, our class, together with Grandma Sara and a couple of other adults, went to visit her. Anna Ivanovna dwelt in a typically Russian impoverished countryside, drab and depressing. In retrospect, her life calls to mind "Matrena's Homestead," but unlike Solzhenitsyn's heroine, Anna Ivanovna was far better educated. Teachers and students alike accorded her much love and a great deal of respect. Once a tall Jewish boy, with a fitting surname, Goikhman, a lazy doofus, became vexed by his poor grade. When he accused Anna Ivanovna of anti-Semitism, all Jewish pupils in the class rejected his calumnious insinuations. For my sense of justice and decency, I am greatly indebted not only to my family but also to Anna Ivanovna.

In my boyhood and early youth, I was mad about soccer. (I still actively follow the English, Italian, and Spanish premier leagues, being an ardent and loyal fan of Chelsea, Juventus, and Barcelona, respectively, and it causes me severe anguish when these teams are pitted against each other in UEFA championships. I was overjoyed when each club became the champion of its respective national league, and Barcelona claimed the UEFA title for the 2014–15 season.) I played left defender and was good at tackling and keeping a tight, terrier-like grip on the forward I was assigned to mark, and in protecting the penalty box. At the time, I was a fan of the CSKA soccer club and closely tracked the country's premier league games. One day, as a boy of nine or ten, I visited my seventy-five-year-old Grandma Zisl and was sharing with her the latest soccer headlines: how Bashashkin inadvertently deflected the ball into his own goal, how Sal´nikov nodded a spectacular header, how the young Strel´tsov hammered a stunning bomb under the crossbar. Grandma was listening rather patiently to my fervent downpour when all of a sudden she asked, with a touch of Yiddish: "Gavrik [the soft "k" betrayed her non-Muscovite origins], do you really want to become a *fisballist?*" (*Gavrik, neuzheli ty khochesh´ stat´ fisbolistom?*)

From my early childhood, I had to stand up for myself. I was very small for my age, a scrawny, freckled redhead—an easy prey for school bullies. (Every time I watch *The Milky Way* and hear the famous phrase by Burleigh "Tiger" Sullivan, portrayed by the incomparable Harold Lloyd, in which he remembers himself being kind of puny as a little boy, it immediately brings my own boyhood to mind.) My peers were creative that way. When referring to my freckles, they would point out that flies had a good night's sleep on my face; and when alluding to my light-blond brows and eyelashes, they would inquire whether I spent the overnight shift working in a bakery. One day, when I was teased and beaten more than usual, I came home in tears and lamented the ordeal to my mother. To my complete surprise, she did not console me at all but instead said firmly: "If you keep crying, I'll punch you too. Go and defend yourself!" That was a valuable lesson. It was not long before I had a chance to apply it. When a tall and corpulent Volodia Dolinsky (the namesake of the well-known Russian actor) resorted to his routine abuse, I smacked him with my tiny fist right in the kisser. The result exceeded all expectations. After I served him the knuckle sandwich, not only did he stop bothering me but all other kids decided to leave "this wild redhead" alone and looked for safer entertainment with easier prey.

The "wee Geordie" of the class (second row, fourth from the right). Moscow, fall 1952.

As a child, I took Grandma Sara's and nanny Polia's care for granted. When Grandma, to whom I was deeply attached, died and Polia got married, I had no choice but to grow up fast. Mother and Father worked extremely hard, and frequently Mother could not find a steady nanny for my toddler sister. At those times, I would try to help as much as I could, occasionally with cleaning but mostly with shopping. I would go to the farmers market to buy fruit and vegetables, or to a bakery to buy bread and pastry. Though there was a bakery across the street, we preferred the one near Clean Ponds, which old Muscovites still called Filippov's after the name of its pre-Revolutionary owner. For some inexplicable reason, after forty-odd years of Soviet rule, this bakery still boasted both a superior assortment and higher quality of breads and pastry.

Father once told me a captivating story about an ambitious young man who arrived from the countryside and started working as an assistant salesman in a bakery. The owner carefully watched his moves and once witnessed this scene: a lady customer came back to the store and groused about finding a fly in her roll. When she showed the contaminated roll to the young man, he quickly snatched the fly, swallowed it, and said: "I think, Ma'am, you mistook a raisin for a fly." The owner liked the young man's quick-mindedness, resourcefulness, and willingness to risk his health for the sake of the business so much that he appointed him the store manager. Eventually, the young man, whose last name was Filippov, became the owner's son-in-law. He not only inherited the store but, endowed with an exceptional business sense, created a successful chain of bakeries that unofficially bore his name long after the Bolshevik takeover. I do not know whether the story was accurate, but I always liked it as the epitome of mother-wit and professional devotion. I read a similar story about Ivan Filippov, as it happens, in Vladimir Giliarovsky's *Moscow and Muscovites* (*Moskva i moskvichi*). Giliarovsky recounts that Filippov regularly supplied baked goods to the dinner table of the Moscow governor-general, Count Arseny Zakrevsky. Once Zakrevsky called Filippov on the carpet and angrily reprimanded him after discovering a baked cockroach in a roll. When Filippov was shown the roll, he ate it and told the governor-general that he mistook a raisin for a cockroach. Filippov revealed that this was an experimental pastry—a roll with raisins. When Filippov returned to his bakery, to exonerate himself, he quickly added raisins to the dough and began making raisin rolls in earnest. The new pastry became so popular with Muscovites that it soon turned into a staple.

Yet another and no less painful challenge was my next transition: from elementary school with one teacher, loved and highly respected, to a middle school with various teachers of different subjects. With what I now realize was ADHD, I was often expelled from class and found myself in the rec room, ready at any moment to hunker down at the sight of the principal or a passing teacher. During these frequent banishments, I had ample time to examine the portraits of classic Russian authors, from Pushkin to Chekhov, which were hanging in the room. Being very visual, I gladly and willingly associated the writers' books with their looks. In any event, I loved reading books and pondering over them, which many years later turned out to become my lifelong vocation. (My career-oriented Department of Chemistry at Moscow University classmate, Grisha P., must have had a crystal ball when he reproved me: "Gavrila, you slob, you! All you do is read books!" [*Gavrila, razgil'diai! Vsë knizhechki pochityvaesh'!*].) In addition to literature, I became fascinated with history, largely because I enjoyed the classes of Elizaveta Nikolaevna Shirokova, our history teacher. Either because of my enjoyment of Elizaveta Nikolaevna's presentations, or because she was capable of keeping me in check, or both, I never misbehaved and was the best student in her class.

Another reason for my fascination with literature and history emanated from growing up in an old Moscow district that had many associations with numerous literary figures of the past. For example, in Crooked-Knee Lane there stands a house that belonged to Pushkin's distant relative, the poet and philosopher Dmitri Venevitinov. In 1826, Pushkin recited his drama *Boris Godunov* there. The house itself and the plaque commemorating Pushkin's reading are among my most vivid childhood recollections. In the adjacent Armenian Lane, so named because Armenians had settled there in the seventeenth and eighteenth centuries, there was the Lazarev Institute of Oriental Languages (which now houses the Armenian embassy to Russia). The institute counted the writer Ivan Turgenev and the director Konstantin Stanislavsky among its students. At the other end of Armenian Lane there is a building that for twenty years served as the urban estate of the Tiutchev family, where the poet Fedor Tiutchev spent his formative winters. I happened to have a friend who lived in the former Tiutchev mansion, which the Soviet regime had turned into a hive of densely populated communal apartments. When I visited my friend, I noticed that the mansion was in deep disrepair both inside and out. It was hard to expect semiliterate Soviet *apparatchiks* to fathom the significance of this illustrious nineteenth-century poet and his legacy.[33] The mansion was eventually restored and since 1988 has been housing the Russian Children's Fund.

Incidentally, my concrete connection to Tiutchev continued after we moved to another Moscow district, where I attended a new school. One of my classmates there was Mitia Pigarev. Because I was already rather well versed in Tiutchev's poetry, I knew that Kirill Pigarev, Tiutchev's great-grandson and Mitia's uncle, was a recognized authority on the poet. Mitia and I became pals, and once I visited him at his residence when he was sick with the flu. His household had a pleasantly old-fashioned atmosphere about it: enormous antique floor-to-ceiling bookcases, filled with volumes in different languages, and antique furniture. Mitia's grandmother treated me to most delicious hot chocolate, which she served in an antiquated navy-blue, golden-rimmed goblet-like cup. Mitia and his family lived in a spacious apartment that originally belonged to his maternal grandfather, by then deceased, who was a Moscow University professor of agrology. (Mitia's father, Nikolai Vasil´evich, was a Timiriazev Agricultural Academy professor of aviculture, an expert on chicken-egg-laying qualities and production.) I do not remember whether Mitia stood out in any specific subject, but I do remember that he drew well and helped me with my draftsmanship assignments. I, on the other hand, helped him with his English homework. Aside from this symbiosis, I was fond of Mitia, for he had a noble and independent air about him and a great sense of humor.

Back to school no. 312. I loved Russian language and literature dearly, but I found our teacher, Lidia Sergeevna Yurasova, totally uninspiring. Because of this, I fidgeted and jabbered beyond measure, and Lidia Sergeevna surely found my behavior annoying. I also suspect Yurasova was displeased that a member of a "nonindigenous ethnicity" (*nekorennoi natsional'nosti*), that is, a

---

33 *Apparatchik* is a Russian colloquial term for a full-time professional functionary of the Communist Party or government.

Jew, happened to be one of the best in class in these subjects. (The other best student in Russian language and literature, and also of a "nonindigenous ethnicity," a Tatar, was Gaiar Zhemaletdinov, but unlike me, Gaiar was a boy of exemplary behavior.) All that led to a rather ugly incident. One day, when I was moving about and blabbering in my usual obnoxious manner, Lidia Sergeevna wittily exclaimed: "Shipiro, do not hiss!" (*Shipiro, ne shipi!*), thereby likening me to some sort of reptile. To this insult, I quickly retorted: "*Yurasova, ne iuri!*" A chilly silence spread through the classroom. In my response, I paid Lidia Sergeevna in kind by euphemistically connecting her surname to the Russian *duras* or *durak*, which means "bad," "ugly," and "stupid." Therefore, my Russian phrase carried a thinly veiled message: "Yurasova, don't be a fool!" (As I learned while working on this book, the surname stems from the Lithuanian *juras*, that is, "noisy, loud-voiced." Ironically, it was I who was noisy and loud-voiced.) Naturally, I was instantly suspended, and my mother was summoned by Dmitri Petrovich, the principal. It turned out that while grumbling about *my* "ghastly affront," Lidia Sergeevna neglected to mention that mine was a response to *her* insult. Upon learning this, Dmitri Petrovich showed exceptional impartiality and a great pedagogical talent: although I was a twelve-year-old pupil and Lidia Sergeevna was an adult teacher, he felt—a rare quality in the Soviet Union—that regardless of age and status, human dignity must not be offended. As a longtime educator myself, I unreservedly subscribe to this commendable principle. Dmitri Petrovich dismissed the case, reinstated me at school, and presumably had a serious talk with Lidia Sergeevna, sternly reprimanding her for the insulting remark. At any rate, she never again "mispronounced" my last name.

In addition to being fascinated with literature and history, I also enjoyed studying English. At the age of eight or so, I began taking private English lessons from Mr. Stein, who affectionately nicknamed me Ginger. Mr. Stein, a short, rotund, bald, and bespectacled man in his early sixties, hailed from London. A member of the British Communist Party, Mr. Stein enthusiastically moved in the early 1930s to the Homeland of Socialism. His euphoria did not last long. Soon, sure enough, he and his wife were sent off to the Gulag, which they both managed to survive. I was taking lessons from Mr. Stein together with Zhenia Vornovitsky, my distant cousin (our maternal great-grandmothers were sisters), six months my junior. Zhenia was habitually late to the lessons. Finally, Mr. Stein lost his cool and asked Zhenia as to why he was always tardy. "I need to walk around puddles," (*Mne nado obkhodit′ luzhi*) was Zhenia's ingenuous reply. Since then the phrase has become one of our family proverbs. "She was late for the meeting." "But of course—she needed to walk around puddles."

Subsequently, I took private English lessons from Amalia Evgen´evna, a vivacious, mousy-faced spinster in her mid-fifties. Amalia Evgen´evna had lived in the United States before World War II and taught me and my classmate Sasha Lebedev the American English pronunciation that served me in good stead in later years. She inculcated in me a great love for Edgar Allan Poe and Mark Twain. Sasha and I read *The Adventures of Tom Sawyer* with her and even staged the dead cat scene for the entertainment of our families. Under Amalia Evgen´evna's influence and with her encouragement, I submitted an application to a newly founded English school, so called because most of the instruction therein was conducted in English. As a Jew, I had a very slim chance of being accepted there. Moreover, for my examination, I wrote an essay on Poe, "a decadent American writer," instead of a conventional Soviet writer, such as, say, Alexander Fadeev or Mikhail Sholokhov. Unsurprisingly, I was denied admission to this specialized, highly privileged school. I was not too upset about it because I knew that the school was intended mainly for children of high-ranking Party officials, who then went on to study at the Moscow State Institute of International Relations (*Moskovsky Gosudarstvennyi Institut Mezhdunarodnykh Otnoshenii*, or MGIMO for short). That institute trained the cadres of Soviet diplomats and overseas KGB functionaries, and a Jewish boy like me had no place in such an "elite" establishment. Although the reason for rejecting my application to the English school was not given, aside from my Jewishness and not belonging to the high stratum of the Soviet society, it was no doubt the Poe essay, which the school administration viewed as "groveling before the West" (*nizkopoklonstvo pered Zapadom*), that sealed my fate.

Needless to say, when English was offered in the fifth grade (I was eleven at the time), it became one of my favorite subjects—to no small degree because I was secretly enamored of the teacher, Liubov´ Yakovlevna Feigina. She had a kind, intelligent, classically proportioned face, almond-shaped brown eyes, dark slicked-back hair, a tall, slender figure, and was apparently in her mid-thirties. All I could do to express my affection for Liubov´ Yakovlevna was to be the best in class, which was not so hard after my studies with Mr. Stein and Amalia Evgen´evna, and to blush profusely, which was even easier because of my redheadedness. Liubov´ Yakovlevna no doubt discerned my feelings for her; she treated me with great gentleness and always called upon me when nobody else could answer a question.

Called upon in English class. Moscow, 1957.

I did not fare so well with the Home Room teacher, Isaak Lazarevich Segal, who also taught math. Mr. Segal was a teeny man with snow-white hair, a vinegary facial expression, and a poor sense of humor. Isaak Lazarevich viewed my hyperactive behavior in his class, which I found quite vapid, as utterly disturbing. To make things worse, Isaak Lazarevich received reports from other teachers about my sabotaging pranks. On one occasion, the blackboard was soaped; on another, sugar was poured into inkwells before a quiz, making the ink unusable. I was rightly suspected of these pranks, but, I am sure, no classmate squealed on me. These antics certainly did not warm Isaak Lazarevich's heart toward me. When I was ready to transfer to another school at the end of my eighth grade, Mr. Segal channeled all his frustration with me into the letter of reference. With this letter, which depicted me as a juvenile delinquent, I could have only been dispatched to a correctional institution. My mother intervened, Isaak Lazarevich softened his stance, and I was admitted to the new school, where I studied for a year. Because of its proximity to Moscow University and to the building in which many families of the university personnel lived, the school (then no. 14, now no. 26) had a slew of first-rate teachers and an above-average contingent of students. One of them was the soon-to-become-famous actress Inna Churikova, two years my senior, who also happened to reside in our enormous building. As before, my favorite classes were Russian literature, history, and English. A new subject, chemistry, albeit a distant fourth, joined that list, owing, no doubt, to the influence of the school's chemistry teacher.

Before I turned sixteen, my parents and I began discussing my future. Had I not lived in a totalitarian state and had had my druthers, I would have pursued my calling in literature or history. But this was not a given. I did not wish to subject myself to an interminable torrent of Soviet ideological gibberish, as would have been the case with the humanities, and decided to choose a relatively neutral field instead. For a while, I wanted to follow in my mother's footsteps: I aspired to become a doctor because, as lofty as it may sound, I entertained the idea of, if not saving people's lives, at least alleviating their suffering. I also wished to become a physician because I liked the atmosphere of the university hospital in which my mother worked and which I frequently visited. I was aware, of course, that doctors toiled long hours, might be paged at any time, and were expected, as I knew my mother was, to work night shifts. My parents were concerned, however, that as a Jew I might have difficulties getting in. When not long before, in late 1958, the Khrushchev administration announced that those, with two or more years of work experience would have an easier time entering universities, my parents decided that I should pursue this track. My father, who worked as an engineer at the industrial plant, arranged for me to be admitted there as an apprentice welder.

Most employees in the department in which I worked for the next two years were in their early to mid-thirties. They had been orphaned in their teens during World War II and were sent to special trade schools to acquire practical occupations—locksmith, lathe turner, or welder. From what I gathered, their labor morale was low and their productivity was at the bare minimum. As it turned out, they had no incentive to act otherwise. One of them explained that if they worked harder, they would receive a one-time small bonus for extra production but then their monthly quota would be permanently increased. "Not worth the effort," he remarked. These men were skillful workers, but the system corrupted them to the point that they preferred to play dominoes in the locker room rather than exert themselves for their measly wages. Or as the popular Soviet saying went: "They pretend to pay us, and we pretend to work" (*Oni delaiut vid, chto nam platiat, a my delaem vid, chto rabotaem*). They treated me fairly well, except for occasional "good-natured" anti-Semitic slurs, such as, "After finishing high school, are you going to work in a store?" (*Konchish´ shkolu, poidesh´ v lavochku torgovat´?*), or "Abrasha, try some chicken broth" (*Abrasha, poprobui kurinyi bul'ion*). When voicing these phrases, they overdid the interrogative inflexion and exaggeratedly rolled the *r*'s the "Jewish" way. They also persistently but unsuccessfully tempted me to have a drink and a smoke.

As a trainee, I was assigned to Volodia Lobanov, a man twice my age. Volodia was married and had a daughter. He always referred to his wife, who worked at the post office, merely as "my woman" (*moia baba*). Though in no way burly, Volodia was a gymnast in his youth, had powerful biceps, and was the arm-wrestling champion of our department. He did not smoke and seldom drank alcohol—a rare exception among his peers. Volodia was an experienced worker, from whom I was supposed to learn the intricacies of welding. In spite of my mentor's angelic patience and desperate attempts, I remained, as he put it, "weldingly inept" because my fingers are all thumbs, and clumsy thumbs at that. I was prudent enough to wear goggles, but every now and then I forgot to put on welding gloves. As a result, I ended up with a few metal chards in my hands. These dark-blue "pellets" have served as mementos of my far-flung past. It looked as though I had already been, albeit unwittingly, in the service of the "Israeli military machine" (*izrail'skaia voenshchina*). Let it be known that the industrial plant where I worked designed and produced engines for MIGs, Soviet military aircraft. These aircraft most likely were used a few years later in the Six-Day War against Israel. Those Soviet MIGs did not do very well in the dogfights against French Mirages. I suspect that was primarily because of the superiority of Israeli pilots, but also perhaps, I like to think, because of my abysmal welding skills.

While working by day, I was studying by night in the tenth and final grade at the so-called School for Working Youth (*Shkola Rabochei Molodezhi*). Most pupils, except for a couple of guys like me, were regular workers who for the most part were ill-prepared and not too studious. They simply needed a school diploma that would entitle them to a promotion and a pay raise. The teachers at that school were of the same substandard caliber. I vividly remember the school principal and history teacher, Makushkin, who kept using one and the same quip. Whenever it became stuffy in the classroom, he would say, "Let's open the window and each drink a cup of fresh air." Makushkin also liked to ask the class for the definition of the "party" (having in mind, of course, the ruling Communist Party) and would always proffer the answer himself with a grin of triumphant glee across his unintelligent face: "Party is the leading, mobilizing, and organizing force of the working class." No wonder that without studying too hard I managed to receive a fairly decent high school diploma, consisting mainly of As and only of two or three Bs.

In the spring of 1962, when I was about to finish high school, Mother told me that I should forget about becoming a physician: because of the severe shortage of military doctors, medical schools' entire classes were expected to fill this gap. There was a truly dreadful prospect of ending up in the middle of nowhere, not to mention having virtually no chance for professional advancement. Being mildly interested in chemistry, I decided to apply instead to the Department of Chemistry at Moscow University.

While making this last-minute decision, I had to face a serious problem: one of the Department of Chemistry entrance exams was in math, which at the time was not required by medical schools. As a result, I found myself insufficiently primed for this subject and received merely a

C for it, while scoring As in chemistry and physics, and consequently was not admitted. With this Moscow University score, I could have easily entered several available chemical institutes, such as the Moscow Institute of Chemical Technology or the Moscow Institute of Oil and Gas (ironically, all these were upgraded to "universities" in the post-Soviet era). Although not as prestigious as the Department of Chemistry at Moscow University, they all the same provided a decent higher education. The entrance exams at these institutes were deliberately held a month later than at Moscow University, allowing for such an eventuality. But for some strange reason, I felt too proud to settle for what I perceived as second best and decided to devote another year to preparing for the Moscow University exams, especially in math.

I continued for one more year as a welder at the industrial plant and spent all my free time studying for the exams. My parents, who were surprised at my decision to forgo the institutes, never before saw me applying myself so seriously to any task. (As a matter of fact, after I finished cramming for the exams, math first and foremost, I threw out a cartful of prep materials.) The next year, 1963, the entrance exams consisted of five subjects: math, physics, chemistry, English, and literature. I got As (fives) in all subjects but literature, in which—O irony of ironies—I received a B (a four). Since the overall passing requirement was 23 and I scored 24 points, I became a Moscow University student.

My being admitted should by no means suggest an absence of anti-Semitism in the decision-making process. At that time, the Soviet government passed a secret resolution, to which Mother was privy as a medical school faculty: the number of accepted Jewish students had to be apportioned, give or take, to the Jewish population in the country and thus should not exceed 2 percent. This policy was more wicked by far than in Imperial Russia, where the *numerus clausus* against the Jews was official and amounted to 5 percent at institutions of higher learning. I vividly remember witnessing the following heartrending scene: a Jewish teenager, whose last name was Vol´fson, a native of Odessa, stood sobbing while his father inquired at the Admissions Office for the reason the young man was not let in. The youngster graduated from high school with great honors (as a straight-A student, he was awarded a gold medal) and was a prizewinner at chemistry olympiads. The admissions official replied that indeed the applicant had received As in entrance exams on all subjects but literature, for which he had received an F. When the father asked to see his son's literary composition, the official refused. This was a blatant case of ethnic discrimination, plain and simple.

Soon after I matriculated at Moscow University, I received a surprise invitation to the reunion of my classmates from school no. 312. As I mentioned earlier, I had been extremely small for my age: at thirteen, I was barely five feet tall. Having short parents—Father was five feet three, and Mother five feet two—I was not expected to be much taller than they. Mother's forecast for me was five feet four, five feet five, tops. I remember sitting and praying, sitting and praying not to be so short and to grow at least as tall as Mother's cousin, Kuba, who was five feet eight. To be as tall as my cousin Gera, ten years my senior, who was five feet ten, was an unthinkable dream.

At that juncture, I saw *Wee Geordie*. This charming British film, by now almost completely forgotten, is about a Scottish boy who was so little that he had to climb up on a stool to reach the blackboard. Having been constantly teased by his classmates for his diminutive figure—hence the movie title—Geordie mail-ordered a set of bodybuilding exercises that turned him into a tall and powerfully built young man (played by Bill Travers, who was six feet six), so much so that he represented the United Kingdom in the hammer throw at the Melbourne Olympic Games. Funny as it may sound, the movie provided me with a great encouragement and motivation. In addition to prayers, I began cross-country skiing and skating in wintertime, playing volleyball and basketball, running track and field, and rowing. Rowing, in which I was engaged for a year, between the ages of fifteen and sixteen, was particularly enjoyable and greatly contributed to my physical development. It so happened that one of my mother's patients was a rowing coach. As a token of gratitude for Mother's successful treatment of his asthma, he invited me to join the club. It was great to exercise indoors and even more so to row with a crew on the Moscow River. Unfortunately, I had to quit all this as soon as I began working at the plant by day and going to school by night and thus had no time for physical training. These athletic activities did not turn me into a hefty giant, but the results exceeded all my expectations. Between the ages of thirteen and fifteen, I grew eight inches. I ate so ferociously—mainly beef and fried potatoes—that, as my Great-Aunt Sofia commented, Mother needed a second job just to feed me.

At the age of eighteen, I was a rather well-built young man and stood five feet eleven. In 1963, my former classmates invited me to their reunion, but we had not seen each other in three years or so. When I entered the room, everyone gasped. Nobody could believe it was I and recognized me only by my red hair. Fifteen years later, I recalled this incident when watching a somewhat similar episode from the sitcom *Taxi*. There, Louie De Palma, played by Danny DeVito, does not want to go to his school reunion because he is short and unsightly. As a schoolboy, he was constantly ill-treated by his classmates, and the only thing that kept him going was his desire to get even with them at some point in the future. That is why he ultimately agrees to the suggestion of Bobby Wheeler, played by Jeff Conaway, a tall and handsome fellow and an aspiring actor who learns to impersonate Louie by emulating his speech patterns and mannerisms to perfection. Posing as Louie, Bobby makes a splash at the reunion and gets even with Louie's tormentors. Additionally, Louie comes unrecognized to watch how everyone reacts to his ruse and inadvertently—by touching the hair of his one-time classmate Sheila, played by Arlene Golonka—turns the party into a complete disaster. In the instance of my own reunion, I had to impersonate myself, as it were—that is how unrecognizable I had become. All the girls, of whom I had been enamored over the years and who had rejected me one after another, surrounded me, vying for my attention. One of them was so bold as to ask me out. At that time, I was already dating a young woman and therefore politely declined the offer.

Our Department of Chemistry class of 1968 contained about four hundred freshmen divided into smaller groups of twenty to twenty-five students. Unlike a four-year college system in the United States, the Soviet higher education system was five years long, its last year focused upon conducting experiments and writing a diploma thesis. There were some older students who either had served in the Soviet army or had been employed for a few years in industry and were admitted under conditions favorable for veterans and workers. Some of them were intelligent, studied hard, and in due time became excellent specialists. But there were others, not so terribly bright, such as Ivan Kartashov, the laughing stock of the entire class, who did not speak proper Russian and was virulently anti-Semitic. I remember one of his Judeophobic diatribes. While talking to another ethnically Russian older student, he said, "We had worked our butts off at machine-tools, whereas dese . . ." (*My vkalyvali u stanka, a enti . . .*), and with those words he pointed his accusatory finger at several Jewish students, myself included. Kartashov either did not know or conveniently forgot that I too had "worked my butt off" as a welder for two years before entering university. It is true that my working experience was more of an anomaly. The vast majority of students, regardless of their ethnicity, entered the university right after high school, and so Kartashov's slur was foolish and completely off the mark. In Russian, Kartashov used the substandard *enti* instead of the correct *èti* ("these") and was duly nicknamed Enti and Vania Kursky, the latter because he hailed from the Kursk province.

I also encountered anti-Semitism among professors, albeit in a more genteel form. While at university, we were expected to study an additional foreign language to enable us to read specialized literature. Those who had studied German, French, or Spanish in high school were supposed to study English; those, like me, who had studied English, were supposed to study German. Oddly, our German-language instructor, Galina Khristoforovna Kniga—her surname incidentally signifies a "book" in Russian—attributed my being best in the class to my good command of Yiddish. No matter how many times I told her that I did not know Yiddish—only a slim smattering of words and phrases, which obviously should not count—she kept insisting otherwise. It seems that she had a problem accepting the idea that a Jewish student could be so good in her beloved subject. My putative proficiency in Yiddish, which was supposed to give me a head start in German, was the only way she could reconcile with that fact.

In addition to Soviet citizens from all over the country, there were some foreign nationals, mainly from the "brotherly socialist countries" (*iz bratskikh stran sotsializma*), such as Hungary and North Vietnam. These close-knit groups of ten to fifteen students each habitually kept to themselves and interacted very little, if at all, with their Soviet peers. Not all foreigners were from the Soviet satellite states, though. There were also a handful of students from Western countries, presumably belonging to families with pro-communist leanings. I remember one such student, Nadine, in our group. Her father was a wealthy businessman, originally from Algeria, but the family relocated to France and resided in Paris. She was apparently smitten with me, but I did not find her attractive in the least. Even though Nadine resided in Moscow, she lived in a bubble. She presumably stayed in some fancy, privileged dorm, or even a ritzy hotel, and was blissfully ignorant of what it meant to be a Soviet citizen. Once, in lab, Nadine all of a sudden approached me and invited to join her for the weekend. When I inquired as to where she would like us to go, Nadine matter-of-factly told me that she was planning "to hop over to Helsinki." As a foreign national with a French passport, she did not have the slightest idea how preposterously unattainable for me her invitation was, even if I wished to join her. I did not want to get into explaining the sheer impossibility of my going abroad at any time, let alone on such short notice, and simply told Nadine that I was busy that weekend.

In mid-October 1964, soon after I began my sophomore year, Nikita Khrushchev, the Communist Party chairman and head of the Soviet government, was deposed. Khrushchev's rivals found many of his foreign and domestic policies erratic and harmful, but the official explanation, at least in the beginning, was that he left the office "for health reasons" (*po sostoianiiu zdorov´ia*). These policies ranged from threatening "to bury" Western countries and quarrels with China to attempting to grow corn in regions with the unsuitable climate, for which Khrushchev was dubbed "the Corn Man" (*Kukuruznik*). He was also accused of unduly bragging that "the Soviet Union will overtake and surpass the United States in per capita production of meat, milk, and butter" (*Sovetsky Soiuz dogonit i peregonit Ameriku po proizvodstvu miasa, moloka i masla na dushu naseleniia*) and that "The current generation of Soviet people will live under communism" (*Nyneshnee pokolenie sovetskikh liudei budet zhit´ pri kommunizme*), whatever that was supposed to be. Khrushchev's removal from office ended a brief and relatively relaxed period of the so-called Thaw. It commenced the twenty-year epoch, during which Leonid Brezhnev, that thick-browed boar of a man (*brovastyi borov*, as I had alliteratively nicknamed him in

Russian in 1970), and his minions tried to turn back the clock in an effort, quite successful I might add, to re-Stalinize the country. There were many jokes alluding to this. One of them came from the fictional Armenian Radio series.[34] The Armenian Radio was asked to define the state of affairs in the Soviet Union. The Armenian Radio answered: "*Po-brezhnemu.*" This portmanteau locution plays on *po-prezhnemu* ("as before") and Brezhnev's last name, thereby suggesting, perhaps a trifle exaggeratedly, that things remained unchanged from Stalin's times.

The day after Khrushchev's dismissal, Party bigwigs instructed the university administration to conduct informational sessions with students and sent ideologues to all its colleges and departments. We students were assembled in the main auditorium. The lecturer who was assigned to enlighten us bore a fitting surname—Iezuitova. In Russian, "*iezuit,*" aside from denoting a member of the Roman Catholic order, figuratively implies a "deceitful, duplicitous person," evidently reflecting the age-old conflict between the Russian Orthodox and the Roman Catholic churches. Comrade Iezuitova explained that Khrushchev had been removed from office because, among other things, he had aspired to build up a cult of personality around himself, thereby deviating from the Party line. After the lecture, Comrade Iezuitova graciously agreed to take some written questions from the audience. The very first note that Comrade Iezuitova, not anticipating any pitfalls, rather imprudently read aloud, stopped her dead in her tracks. The note contained an ostensibly innocuous query: "In view of your explanation of the reasons for Khrushchev's removal from the office, is it possible that striving for a personality cult is inherent in the Soviet system?" The question made a lot of sense: after all, the Stalin era exemplified that repugnant phenomenon, and although Khrushchev debunked Stalin's cult of personality, he slowly but surely created one of his own. Upon reading the note for all to hear and realizing its implications, Comrade Iezuitova gasped. The note incensed her to such a degree that her face turned beet red. Instead of answering the question, Comrade Iezuitova went completely berserk. She banged the podium with her fist

---

34 A series of jokes presented in the format of the imaginary radio station answering questions asked by its listeners.

and demanded to know who wrote it. When no one stood up to acknowledge the authorship, she threatened us in a typical totalitarian fashion: "Don't you worry! We have handwriting experts. We'll find out who wrote the note!" And she flounced out of the auditorium in a fury.

After my first year, I came to the realization that chemistry was not my cup of tea. I decided to do just the bare minimum that would keep me afloat to allow for satisfactory grades and spent most of my time reading works of literature. For a while, I was captivated by Boris Pasternak's poetry. However, I was greatly disillusioned by his novel, *Doctor Zhivago*, which was officially banned from the Soviet Union but circulated in *samizdat*. Even at the age of twenty, I found Pasternak's narration disjointed and contrived, his characters stock and stale, and his jabs at Judaism offensive and objectionable. However, the man of letters who has invariably captivated my imagination and has never disappointed me was Osip Mandel´shtam—in my view, the greatest Russian-language poet of the twentieth century. I was entranced and deeply moved by his *Voronezh Notebooks* (*Voronezhskie tetradi*), which I also read in *samizdat* because the Soviet regime did not dare to publish the poems. As for prose, I was spellbound by Mikhail Bulgakov's *Master and Margarita*, which appeared in the monthly *Moscow* in the late 1966 and early 1967 issues, albeit with considerable censorial excisions, as I later found out. Other eye-openers for all of us at the time, regardless of their inferior literary merit, were Alexander Solzhenitsyn's *In the First Circle* (*V kruge pervom*), *The Cancer Ward* (*Rakovyi korpus*), and *The Gulag Archipelago* (*Arkhipelag GULAG*), all of which I also read in *samizdat*.

In addition, I frequented literary events, in particular at the auditorium of the famous Polytechnic Museum, where I attended the memorable poetry readings of Andrei Voznesensky and Bulat Okudzhava. I also remember an evening of Evgeny Evtushenko's poetry at the Variety Theater on a bitterly cold wintry night in early 1966, if my memory serves me right. On that occasion, the poet most fittingly read, with characteristic ululations fashionable at the time, his then freshly written "The White Snows Are Falling" ("*Idut belye snegi*"). Voznesensky, Okudzhava, and Evtushenko were the literary idols worshipped by the youth of the 1960s.

Here I allow myself a slight digression. I never met Voznesensky or Okudzhava in person, but I did meet Evtushenko many years later, in the spring of 2006, when he visited Cornell. Evtushenko gave a poetry reading, which he titled "Walk on the Ledge" (*Progulka po karnizu*) after his then newly published bilingual collection of poetry. In this recitation, Evtushenko proved himself a good pop art entertainer and showman. In spite of being in his early seventies, Evtushenko moved with great vigor. Although not a great fan of his poetry, I was quite taken with his performance as his gangly, agile figure in a flashy jacket and a clownish cap darted to and fro, covering the entire stage. Evtushenko also impressed me as an ultimate egocentric. When I struck up a conversation with him in the intermission, any topic upon which we touched he would turn around to himself. When he heard that I taught Russian literature and was a Nabokov scholar, first thing he blurted out was: "Have you read my essay on Nabokov?" Over dinner at a local Greek restaurant, Evtushenko talked to everyone, including the proprietor, with whom the poet exchanged a couple of phrases in Greek, which he, by his own admission, picked up when visiting Cyprus. Evtushenko resides with his fourth wife and their children in Tulsa, Oklahoma, where he teaches part-time at the city university. He quizzed me and other fellow diners on the Cornell admission process because one of his five sons was a high school junior at the time.

To return to my main narration, in the mid-1960s, I began writing and translating poetry. I tried my hand at rendering poems by Robert Frost, Langston Hughes, and Archibald MacLeish into Russian. A couple of times, my original poetry and translations were printed in *Moskovsky Universitet*, the Moscow University student newspaper. On occasion, I attended the Translators' Wednesdays at the Central House of Literati. There, I witnessed the symposia of such remarkable stars as Sergei Shervinsky, Vil´gel´m Levik, Margarita Aliger, Asar Eppel´, Shimon Markish, Rakhil´ Baumvol´, and Zinovy Telesin.

Several years later, I became aware of Baumvol´ and Telesin's son, Julius, a mathematician and chess player, and a known dissident. For his prominent role in the dissemination of *samizdat*, Julius was nicknamed the Prince of Samizdat (*Prints Samizdatsky*), an obvious play on the royal title of Hamlet, *Prints Datsky*—Prince of Denmark. Julius himself was not devoid of literary sensibilities, which he most likely inherited from his parents: he translated poetry and prose. While still in Moscow, he reportedly adorned his apartment with an enormous official poster—"FIFTY YEARS OF THE SOVIET CIRCUS" (*Piat'desiat let sovetskogo tsirka*). Its copy had adorned the pediment of the Moscow circus building, but even humorless Soviet bureaucrats soon understood the slogan's equivocal nature—"circus" as institution and art form and "circus" as an allusion to the chaotic and malfunctioning hubbub of the entire Soviet system—and the poster was taken down.[35] Upon his immigration to Israel, Julius compiled and published a collection of Soviet political jokes, *One Thousand and One Anecdotes* (*Tysiacha i odin anekdot*), some of which, I suspect, he himself composed. His witticisms circulated widely. When asked what he thought of Israel, Julius reportedly declared—hyperbolically but not totally without foundation—"Everything's the same, only in Hebrew" (*Vsë to zhe samoe, tol'ko na ivrite*).

In the 1960s, Moscow University was still geographically divided: the sciences were located on Sparrow Hills in the southwestern part of Moscow, whereas the humanities were housed in the original downtown compound on Mokhovaia Street. I very much wanted to attend classes on literature, but for that I needed special permission because my chemistry student ID card did not entitle me to do so. Whenever I tried to obtain such permission at the Dean's Office, I would be told that if I had spare time on my hands, I should spend it in chemistry lab. In general, the Soviet educational system discouraged well-rounded learning and was geared instead toward producing narrow professionals, or in the parlance of my physician mother, "left nostril specialists." It proved to be a great handicap for many émigrés. Finally, in my third year, after numerous applications, denials, and appeals, I received the coveted permission to audit classes on Mokhovaia Street. I distinctly remember the presentations of Sergei Mikhailovich Bondi, a great authority on Pushkin. In his brilliant lectures, sparkling with wit and humor, Bondi recited Pushkin's poems and sang *romansy*, their lyrics set to music, while accompanying himself on the piano.

I also enjoyed going to a variety of musical events, notably the International Tchaikovsky Competition, which I attended diligently

---

35   See Alexander Podrabinek, "Tsirk uekhal, a klouny ostalis'" ["The Circus Had Left but the Clowns Stayed"], http://podrabinek.livejournal.com/16850.html.

throughout most of the 1960s. I vividly recall the 1965 Isaac Stern recital and the 1969 Herbert von Karajan concert as the pinnacles of the Moscow musical life of the decade. At these epochal events, the public, disgruntled by the scarcity of tickets, literally broke down the doors and thronged into the Moscow State Conservatory, and the mounted police were called in to restore order.

Initially, I had no ticket for the Stern recital and started asking passersby for an extra one, which in the end I luckily obtained. One person I asked was a tiny old man in his mid-seventies, smartly dressed, who wore gold-rimmed glasses and exuded a professorial air. He had a well-matched old woman by his side, diminutive and festively clad. As I stood on the corner of Granovsky and Gertsen Streets (as they were known then), the couple was walking slowly toward me in a stately, self-important manner. When they approached me, I asked them for a spare ticket. The man, visibly annoyed, glared at me disapprovingly. He did not dignify me with a response, and the couple proceeded with great pomp toward the conservatory. The elder's face looked vaguely familiar. A bystander who witnessed the scene solved the puzzle: "Don't you realize that you just addressed Molotov himself?" he asked. So that is who this old man was! Thank heaven, this was my single encounter, and under such innocuous circumstances, with one of Stalin's closest henchmen, the chief negotiator of the notorious Ribbentrop-Molotov Pact between Nazi Germany and the Soviet Union, a signatory to numerous execution lists—one of the greatest villains of the twentieth century!

I have also always loved the fine arts, even though on my first visit to the Tret´iakov Gallery at the age of five or six I ran around from one room to the next and counted paintings. But while running and counting, I evidently became fascinated with art and later regularly attended museums and art exhibits in my boyhood and youth. When I was ten, my parents went to see the farewell exposition of the Dresden art collection, which the Red Army captured as a war trophy in Nazi Germany. In 1955, the Moscow government was returning these art treasures to the Saxonian capital, which was part of the Soviet-controlled East Germany. My parents considered themselves extremely fortunate to obtain two tickets. For my part, I vividly remember how crestfallen I felt that I could not join them. But even if they had an extra ticket, I would not have been allowed to attend the exposition because it was off limits to little children like me. I became somewhat cheered up when my parents brought home the catalogue. Although it contained poor-quality black-and-white reproductions, I was mesmerized by these celebrated works of art. (Forty or so years later, upon visiting Dresden, I went to see my old acquaintances and was intoxicated by their remarkable splendor.) During my student years, in 1966, I remember going to the posthumous display of Robert Fal´k's paintings in a small exhibition hall on Begovaia Street. The same year, there was an exposition of Alexander Tyshler's works at the Pushkin State Museum of Fine Arts. Both caused quite a stir among the visitors, and the horde at Fal´k's exhibit was so tumultuous that order, once again, had to be maintained by the mounted police.

Aside from my predilection for reading, writing and translating poetry, and my fondness for music and the fine arts, I also took an interest in the stage and frequently attended avant-garde productions at the Taganka and Sovremennik Theaters, which naturally were a source of great concern and consternation for the regime. In 1967, I went so far as to join the university theater troupe. I was thrilled to learn that it planned a production of *Rhinoceros* by Eugène Ionesco, whose dramaturgy I greatly admired. I was excited when the play parts were distributed, and we the cast began reading them out. My excitement, as it turned out, was premature and short-lived. The production was soon closed down after the Soviet censorial guardians had discovered Ionesco's resolute anticommunist and pro-Israel stance. The ideological watchdogs decided that Vladimir Maiakovsky's jingoistic propaganda poem *150,000.000* should be staged instead. I immediately quit the troupe in protest.

Equally unsuccessful were my cinematic pursuits. To familiarize myself with movie-making, I signed up as an extra at the Mosfilm Studio and was assigned to the production of *Anna Karenina*, the screen version of Leo Tolstoy's novel set in the late nineteenth century. I remember how irked I was when an assistant director told me that my face was "too modern" for the front seating in the opera house scene and relegated me to the back row, completely out of sight. Even more disheartening was my experience with another movie, *Arena*, set in Nazi-occupied Europe. This shabbily made film attempted to show how the international circus, staffed with artists from different countries, successfully resisted the Nazis, even at the expense of their own lives. I was offered the role of a Nazi soldier because of my "Aryan" appearance, red-haired and blue-eyed. Although I perfectly realized that it was just a movie, as a Jew I adamantly refused to impersonate a Nazi under any circumstance and was summarily dismissed from the set. Thus, my movie "career" was abruptly and ingloriously nipped in the bud.

"Starring" in the movie *The Grandmaster*. Pärnu, Estonia, August 1972.

Five years later, I was given a chance for its revival. In August 1972, after the trial at which I was sentenced to one year of "corrective labor" and before serving the sentence (see Chapter 5), my parents took me to recuperate to the Estonian town of Pärnu, the Baltic Sea resort. There I was approached by the assistant director of *The Grandmaster* (*Grossmeister*), a movie about a chess player, with Andrei Miagkov in the title role. The movie contains a brief tennis court episode, and I was asked to don a white tennis shirt and white shorts and to sit in the stands. My prison buzz cut, which had grown out somewhat, looked more like a sportsman's close-cropped hairdo. The assistant director thought that my athletic and "Nordic" physical appearance—red hair, blue eyes, and light-blond brows and eyelashes—would help to convey the Baltic *couleur locale*. My bad cinematographic luck, however, continued to haunt me. The film was premiered in 1973, about a year after I left Soviet Russia for Israel, and, following a brief showing, was expunged from circulation and shelved for many years. This was because Viktor Korchnoi, a distinguished chess player, who had a supporting role in the movie and who acquitted himself admirably as an actor, fell out of favor with the Soviet regime and finally, in 1976, defected to the Netherlands. I recently watched the movie on YouTube and did not find myself in the tennis court episode. It is possible that vigilant Soviet censors recognized me prior to the movie release and insisted on cutting out the footage with the "Zionist traitor."

Aside from a slew of courses in chemistry, physics, and advanced math, there was the inevitable evil of obligatory ideological courses, but thankfully their number was far fewer than for the humanities students. Among them, there was a course on the history of the Communist Party, not to mention an oxymoronic, and moronic, monstrosity called "The Foundations of Scientific Communism," for which I proudly received a well-earned C. In addition, we had mandatory military classes (the Soviet equivalent of ROTC) in chemical warfare. Our instructor, who bore the Chekhovian surname, Captain Telegin, was a tall, dark-blond man in his late thirties, good-natured and fair-minded.[36] On occasion, Telegin was replaced by Colonel Dvorkin, a man in his mid-fifties. Although small in stature, Dvorkin carried himself with dignity and was a great stickler for the Russian language. Whenever a student would make a grammatical mistake, Dvorkin would be visibly annoyed and would go on a linguistic binge to explain the mistake and to correct it.

After the fourth year, all male students who had not previously served in the army were sent to boot camp under Captain Telegin's supervision. Upon completing a two-month course, we were expected to receive the lowest officer rank—third lieutenant in reserve. The camp was situated at

---

36   Telegin, nicknamed Waffles, is a minor character in Anton Chekhov's play *Uncle Vanya*.

a military base in the Briansk Province, about two hundred miles southwest of Moscow. We were lodged in big tents, each accommodating up to eight people. The tents were set up right on the edge of a thick forest, resplendent with blueberries, of which I have always been so fond. I set my eyes on the berries, eagerly awaiting an opportunity to sink my teeth into them. One day such an opportunity presented itself. I managed to play hooky from the studies and went to the nearby woods instead. I sat down on the ground, took off my belt and forage cap, and started devouring these magnificent berries. Just as I was in the middle of my blueberry spree, Captain Telegin and other officers passed by. It was no doubt quite an amusing picture: a redheaded youngster, with a face crimson from being caught red-handed, with his hands and mouth all ablue. Captain Telegin, the only one who acknowledged my presence, genially smiled, facetiously waved a scolding finger, and kept walking.

My other transgression was far more serious. It is common knowledge that drinking runs rampant in Russia, and my classmates were no exception. The closest grocery store that sold vodka was about a mile and a half from camp. Since I was a middle-distance runner and the grasshopper-built Serezha Torbin was a steeplechase runner, we were delegated to fetch alcohol for the guys. For the two of us it was a nice cross-country jog through the woods, and for the rest it was supposedly a much-needed fix after a day of drills and exercises. If Serezha and I had ever been caught carrying alcohol to the camp, we would have faced serious repercussions. But apparently the Almighty guarded over all of us, young and foolish: Serezha and I as well as the boozers came out of these symbiotic operations totally unscathed.

Another memorable incident, in which I was heavily involved, occurred when a semiliterate and anti-Semitic drill sergeant was picking on Fima Gottlieb, a meek Jewish fellow from Riga. I alerted the other students to what the drill sergeant was doing, and they supported me in my protest against his despicable behavior. I spoke my mind to the sergeant in front of the fellow students and told Captain Telegin about this ugly matter. He conducted himself in this affair honorably and efficiently and saw to it that the drill sergeant was instantly replaced.

In 1967–68, in the fifth and final year of my studies, when all the students in our class were sent off to all kinds of research institutions to work on their theses, I found myself in the catalysis lab of the Institute of Chemical Physics. The institute was commonly known as "Semenovka" after the name of its founder, the Nobel Prize chemistry laureate Nikolai Nikolaevich Semenov. Liah Yakovlevna Margolis, a gaunt, dark-haired, swarthy-skinned woman of small stature in her late fifties, one of the lab's leading scientists, initially took me under her wing. It did not take her long to size me up: "Shapiro has a good head on his shoulders, is quick-witted and sharp-tongued, but his hands . . . ," and with these last words Liah Yakovlevna would roll her small but expressive dark eyes. Hands or no hands, Liah Yakovlevna quickly discerned that I was not putting my whole mind to the project, and as a result, my progress was slow. In my specious self-defense, I tried to comfort myself by thinking that I was not the only one whose attention was distracted by extraneous matters. Indeed, the proximity of the retail store "Moscow" to the Semenov Institute caused mass distraction for its female lab personnel. At the time, ladies boots were, in the contemporary Soviet lingo, "the last scream of fashion" (*poslednii krik mody*). Women, who constituted the vast majority of the lab personnel, were keen on buying them, even though their average cost of about 60 to 70 rubles amounted to more than a half of their monthly earnings. Predictably, it was hard for these women to keep their mind on test tubes, flasks, and vials in the fear of missing the coveted boots. To prevent this from happening, they now and then took turns checking out the boot situation at the store, which greatly disrupted their teamwork.

As I was inwardly scoffing at these women for their mundane, materialistic pursuits, I had the audacity while in the lab to write poetry instead of working on my thesis. I did so in the sincere belief that *my* distraction was well justified because of its lofty nature. I am still grateful to Liah Yakovlevna for not throwing me out of the lab, which would have spelled my doom. I would have been summarily kicked out of the university and would have been immediately drafted into the Soviet army for at least three years. Instead, Liah Yakovlevna banished me—out of sight, out of mind—to another research institute and placed me under the care of a young ambitious Ph.D. student, a tall towhead from the northwestern city of Vologda, several years my senior. He and I forged an agreement: in exchange for his taking care of my master's thesis, which was a small portion of his doctoral dissertation anyway, I would translate English articles for him. With this arrangement, I had all the time in the world to read, write, and translate poetry. The hour of reckoning was rapidly approaching, however. Although my thesis was all written and nicely typed up, I had not the slightest idea of its essence and surely was ill-prepared to defend it before the university committee. Finally, my advisor sat down with me for half an hour and patiently explained the project. I tried to keep his explanations tightly in my head so as not to splash them out and rehearsed the delivery once or twice. As a result, I defended my thesis with flying colors. Naturally, I gave the advisor a bottle of the best available cognac for his pivotal role.

Earlier Liah Yakovlevna made a prediction that I would flunk the thesis defense. When I saw her shortly afterward at a concert of classical music and warmly greeted her, she deliberately turned her head away. Perhaps Liah Yakovlevna could not forgive me for proving her wrong and furthermore for making a farce out of what was supposed to be a scholarly presentation. In the early 1990s, by which time I taught Russian literature at Cornell, I chanced upon a visitor, a fellow graduate of the Department of Chemistry at Moscow University, who happened to know Liah Yakovlevna well. I asked her to pass on to Liah Yakovlevna my Cornell business card along with my warm regards. I do not know if she did, but I have not heard from my erstwhile momentary mentor. Liah Yakovlevna was a talented chemist who devoted all her long and industrious life (she died in 2007 at the age of ninety-seven) to research, and I genuinely regret if I offended her sense of scholarly duty with my juvenile mindlessness. I am immensely grateful for her supreme tolerance and nobility of heart. I can only imagine how I would have felt having a student uninterested in my beloved discipline and thus wasting my time.

Sometimes I am asked whether I regret spending five years on the subject that in the end turned out not to become my profession. Has it been of any use? Definitely! Learning always is. I enjoyed gaining an in-depth knowledge of the natural sciences, the classroom and the lecture-hall atmosphere, less so the unpredictably long hours in labs that to a great extent are what experimental chemistry is about. Chemistry also appealed to my visual sense and reinforced my imagination. I am certain that many of the research methods I acquired while studying chemistry have served me in good stead in my philological pursuits. Finally, unlike many of my fellow humanists, I have no inferiority complex toward scientists.

※ ※ ※

Even though I was born and raised in Soviet Russia, as a Jew I never considered it my homeland. Why? Because I never felt at home there. In my family, there was always a clear distinction between "us" and "them," and the government was characterized by the Yiddish word *di melukhe* (literally, "the kingdom"). Any Jewish religious and cultural education in the country was strictly prohibited. Like *conversos* in Inquisitional Spain, we observed Jewish holidays in secret lest our neighbors find out and report us to the authorities. Needless to say, it was even more dangerous to go to a synagogue full of informers and plainclothesmen. In Stalin's carnivorous times, this meant a labor camp and death, and in times more vegetarian—loss of a job.

Although my Jewish religious and cultural education was extremely meager, my ethnic education began at an early age and advanced at a rapid pace. This was thanks to the beneficial climate of the "friendship of nations" (*druzhba narodov*), charted by Joseph Stalin, the greatest expert on nationalities, who was also known as the Father of Nations (*Otets Narodov*). On that score, an exchange from the Armenian Radio series comes to mind. Asked to define friendship of nations, the Armenian Radio answered: "Friendship of nations is when Armenians, Russians, Ukrainians, Tajiks, and Estonians all join together to beat up Georgians."

My very first introduction to Jewishness occurred when I was just about five years old. My kindergarten mate, a Russian girl of whom I was secretly enamored, asked me why my last name did not end with "in" or "ov," like most Russian surnames. (Such shrewdness on the part of the little girl suggested that she was destined for greatness in human resources, personnel administration, or, who knows, even in the KGB.) I was puzzled by the question and sought an explanation from my mother. She then told me that it was because we were Jews, not Russians. I doubt I fathomed at the time what it meant but realized that we were different, other.

Two years later, my Jewish education progressed dramatically when on the very first day of school my deskmate, Zhenia Mukhin, welcomed me and Alik Gvirts, who was seated right in front of him, with "You're a Yid!" (*Ty zhid!*). Not knowing what this succinct salutation meant but sensing from Zhenia's tone that it was derogatory, both Alik and I, to Zhenia's great astonishment, returned the greeting with "You're a Yid yourself!" (*Ty sam zhid!*). That evening, my mother, her face turning sorrowful, explained what that "term" signified, one that I, alas, heard many times afterward in the Land of the Soviets.

Zhenia Mukhin was not a bad kid; he simply regurgitated what he heard at home from his semiliterate parents. Zhenia had a flair for the fine arts and as a child could already draw skillfully. He answered his calling and became an artist. Years later, when we were both in our late teens/early twenties, we would occasionally bump into one another and would have a nice friendly chat. Curiously, more than twenty years later, as if to compensate for Zhenia Mukhin's juvenile anti-Semitism, fate sent my way an attorney named Israel Mukhin, who notarized the Hebrew translation of my Moscow University diploma certificate in Jerusalem in 1975.

I was not the only Jewish boy in our class. There were also the earlier mentioned Sasha Goikhman and Alik Gvirts, along with Lenia Abramovich, Sema Pevzner, and Lenia Vizel′man. Once when a Russian kid made an anti-Semitic remark and assaulted Pevzner, a fight broke out between the Russian and the Jewish classmates. The fight ended as abruptly as it started when the powerfully built Vizel′man grabbed one of the opponents and threw him out the wide-open window into the school garden. Fortunately, the classroom was located on the first floor, and the lad got off with only a broken arm. When our teachers tried to find out what had happened, no one told on Vizel′man, and what is more, the anti-Semitic rants from our classmates ceased.

In my family, Stalin was loathed and despised. That is why in early March 1953, as a seven-and-a-half-year-old boy, I would listen to the bulletins of Stalin's failing health on the radio and would repeat as a mantra: "Drop dead! Drop dead! Drop dead!" (*Chtob ty sdokh! Chtob ty sdokh! Chtob ty sdokh!*). Little did I know that my wish was already answered because by then the dictator had kicked the bucket. Many years later, I found out that those in Stalin's entourage were so terrified of him and so badly wanted him dead that they did not call for medical assistance when he had a brain hemorrhage. As the vast majority of Soviet citizens were devastated by Stalin's death and were sobbing their hearts out, my father went to the famous pastry shop in Stoleshnikov Lane and bought its scrumptious chocolate torte and a score of its delectable pastries. Father's unpatriotic act raised a lot of eyebrows, but he was not swayed, and thus began the family tradition of celebrating the dictator's demise. Last time we marked it was in Jerusalem in 1978, on the twenty-fifth anniversary of the accursed tyrant's miraculous downfall.

As a physician, Mother was affected by the virulent anti-Semitic campaign of the late 1940s and early 1950s that the authorities dubbed "the struggle against cosmopolitans," "cosmopolitans" being a euphemism for Jews. The campaign culminated in the so-called Doctors' Plot (Stalin's attempted purge of Jewish doctors, who were falsely accused of plotting to assassinate Soviet leaders). Furthermore, one of the arrested physicians, Vladimir Nikitich Vinogradov, was the head of the department in which my mother worked. The Doctors' Plot was directed against Jews, but to avoid being accused of anti-Semitism, the regime detained a few non-Jews, one of whom was Vinogradov. Although ethnically Russian, Vinogradov too was "libeled" as a Jew: it was insinuated that his real name was Vaintraub (the German *Weintraube*, "grapes," is *vinograd* in Russian). Mother told me that Vinogradov was absolutely indifferent to the ethnicity of his personnel and cared only about their expert qualifications and capabilities. Vinogradov was an exception in another important respect: despite obvious pressures from the regime, he remained apolitical and never joined the Communist Party. Mother remembered how in one of his speeches Vinogradov called Lenin "Vladimir Ivanovich" instead of "Vladimir Il′ich." This slip of the tongue, at the time when all Soviet citizens were expected to worship and deify "the Founder of the First Socialist State in the History of Mankind" and "the Leader of the World Proletariat," could have been viewed as a serious transgression. After Stalin had died, the Doctors' Plot was repudiated by the new leadership, and all charges against the accused were dropped. Upon his release from jail, Vinogradov told his personnel that he, a seventy-year-old man, was put in irons and was badly beaten during interrogation as long as he continued to deny being part of the plot to murder Soviet leaders, Stalin first and foremost. The pummeling ceased when Vinogradov realized that the secret police would stop at nothing until they elicited, or more precisely beat, a confession out of him. He, therefore, admitted to the most bizarre accusations. He "confessed" that he was a quadruple spy—German, British, American, and Japanese. According to Stalin's script, the doctors were to be publicly executed in Red Square. There were widespread rumors that the Doctors' Plot was supposed to pave the way for the mass deportation of Soviet Jews.[37] If it was indeed the case, only Stalin's sudden but timely death saved the Jews and the indicted doctors from this diabolical scheme. Several months after his release from jail and after recuperating somewhat from this dreadful ordeal, Vinogradov returned to his duties. Mother told me that when at the beginning of a new school year, in the fall of 1953, he entered the auditorium to give a lecture, the medical staff and students alike greeted him with long standing ovations.

After Stalin's death, despite the risks, Father every now and then would go on Jewish holidays to the Moscow Choral Synagogue in Major Spasoglinishchevsky Lane (*Bol'shoi Spasoglinishchevsky pereulok*). (In 1961, the lane was renamed Arkhipov Street after the realist painter Abram Arkhipov, only to regain its previous appellation after the collapse of the Soviet regime. Jews used to joke that although Arkhipov was of peasant stock and ethnically Russian, his first name, Abram, a proverbial Jewish name in Russia, sealed the deal for the regime to name the street after him.) On one such occasion, in 1955, and fittingly on Purim, Father took me along with him. This was the first time I set foot in a Jewish house of worship. I vividly remember the imposing figure of the Israeli ambassador, General Iosef Avidar, who like Iosef Trumpeldor, his legendary namesake, lost his arm in the military. At this festive service, all children were called to the stage (*habima*) and made a lot of noise with ratchets (*raashanim*) each time Haman's name was uttered. Curiously, when I

---

37 See Roman Brackman, *The Secret File of Joseph Stalin: A Hidden Life* (London: Frank Cass, 2001), 388; Jonathan Brent and Vladimir P. Naumov, *Stalin's Last Crime: The Plot against the Jewish Doctors, 1948–1953* (New York: HarperCollins, 2003), 298–300.

shared my impressions of that memorable night of sixty years ago with my relative Shifra Katz, they sparked off a reminiscence of her own. Shifra recalled that her friend Rama, the elder daughter of General Avidar, had told her about this very Purim celebration in the Moscow synagogue. This was the earliest festivity Rama attended in the Soviet capital after her father assumed his ambassadorial post.

In the Soviet Union, at the age of sixteen one was supposed to receive an internal passport stating one's ethnicity. Since the ethnicity was listed on the fifth line of the passport, Jews semijokingly and self-deprecatingly dubbed themselves "invalids of the fifth group" or "invalids of the fifth paragraph" (*invalidy piatoi gruppy* or *invalidy piatogo punkta*). The passport was a crucial factor in official situations, such as applying to universities or looking for a job. But as the Soviet saying goes, "one is hit not on one's passport but in one's mug" (*b'iut ne po pasportu, a po morde*). So in street situations it was enough to be *perceived* as a Jew, without necessarily being one. My classmate Sasha Lebedev, with whom I took private English lessons, experienced this firsthand. Although ethnically Russian, he was regarded by the neighborhood urchins as a Jew and was often teased and beaten. My sister told me that when she briefly worked in some office before immigrating to Israel, her co-worker, an ethnic Russian, lamented her miserable fate. Ironically, the wretched girl had a "Jewish look" and was often called a "kikess" (*zhidovka*). It was all the more ironic because the girl was pouring her heart out to my sister with the last name of Shapiro. This surname is common among Ashkenazic Jews, unequivocally establishes the ethnicity of its bearer, and was used in anti-Semitic slurs in Soviet Russia. It appears in one such dig, which insinuated that Jews overpopulated Moscow and took over its prestigious downtown district, called Arbat. The story goes that two Jews ran into each other in the street, struck up a conversation, and one of them, an Arbat resident, invited the other over. The other Jew naturally asked for the address. "There is no need," his new pal replied. "Just come up to the middle of the district and shout 'Abramovich!' All windows will open, and one window will not. That's where I, Shapiro, live." Sadly, such anti-Semitic gibes, specifically those using my surname, are not confined to Soviet Russia. They can happen even in the United States, and even today, as the

"Theodore Shapiro" incident at the 2013 Academy Awards ceremony vividly demonstrates.[38]

It is owing to this "education" that I never considered Soviet Russia my homeland, and so leaving it behind was not hard for me in the least. Departing from Soviet Russia, on the other hand, was a different matter—a most difficult task indeed. In any civilized country, to go abroad, all one has to do is to obtain a passport and to pay the travel fare. But in Soviet Russia—that "One Sixth of the Planet Earth," as the Soviet propaganda liked to brag when speaking about vastness of the country's territory—I felt like a prisoner in a colossal labor camp. The only fleeting consolation for being trapped in that enormous open-air dungeon, dank, dreadful, and dreary, was to travel westward, to the Baltic Sea. On a crisp sunny day, I could see, or perhaps imagined seeing, Helsinki or Stockholm, and my heart would sail there for a brief visit and would come back refreshed with a new hope.

Here I permit myself another small digression. The Baltic countries have always occupied a special place in my heart. To some extent, it was because Grandpa Gavriel was a native of Latvia, and my paternal grandparents, Hirsch and Zisl, had lived in the Latvian capital for over ten years. But more important, because for us, living behind the Iron Curtain, these countries were the only window, or rather window vent, to the West. I was enthralled by the medieval atmosphere of Tallinn, the Baroque milieu of Vilnius, and the elegant ambiance of Riga with its plethora of art nouveau buildings. When Father bought a car, we frequently traveled to the Baltic Sea on holiday and would habitually stay in Estonia. On one such visit, we rented part of the house from a fisherman's family in Häädemeeste, a small coastal village near the border with Latvia, into which we would usually foray to have lunch or dinner. We traveled inland to Viljandi, Estonia, to see the impressive hilltop ruins of the once-powerful Hanseatic castle. On the way to the town, I gathered in the nearby

---

38 The teddy bear (named Ted and the title character of the movie directed by Seth MacFarlane), voiced by MacFarlane, the host of the ceremony, while claiming that he was born a Jew as "Theodore Shapiro," announced that he "would like to donate money to Israel and continue to work in Hollywood forever." Whether MacFarlane did it deliberately or not, his sketch contributes to the revival and legitimization of anti-Semitic stereotypes.

woods the best raspberries I have ever had in my life. Häädemeeste is about twenty-five miles from Pärnu, Estonia, which we visited every now and then to hobnob with numerous vacationing Jews from Moscow and other cities. Because of the high percentage of Jews on holiday, the Pärnu beach was facetiously dubbed "the Wailing Wall" (*Stena Placha*). I remember an older woman saying to her grandson, with that inimitable Jewish intonation, her *r*'s rolling: "Boria! If you eat a little bit of millet porridge, you will get half a watermelon" (*"Boria! Esli ty s˝esh´ nemnozhechko pshennoi kashi, ty poluchish´ pol-arbuza"*).

Initially, our Estonian landlord and his family were impeccably civil but kept us at arm's length. All that changed one day when we were looking at and admiring their attractive Swedish wall calendar in the kitchen. At that point, they told us that they had relatives in Sweden, and we told them that we were Jews—they assumed that we were ethnic Russians because we were from Moscow and spoke Russian—and that we had family in Israel. After we compared notes about the ill-treatment of our peoples by the Soviet regime, the family completely changed its demeanor toward us, from icily polite to warm and amiable. The head of the family even invited me to go fishing with him and his two sons. He kindly supplied me with all the necessary gear, and we sailed out to sea before dawn. It was an unforgettable experience!

I greatly sympathized with the Baltic States for being annexed to the Soviet Union. I vividly and gladly remember the January 1991 TV footage that showed Lithuanian youth confronting Soviet tanks in Vilnius with their national flags. I was delighted when the crumbling Soviet empire balked under international pressure, and the Baltic republics, at long last, reclaimed their independence.

As Jews and non-Party members, my family belonged to the category of so-called *nevyezdnye*—restricted from traveling abroad. I remember one day in the mid-1960s when my mother, an eminent pulmonologist, came home excited about the prospect of going to Japan for an international congress of lung specialists. Her euphoria did not last long. Mother brought home from her personnel office a questionnaire to be filled out. It asked about her nationality, to which, as in the well-known Soviet anecdote, she responded in the affirmative: "Yes, indeed" (*taki da*)—"Jewess," that is. Then the questionnaire inquisited if she or other members of the family had relatives abroad. That question was loaded and highly explosive—Mother had an uncle in New York City, and Father had an extensive family in Israel. Since responding to these questions in Soviet Russia would have been tantamount to political self-incrimination, just short of suicide, there was nothing left for Mother to do but to toss this hazardous form into the circular file. Her dream of seeing the world and her hope for global professional collaboration had to be put on hold for another decade.

The inquiry about relatives abroad brings to mind an amusing tale. Abramovich is summoned to the KGB headquarters for a talk. Without mincing words, a KGB official reproves him: "Comrade Abramovich! We find it disappointing that you lied to your homeland. It was your civic duty as a Soviet citizen to inform us that you have relatives abroad. We know for a fact that you have a family in Israel." "No, I didn't lie," 'Comrade' Abramovich replied. "It's my relatives who live in the homeland, and it's I who lives abroad."

In my childhood and early youth, I had a few "rehearsals" of departing from Soviet Russia, even though I did not realize it at the time. The first one occurred at the age of five when I was still in kindergarten, which was situated on the same side of Crooked-Knee Lane as our communal apartment house, no more than two hundred of my small steps away. Between them, there was a fenced yard, with some sparse wilted greenery, in which we kids had our daily ration of outdoor activities. One late morning, I decided not to return to kindergarten. The supervision was lax, and I easily snuck out and walked undetected in the opposite direction. When I showed up on our doorstep, Grandma Sara and nanny Polia were surprised at the kindergarten's early dismissal and grew quite concerned when I told them of my getaway. Soon thereafter, my kindergarten teacher, the aforementioned Klavdia Ivanovna, came to fetch me. She carried me face down under her mighty arm, and I remember seeing through a thick film of tears how the cobblestones, with which Crooked-Knee Lane was paved at the time, were rapidly running toward me.

The second "rehearsal" occurred soon thereafter when I was six or so. An unruly child, I frequently acted up and was disobedient. Admonished by my mother, I responded in a brazen manner and refused to apologize to her. Having reached the end of her patience, Mother impetuously suggested I get out. A stubborn boy, I did just that. Mother thought that I went to the enclosed courtyard. I decided, however, to go to my paternal grandmother's residence, about a mile away. I was quite familiar with the itinerary that for the most part consisted of lanes and alleys, with almost no traffic. The only time when there was a larger street to cross, Pokrovka, I had enough prudence to ask an adult woman for assistance. Grandma Zisl and Aunt Niuta were astounded to see me and immediately phoned my worried family to let them know that I arrived safely. I stayed with Grandma Zisl and Aunt Niuta for a couple of days but never modified my obnoxious noisy behavior. My much too tolerant Grandma did not reprimand me for misbehaving, but, as it turned out, her quiet suffering seeped through. When I heard Grandma scream in her sleep and asked her the next morning for the reason, she told me that she had a nightmare: she envisioned a little boy aiming at her with a rifle.

The third took place at summer camp when I was in my early teens. I was a scrawny, freckled redhead, an easy prey for bullies. They teased me, picked on me, and dubbed me a "rusty Yid" (*rzhavyi zhid*), a moniker that contained an admittedly clever alliteration in Russian. The most hostile among them was Vit'ka Chugryshin, the son of a hospital custodian. Chugryshin, a year or two my senior, already smoked, drank, and generously peppered his speech with swear words. His animosity toward me was absolute. He detested me not only for being Jewish but also for being a doctor's son. To top it off, Vit'ka could not forgive my being a better athlete than he, which clashed with his Archie Bunker worldview. At track-and-field competitions, when we were running 1,500 meters, I easily passed him by on the final curve, despite his desperate attempts to prevent it by zigzagging in front of me. What irked Chugryshin the most and what he found highly unforgivable was my scoring the decisive goal in an important intercamp soccer match, in which I played left defender and he played right winger. More than fifty-five years later, I still remember how it happened. Toward the end of the match, when it appeared that a 1–1 draw was inevitable, I had a strange sensation that I should take matters into my own hands. I asked the central defender to cover for me and, to his complete surprise, told him that I was going ahead to score a goal. Our squad had been awarded a corner kick on the other side of the pitch, and just as I reached the opposing team's penalty box, the ball rolled along the goal line, miraculously evaded the rest of the players, and ended up right in front of me. All I had to do was to stretch and slide my right leg to tap the ball into the net.

When I could no longer take the harassment from Chugryshin and his cronies, I fled the camp, boarded a Moscow-bound train, and stunned my parents by showing up long before the end of the term. I remember how saddened they became when I told them what had happened, and Mother filed a complaint with the camp administration. But what could the camp administration do when the whole country was pervaded with anti-Semitism and lawlessness? In retrospect, I suppose these early "rehearsals" psyched me up for my real departure from Soviet Russia many years later.

CHAPTER 4

EMERGENCE OF NATIONAL AWARENESS AND THE STRUGGLE FOR IMMIGRATION TO ISRAEL

> Dr. Herzl awakened the Jewish people
> from their long sleep.
> —Iosef Menachem Ashbel, "Zionism and
> the Balfour Declaration"[39]

In my family, primarily on the paternal side, there were constant talks about Israel. Grandma Zisl corresponded on and off with our relatives there, depending on how vegetarian were the times. She told me that friends of our Israeli kith and kin would come to Moscow as tourists and would stop by to convey greetings from our family there. During my boyhood visits to her, she would show me envelopes with Israeli stamps, which looked very exotic and enchanting. I remember one such stamp, issued in 1956 on the occasion of Israel's eighth year of independence: it showed a figure-eight-shaped blue-and-white pennant hoisted from a flagpole carrying the national symbol—Menorah—on its top. It later occurred to me that if the stamp is turned ninety degrees, the eight will morph into what is known as the

---

[39] In a letter to Baron Lionel Walter Rothschild, a leader of the Jewish British community, of November 2, 1917, British foreign secretary, Lord Arthur James Balfour, wrote: "His Majesty's Government view with favour the establishment in Palestine of a national home for the Jewish people" (*Times of London*, November 9, 1917, 7).

A stamp commemorating the eighth Independence Day of the State of Israel, 1956.

lemniscate of Bernoulli, the symbol for infinity, colloquially referred to in Russian as "the figure-eight on its side" (*vos´merka na boku*). Whether or not the artists had this meaning in mind, I wholeheartedly wish the State of Israel to be forever well and thriving. Amen!

Our family talks about Israel were not just pointless prattle. As long as I remember, my father repeatedly spoke about us going to Israel someday. Throughout my studies at school and university, Father kept badgering me about learning Hebrew in earnest. I was about seven or eight when he taught me the alphabet, which proved to be the key to the language. In the 1950s and through most of the 1960s, immigration to Israel from Soviet Russia, especially from Moscow, was as realistic and relevant as going on a trip to another galaxy. And so I dismissed Father's off-the-wall projects as wild fantasies and used various excuses—lectures, lab, homework, exams, dating, anything—to dodge studying the language, for which I felt no need, and to steer clear of this entire hokum altogether.

A crucial change in my attitude toward Israel gradually occurred throughout the 1960s, even though the country began to find a unique place in my heart much earlier. I remember how in the mid-1950s, Father and I chanced upon Israeli oranges displayed in wooden crates outside a grocery store, each fruit carefully wrapped in white tissue paper, with the name of the Israeli port city "Jaffa/Yafo" embossed in both English and Hebrew. My family savored these delicious and fragrant fruits, and I treasured the tissue paper with the English and, above all, Hebrew lettering for a long time. These fruits, consigned to the back of my memory, were merely produce, and while representing the country, they did not make an indelible mark on my psyche. It occurred to me years later that these oranges could have come from the citrus grove of my great-uncle Moshe, or, at the very least, could have been packed under his supervision. As I discovered later, Uncle Moshe, a great expert in fruit packing, worked at the time for the Tnuva Export (as mentioned in Chapter 1). The company conducted trade with Soviet Russia in the mid-1950s, and Uncle Moshe once or twice accompanied the merchandise to Odessa. In retrospect, these oranges may be perceived as a sweet and fragrant "hello" from him and, by extension, from the rest of our Israeli relatives.

In the summer of 1963, shortly after I entered Moscow University, Father's cousin Alex paid us a surprise visit. Alex was en route to Tashkent, the capital of Uzbekistan, where she was going to take part in an international congress. Regrettably, Father and Luba were out of town on vacation in the Crimean resort of Eupatoria. It was amazing how much Alex and I looked alike: both red-haired and blue-eyed like Iosef Menachem Ashbel, her grandfather and my great-grandfather. (Nine years later, when I arrived in Israel while Alex was on sabbatical in the United States and Canada, people would come up to me in the streets of Jerusalem to inquire if I was related to her.) For the first time in my life, I saw an Israeli up close and personal, and my own relative at that—intelligent, independent, and free. Alex's visit was an important landmark on my path toward Israel.

Another essential step in this direction took place in the early summer of 1965. The European Basketball Championship, also known as EuroBasket, was held over the first ten days of June in both Moscow and Tbilisi, the capital of Georgia. I was delighted to learn that the Israeli team, which made it to the final stage, was part of Group A and would be playing all its games in Moscow. In the Soviet capital, the games were held at the Luzhniki Sports Palace, which seated approximately twelve thousand people. An avid basketball fan, I was spellbound by the participation of the Israeli national team and tried to attend every one of its games. When I saw the Israeli athletes that memorable summer, I began to realize that for me Israel was not just another state but the country where my brethren, fellow Jews, lived. The team's excellent performance filled my heart with enormous pride. It finished sixth among the sixteen teams, triumphing over Hungary, Romania, Finland, East Germany, and Greece in the process. The Israeli squad demonstrated a great will to win, repeatedly beating its rivals by merely one or two points. Each victory brought about the most desirable, highly anticipated, and long-cherished treat, the performance of "Hatikvah," to which I listened, along with many other Soviet Jews, with enormous excitement and jubilation. Yes, indeed, the unimaginable was happening before our very eyes and ears: a Soviet orchestra was performing the Israeli national anthem in the jam-packed Sports Palace, in the capital of anti-Semitic and anti-Zionist Soviet Russia, day in and day out! (Since then, whenever I hear "Hatikvah," I mentally migrate to the distant past and visualize that memorable tournament of half a century ago.) This was the first time I actually felt that Israel was my country. When the Israeli squad played against the mighty Soviet team and was crushed by it (88–50), my sympathies of course lay with the blue and white. By comparison, nine years earlier, in July 1956, when I was eleven years old, my father took me to a qualifying match for the Melbourne Olympics between the Soviet and the Israeli national soccer teams. The Soviets demolished the Israeli squad 5–0. I remember being upset over this devastating loss but did not yet feel that Israel was my country.

The names of the Israeli basketball players still resonate in my ears fifty years later: Tanchum Cohen-Mintz, Tzvi Lubetzky, Ig'al Volodarsky, David Kaminsky, Chaim Starkman, Avraham Hoffman, Ofer Eshed, Ilan Zeiger. At the Luzhniki Sports Palace, I noticed a teeny-weeny old Jew, always present at the games of the Israeli team, who would occasionally shout out "*Kadima!*" My father, who together with my kid sister joined me for a couple of games, explained that this word meant "Forward!" in Hebrew. I did not dare to join the elderly fan and to shout "*Kadima!*" but merely muttered it under my breath. Furthermore, when after one game David Kaminsky made a welcoming gesture toward me, inviting to come down from the stands, as painful as it was, I chose to ignore the invitation. I was concerned that I would be expelled from Moscow University for consorting with a foreigner and that as a result my parents too might lose their jobs. In the Soviet Union, permeated with the mania of espionage, such contacts were viewed as a serious political crime.

It so happened that the championship overlapped with my university exam session. Even though I spent little if any time on preparation for the tests, I managed to pass them nicely, except for math, which I badly flunked. The instructor was surprised at my poor showing since I had been doing fairly well in the class throughout the semester. His surprise grew even larger when a week later, after the championship was over, I retook the exam and scored an A. The instructor expressed his astonishment about the reversal in my exam performance, apparently expecting some explanation. Obviously, I could not divulge the true reason and mumbled something about the family circumstances.

It is well known that the vast majority of Soviet Jews felt jubilant upon learning about the Israeli victory in the Six-Day War. Indeed, it was the fateful turning point which made us realize that our hearts and our loyalty belonged to the Jewish State. I remember how all within our family and circle of friends were hugging, kissing, and celebrating. And yet there were some, such as my university classmate Grisha P., whom the Israeli victory did not make in the least bit happy. I remember him apprehensively saying, "Now that Israel has won, the Soviet Union will retaliate against its own Jews and will make our lives even more miserable." Grisha's prediction proved to be accurate as the Soviet regime did indeed become even more hostile to its own Jews than before. What Grisha failed to wrap his mind around, though, was that the existence of a vital, vibrant Israel is the only guarantee of the collective survival and continuance of Beit Israel—the entire Jewish people.

Three years later and a couple of years after our graduation from Moscow University, Grisha phoned me and suggested we get together. By then, he was working on his Ph.D. at one of the prestigious Academy of

Science research institutes. I, on the other hand, had already become involved in Zionist activities and was on the regime's blacklist. I agreed to meet with him at a nearby subway station and decided to let him know of my current situation right off the bat. As we passed through the turnstile and were walking toward the train, I quickly told Grisha about the essential changes in my life. I noticed that his face turned paler and paler with each new sentence. When we finally reached the platform, he said in a demonstratively loud voice before boarding the train: "I don't share your views and don't wish to have any contact with you ever again." Grisha's words saddened me, even though I understood perfectly well that they were prompted by fear of jeopardizing his academic career and were intended for the KGB secret agents who, as he rightly suspected, were shadowing me. Nonetheless, before the train took off I said in response: "I feel sorry for you and am absolutely certain that we'll eventually resume our contacts." And that is exactly what happened about thirty years later. After the collapse of the Soviet Union, Grisha resided in a few countries, including the United Kingdom and the United States, where he worked for companies selling oilfield equipment. He eventually embraced and became attached to his Jewish heritage and even enrolled his daughter in a Hebrew Sunday school. Although we have yet to see each other after all these years, we maintain a regular telephone and electronic communication and exchange the High Holidays greetings. In 2008, Grisha went to the fortieth class reunion of the Department of Chemistry at Moscow University and told me that many of our classmates knew about my emigration from the Soviet Union and my career change from chemistry to Russian literature. Most recently, Grisha admitted that he received the basics of a Jewish education from me fifty years ago. I am exceedingly happy to hear that, even if there is a considerable degree of exaggeration in his statement.

I have stayed in much closer contact over the years with two other former classmates. One of them, Misha Sinyakov, wished to immigrate to Israel in the 1970s but was prevented from doing so by family circumstances. He arrived in Israel in the fall of 1989 and found work as a research fellow at Bar-Ilan University. The other classmate of mine, Fima Vinnik, dropped out after three semesters. (He had a heart condition and therefore was not subject to the mandatory military conscription.) Fima worked for a while as a chemistry lab technician until one day he stumbled upon an announcement about openings in the Department of History. Even though he had virtually no time to get ready for the entrance exams (history, literature, Russian language, and English), he took them and scored well enough to be admitted to the program. After hearing the introductory lecture, Fima realized that he found the subject to which he could devote his professional life. Fima has remained in Moscow and until his recent retirement taught history, first at high school and then at a lyceum. Fima regularly visits Israel, where his sister's family has lived for many years. It is a rare treat when the three of us meet to touch base and to recollect the good old days at Moscow U. Last time we met in January 2014 to celebrate fifty years of our friendship—a remarkable jubilee indeed!

The Soviet regime's attitude toward Jews drastically changed for the worse in the late 1960s, and in particular in 1968 when I graduated from Moscow University. It proved to be an exceptionally bad year. Having been deeply humiliated a year earlier by the resounding defeat of their Arab clients in the Six-Day War, the Soviet authorities decided to turn the screws on their own Jews. The Soviet government broke off diplomatic relations with Israel in the wake of the war and launched an intense anti-Zionist propaganda campaign inside the country. Zionism was proclaimed a form of racism and was equated with fascism and Nazism. The Communist Party ideologues gave the green light to the broad dissemination of Trofim Kichko's vituperative *Judaism Without Embellishments* (*Iudaizm bez prikras*, 1963) and Yuri Ivanov's vilifying *Beware: Zionism!* (*Ostorozhno: sionizm!*, 1969). These pamphlets essentially repeated the tall tales of *The Protocols of the Elders of Zion*, the notorious fabrication alleging the existence of a Jewish conspiracy to conquer and rule the world. The events in Poland and Czechoslovakia, two countries still held tightly in the Soviet grip, exacerbated the situation. The Soviet propaganda machine squarely blamed political dissent in Poland and the remarkable Prague Spring in Czechoslovakia on local "agents of Zionism."

So when I began looking for a job in the late summer of 1968, the outcome was invariably the same. For several months, I went from one research institute to another (altogether, I believe I visited more than twenty of them), but to no avail. It was pretty much the same everywhere I went, even if the responses slightly differed. They ranged from "Oh, we've hired someone we needed just a moment ago" to the infamous and proverbial "Your profile doesn't suit us" (*Vy nam ne podkhodite po profiliu*), reminiscent of a joke regarding the stereotypical Jewish appearance. There were occasions when I received an honest, albeit off-the-record response: "With your last name, you realize, we can't hire you!" The latter reaction created a sense of helplessness and hopelessness. It made me feel as though I had a hideous, disqualifying physical impediment: being armless and yet trying to enter a weightlifting competition. These discriminatory hiring policies are reflected in the following funny story. Two Jews come to a personnel office looking for a job. One of them, brash and talkative, asks about the eligibility criteria. In his inquiry, he refers to common Russian surname endings (of which already my kindergarten classmate was aware):

> "Do you admit people with 'ov'?"
> "Yes, we do."
> "And with 'in'?"
> "But of course."
> "And what about 'ko'?"
> "Naturally."
> "Kogan, come over here, you got the job!"

The point of this funny story is that the personnel officer expects the applicant to have a Ukrainian last name, which often ends with "ko," and not a typically Jewish one that begins with that syllable.

Ultimately, after pounding the pavement for five months, I found a job as a chemical engineer, for which, with my Moscow University diploma, I was completely overqualified: most of my colleagues received a specialized chemical education only a tad above high school level. My work consisted of servicing boilers at industrial plants. This work gave me no satisfaction whatsoever, and I quickly realized that I had no future in the Land of the Soviets. It was the straw that broke the camel's back.

At that same time, I started listening to foreign radio stations in Russian and became aware that there were Jews out there who wished to leave for Israel. Soon I became acquainted with some of them and realized all of a sudden that my father's idea, which sounded so bizarre only a few years earlier, now made a lot of sense. I began studying Hebrew in earnest. I obtained a textbook called *Elef milim* (*A Thousand Words*) from an American tourist I met near the synagogue.

I am not blessed with any superior linguistic aptitude, but when I began learning Hebrew in its ancient-modern pronunciation, I got the feeling that I was recalling the language. Such experience was independently shared by some other Russian Jews, such as the late poet Leonid Ioffe. This is what is known as "the call of blood" or "voice of blood" (*zov krovi* or *golos krovi*). When I arrived in Jerusalem, I was overcome by a strange sensation that I had lived in the city long before. Despite my exceptionally poor sense of direction, my feet brought me, seemingly on their own, to the Western Wall. I had the same feeling of déjà vu in the Sinai desert, which I had visited on several occasions in the early and mid-1970s before it was relinquished to Egypt in accordance with the bilateral peace treaty. Therefore, I find preposterous the conjecture of Arthur Koestler, promulgated in *The Thirteenth Tribe* (1976), and of his acolytes, that Ashkenazic Jews were the descendants of Khazars, Turkic tribes who allegedly converted to Judaism in the mid-eighth century. This conjecture has been discarded not only by all serious historians, most recently by Shaul Stampfer of the Hebrew University of Jerusalem, but has also been proven false by DNA research that indisputably demonstrates the Semitic origins of East and Central European Jewry.[40]

Shortly before beginning to study Hebrew, I came across a book about Ármin Vámbéry (born Hermann Bamberger, 1832–1913), a prominent Hungarian linguist of Jewish descent and an explorer of what was then known as the Orient, mainly the Ottoman Empire and Central Asia. Although my knack for languages, of course, is far more modest than Vámbéry's, I adopted his method of self-instruction—memorizing a given number of words per day. Whenever I fell short, I would simply add the

---

40 See Shaul Stampfer, "Did the Khazars Convert to Judaism?" *Jewish Social Studies* 19, no. 3 (2013): 1–72; Harry Ostrer, *Legacy: A Genetic History of the Jewish People* (New York: Oxford University Press, 2012). Incidentally, my own DNA test has established that I have a 97 percent Jewish ancestry, with a 3 percent margin of error.

difference to my next day's quota. I also began listening to the Voice of Israel broadcasts in Hebrew. My vocabulary was steadily growing, and pretty soon I was conversing with my peers and learning from them and from those more advanced. A few months later, I myself began to teach elementary Hebrew but did so surreptitiously. This is because in the Soviet Union, Hebrew was strictly prohibited as the language of "Zionism" and of "the Israeli military machine." (When I tell my Cornell students about it, they have difficulty fathoming how a language could be declared illegal—the natural reaction of people who grew up in a free democratic country.)

Providentially, several years earlier, on one of our weekend strolls in 1963, my father and I chanced upon Felix Shapiro's newly published Hebrew–Russian dictionary and had enough foresight to purchase it. It was the indispensable tool for any Russian-speaking Jew who wished to study the language. Whenever there was a dry spell and no other reading materials were available, I studied words and phrases from the dictionary that frequently served as my main and lone source of Hebrew language knowledge. (At times, fate would provide an opportunity to satisfy my thirst for Hebrew learning in the most whimsical way. This occurred, for example, when I received bouillon cubes that Jewish tourists, primarily from the United States, distributed before Passover among Soviet Jews striving for immigration to Israel. I remember how pleased I was to obtain these cubes, which, first and foremost, symbolized the support that Western Jewry rendered to their brethren behind the Iron Curtain. Another great cause for joy was that these nutritious cubes were made in Israel, and their packaging contained a list of ingredients and sundry recipes in Hebrew, which I perused with utmost excitement and close attention.) But fortunately these dry spells were followed by true feasts. This was when I read the poetry of Chaim Nachman Bialik, Natan Alterman, and Leah Goldberg; newly published prose, such as Aharon Megged's novels *Chedva and I* (*Chedva veani*) and *The Living on the Dead* (*Hachai al hamet*) as well as A. B. Yehoshua's collection of short stories, in which I singled out "The Continuing Silence of a Poet" ("*Shtika holekhet venimshekhet shel meshorer*").

Soon my name began appearing on Zionist activist lists. One day, I received an issue of *Maariv* by regular mail from a total stranger, an Israeli youngster, named Boaz, who studied in West Germany. I viewed getting this newspaper as a sheer miracle since the Soviet regime habitually intercepted all suspicious correspondence, especially overseas packages from Western countries, and I treasured this precious gift for a long time. Boaz surprised me once again. Shortly after my arrival in Israel, I received *Bending over Backwards (Shminiiot baavir)*, a collection of humorous short stories by Ephraim Kishon, the Israeli Mark Twain, with his autograph inscription to me on the title page. This was indeed a great present, which I thoroughly enjoyed when laughter was a much-needed commodity for me at those times of anxiety and uncertainty. I doubt Boaz realized how much his thoughtful gestures meant to me: first sending the *Maariv* issue into the hostile, anti-Semitic Moscow and then posting the Kishon volume during my first weeks in Jerusalem. Recently, I gave the book to my nephew, Tzakhi, knowing full well that he will appreciate and cherish it for years to come.

I endlessly perused the newspaper backward and forward, closely examining its every nook and cranny, including the small print and ads. Scrutinizing this issue greatly enhanced my language proficiency and gave me numerous insights into the life of the country to which I so eagerly wanted to immigrate. Now, when I open a Hebrew newspaper, I quickly skim through the news and every so often read an article or two. When I remember with what exhilaration in my heart I studied every iota in that *Maariv* issue more than forty years ago, I feel at first a bit ashamed for treating a current issue so casually. But then again, each time I pick up an issue of a Hebrew newspaper, it gives me an opportunity to express my gratitude to the Creator, my thanksgiving, for liberating me from Soviet captivity and enabling me to read what I want and as cursorily or carefully as I want.

Come to think of it, there was another important source of my language studies. In 1963, when Alex visited us in Moscow, she brought with her two records. They contained Hebrew songs performed by the incomparable Rika Zarai and by the magnificent Ran and Nama duo. Alas, Aunt Niuta's second husband (she was married four times), Lev Konstantinovich—who had the Pushkinian surname Ezersky—took them away from me.[41] He justified this confiscation by his familiarity with

---

41 Ezersky is the protagonist of Pushkin's unfinished poem (1832–33).

Hebrew, which he remembered from his pre-Revolutionary childhood, and by insisting that the records were useless to me since I did not know the language, which was true at the time. Fortunately, I taped the records before Lev Konstantinovich carried them off. Several years later, these songs were not only a great inspiration to my growing love for Israel but also an irreplaceable means for learning Hebrew. I was listening to such Zarai classics as "Voice of Horologe" ("*Kol orlogin*"), "The Sycamore Garden" ("*Gan hashikmim*"), and "The Kite Song" ("*Shir haafifon*"*)*; and to the duo's very popular "My Sweetheart" ("*Chemdati*"), "Go out!" (*Tzena!*), and "Let Us Rejoice!" ("*Hava nagila!*") over and over again, even daring when nobody was around to sing along. (Once in a while I hum a tune when taking shower and even that I do softly. This is because my singing is so bad that the water, begging not to hear it, runs back into the shower head. Well, sometimes you have to be careful what you wish for. When I was a little boy, I had a nice voice and therefore was compelled to join the school choir, whose entire repertoire consisted of laudatory songs about Lenin and Stalin. I loathed this choir and pleaded with the Almighty to make my voice unlistenable. The Lord granted this wish before I knew it: when my voice started mutating, my singing became so horrendous that I was duly booted out of the choir.)

I also used to jot down the lyrics and thus became familiar with a slew of new words. Some of them, such as "abyss" (*metzula*) or "prankster" (*kundas*), were rather uncommon. Coupled with poring over Felix Shapiro's aforementioned dictionary, it should come as no surprise that when I arrived in Israel I knew some of the rarest Hebrew and Aramaic expressions, which every now and then would roll off my tongue with extraordinary ease.

There were more than a few youngsters who immigrated to Israel about the same time I did and whose Hebrew was as good as mine or better, but still and all, it was quite a novelty for Israelis to see recent émigrés so proficient. That is why when I scored a 97 on the Hebrew University of Jerusalem language aptitude exam after only a couple of months in the country, my performance astounded the proctors and the exam committee alike. That is why when I took a Hebrew proficiency test at the army recruitment office, the sergeant dashed off with it in disbelief to the office manager, and the entire staff gathered round and gazed at me as if I were some sort of exotic bird. I also derived pleasure from playing a fun language game with Aunt Rivka. She would utter a Latin-rooted and commonly used word like, say, *perspektiva* ("perspective"), and I would provide the Academy of the Hebrew Language locution—*tishkofet*—rarely if ever used in ordinary speech.

By keeping me in the Soviet Union against my will for two years, from 1970 to 1972, the KGB most solicitously gave me an opportunity to study the Hebrew language without haste in the comfort of my home. For this considerateness and much more, I am forever indebted to this glorious organization. All joking aside, those two years were not easy because I never knew when, if ever, I would be able to emigrate. Although not prone to despondency, I was now and then seized by a sense of desperation when my friends and brethren-in-cause, for whom I was exceedingly happy, were departing one wave after another as I kept staying behind time and time again, time and time again . . . But such moments of embitterment were brief and did not rend my world asunder. In addition to putting my trust in the Almighty, first and foremost, I always remembered the story about two mice that fell into a bucket with cream. One mouse decided that nothing could be done and drowned, whereas the other started quickly moving its little paws until it churned the cream into butter, and thus survived.

In the late 1960s, there began the Jewish immigration to Israel from the Baltic republics. I knew about it because Leah, the girl I met a year earlier in Vilnius, wrote to me about her family's imminent departure. As important as it was in creating a precedent, this Baltic emigration was quiet and did not resonate across the Soviet Union. The struggle for Jewish emigration received close international scrutiny in the fall of 1969, after eighteen families from Soviet Georgia sent a collective letter to the UN Human Rights Commission; to Iosef Tekoah, the Israeli ambassador to the UN; and to the government of Israel. The letter marked the first public group demand by Soviet Jews for the right to emigrate. Israeli Prime Minister Golda Meir read it to the Knesset, thereby commencing an intensive worldwide campaign to ease up the restrictive Soviet emigration policies toward Jews.

Georgian Jews continued to be at the forefront of the struggle for Jewish emigration to Israel. In July 1971, they held a hunger strike at the Central Telegraph. I distinctly remember coming almost daily, with many other local Jews, to the Central Telegraph building in downtown Moscow to render moral support to these courageous individuals. Georgian Jews set a great example to all their brethren across the Soviet Union of what it means to be a proud Jew and to love Israel. Here is a curious and instructive detail. On one such visit to the Central Telegraph, I espied a tall, blondish young man who watched the Georgian Jews with great interest. Initially, I suspected him of being a KGB agent. I went straight up to the man and brazenly inquired what business he had to watch the hunger strike of the Georgian Jews. His answer: "I am an ethnic German. I came to learn from their experience and to apply it to our struggle for immigration to Germany." This response is very telling. Usually and rightly so, Georgian Jews are credited with extracting from the Soviet regime one of the earliest concessions toward the Jewish exodus. As this recollection demonstrates, the ramifications of their struggle were far-reaching and affected other ethnic minorities in their battles for the right to emigrate.

As heartening and important as these phenomena were, the emigration of Baltic and Georgian Jews was from the periphery, not from the capital. Many Moscow Jews were highly emboldened upon discovering that a group of nine families, including the valorous Tina Brodetsky, obtained exit visas and left for Israel in July 1970. (Before long, I found out that the legendary Zionist David Khavkin emigrated in 1969.) Inspired by these pivotal developments, I decided a month later, on my twenty-fifth birthday, to follow their suit. When I told Father and Mother of my decision, they were visibly distraught and were concerned that my application would have harsh consequences both for me and for them. They keenly supported the idea in principle but were worried that I would lose my job (they were right about that), would end up exiled to Siberia (they were almost right about that), and they would lose their jobs (thankfully, they were wrong about that). I tried to reason with them and maintained that it was as good a time as any. I told Father and Mother about the first group of Moscow Jews who had served as the precedent by receiving exit visas. They were not too convinced by my rationale and were highly apprehensive about the prospects of my emigration. It may sound odd, but it was my teenage sister who tilted the scales when she stated the obvious: "If he doesn't apply, he stands no chance, but if he does, there is always a possibility." This youngster's truism unexpectedly sealed the deal. This reminds me of an amusing story. A Jew repeatedly prays to God, asking the Almighty to help him win the lottery. As he is praying, he hears the Voice: "Please help me to help you! For heaven's sake, go and buy a lottery ticket!"

To set the process in motion, I first had to receive an invitation from an Israeli relative. Under pressure from the United States, the Soviet government recognized repatriation to Israel but only "within the framework of family reunification" (*v ramkakh vossoedineniia semei*). Never mind that I was leaving my parents behind and reuniting with my father's cousin, whom I met only once, but a modicum of legitimacy had to be observed. Curiously, this issue came up in a conversation with the Department of Visas and Registrations officials when they asked me who will fetch my parents a cup of tea after I leave for Israel and they grow old (by then, Luba already lived in Jerusalem). I retorted: "My parents have been working all their adult lives for the benefit of the Soviet Union. The least the Soviet government can do is to provide them with comfortable life at their old age." I obviously could not tell these compassionate bureaucrats that my parents planned to leave Soviet Russia as soon as I did.

I wanted to write to my Israeli relatives to ask for an invitation but was not sure how to find their addresses. Although Grandma Zisl could have helped me since she had corresponded with the relatives on and off in the past, I wanted to keep the whole thing a deep secret. I was concerned that if the ninety-one-year-old Grandma, despite not being known for her loquacity, inadvertently told someone with loose lips about my plans, this might unwittingly jeopardize the effort from the very start and toss us all in the soup. Luckily, the addresses of two of them, Uncle Dov and Alex, were listed in *Who's Who in Israel*. Luckier still, the directory was accessible at the time in the Moscow Foreign Languages Library. A year or so later, the library was instructed to remove this and other Israel-related materials from its shelves.

I chose to write to Alex for a variety of reasons. Uncle Dov was in his mid-seventies, and I did not wish to burden him with this task. Alex, on the other hand, was twenty years his junior, was my father's first cousin, and more important, I had met her in Moscow only several years earlier. *Who's Who in Israel* listed Alex's university address, to which, with trepidation in my heart and much prayer, I sent my letter. Even though Alex's Russian was near perfect, I wrote the letter in Hebrew to show her and other relatives the seriousness of my intentions. In four weeks, the package from Jerusalem, with all the necessary papers, miraculously arrived.

It so happened that I was applying for an exit visa while still working as a chemical engineer. As bizarre as it may sound, among the documents required by the Department of Visas and Registrations (*Otdel viz i registratsii*, acronymed OVIR in Russian, and dubbed TEL OVIR by the emigration-seeking Jews), was a letter of reference from my workplace. One may ask: Why on earth was this document needed for immigration to Israel? This was a sinister move on the part of the regime. It was designed to force a visa applicant to inform the company employer of a "Zionist renegade" in its midst. The outcome of such self-squealing was predictable—job loss. On occasion, this requirement created comical situations—some nitwitted bureaucrats wrote enthusiastic reference letters for prospective émigrés as if they were taking up another position within the Soviet Union. In my case, I was immediately suspended, albeit with pay.

While on suspension, the company administrators summoned me for discussions, trying their hardest to persuade me to change my mind. When I flatly refused, meetings were arranged to denounce my "anti-Soviet actions." It was a bizarre, echt-Soviet case of doublethink. At those officially sponsored gatherings, Jews who held key positions in the organization vehemently condemned me for being a Zionist and dubbed me "a traitor to the Soviet Motherland." Yet when running into me one-on-one in the dimly lit corridors of the office building, after cautiously looking left and right, as if crossing a busy street, they would tell me that they heard about me on the Voice of Israel or the Voice of America and wished me all the best in my emigration endeavors.

Some of my Jewish co-workers courageously abstained from denouncing me in public and even feared for my future. In this regard, I affectionately remember my immediate supervisor, Adol´f L´vovich Iofan, a nephew of Boris Iofan, a distinguished Soviet architect. Boris Iofan was the author of the never-realized Palace of Soviets project that was supposed to be built on the site of the infamously demolished Christ the Savior Cathedral (now rebuilt) and the designer of the elite block-long building commonly known as the House on the Embankment. It so happened that right after my confrontation with the management, Adol´f L´vovich, who had a heart condition, suffered from chest pains (I sincerely hoped not on my account). He was admitted to the university hospital where my mother worked and soon afterward wished to see her in private. Adol´f L´vovich looked pale and distressed and asked my mother point-blank if she knew about my intention to apply for an exit visa to Israel. Mother responded in the affirmative and told him that she unconditionally supported my decision. To that, this nice, caring man, albeit in the fashion typical of a frightened Soviet Jew, exclaimed: "What is he doing! He's going with his bare chest against barbed wire!" Likewise, my father's superior, Georgy L´vovich Shnirman, upon becoming aware of my Zionist activities, exclaimed: "What is he doing! He's laying his head on railroad tracks!"

Another co-worker, whom I fondly and gratefully remember for not pointing the accusatory finger at me—in and of itself a valiant act—was Boris Samoilovich Lubin, head of one of the divisions in the organization. Lubin was a short, bald, bespectacled man in his early sixties. Lubin, who spoke Russian with a detectable accent that betrayed his Belarusian *shtetl* origin, was an excellent and most experienced engineer. I recall how constantly annoyed he was with his subordinates who worked ineffectively, procrastinated, and jeopardized the timely submission of quarterly reports. "Finish [it] off already!" (*Zakanchivaite uzhe!*) he would tell them with that inimitable Yiddish tone of exasperation in his voice. Lubin's poignant phrase also entered the golden fund of our family sayings. Sometimes I will say it to myself if, for whatever reason, my meeting a deadline seems to be in danger.

Yet another decent co-worker of mine, this time an ethnic Russian, was Slava K. I remember how in the summer of 1970 he and I were sent on a business trip to the aforementioned Estonian town of Viljandi. It turned out that the plant at which we were supposed to conduct the work was absolutely unprepared for our arrival. Overall, we spent an entire month twiddling our thumbs and eventually were called back to Moscow. Only in the Soviet Union was it possible to stay in a hotel for an extended period of time and to receive a per diem for not doing diddly squat in return. Slava proved himself a trustworthy fellow. When he noticed my Hebrew books, which I brought with me on the trip, I confided in him that I was studying the language and entertaining the idea of immigrating to Israel. Slava, in turn, revealed to me that his family belonged to the Russian nobility and that they had to hide their origins all these years to escape persecution. Later, when I announced my intention to emigrate and before I was suspended from the job, one co-worker, who in all likelihood did his utmost to curry favor with the authorities, declared that he would not shake hands with me because I was a "traitor to the Soviet Motherland." Slava, who happened to be present in the office, challenged this obsequious declaration by saying that he, on the contrary, would happily shake hands with me. For him, an ethnic Russian who had no prospect of leaving the country, it was a brave deed, and I was greatly touched by his decent, indeed, noble behavior.

Since I had no work to do in Viljandi, I decided to go to Riga for a weekend. Upon my arrival on Friday afternoon in the Latvian capital, I could not find a room available in any of the hotels. As Vladimir Voinovich has graphically shown in his *Anti-Soviet Soviet Union*, these lodgings were reserved for the Party big shots, members of privileged organizations, such as the Union of Soviet Writers, for people on government-authorized business trips (that is why I got an accommodation in Viljandi), and finally for foreigners. Completely desperate and leaving it up to fate, I went to the Riga synagogue for the Friday night service. Since the local synagogue goers were a close-knit group and knew each other well, they were surprised and intrigued to see an unfamiliar face and were all staring at me throughout the service. Afterward, during the *oneg shabbat*, one Jew had the chutzpa to come up to me and

inquire in Yiddish: "Where is the Jew from?" (*Fun vanen iz der yid?*).⁴²
Although my Yiddish was practically nonexistent, I understood the
query and answered in Hebrew. The worshippers gathered around me
and bombarded me with questions in Russian. They were quite impressed
with my proficiency in Hebrew (rather meager at the time, I might add).
When they learned about my lodging predicament, a member of the
congregation invited me to stay with his family for the weekend. Their
hospitality was boundless, their tactfulness immeasurable. They angelically tolerated my incredible ignorance of the kosher eating regulations.
A few years later, when I worked in the Russian division of the Voice of
Israel, I ran into my host's daughter, who told me that, alas, her father
passed away shortly before the family's immigration to Israel.

At the *oneg shabbat*, I also met another local Jew who was born and
grew up in interwar Latvia. In retrospect, I realized that he had gone
through numerous horrific experiences, most likely losing family members
in the Holocaust. He himself evidently survived the unspeakable ordeal
by managing to escape the Nazi occupation. At the same time, he was
subjected to the protracted Soviet occupation and, in all probability, knew
the bitter taste of exile to Siberian labor camps. Nevertheless, the man
preserved his Jewish identity and retained his West European demeanor.
This lanky middle-aged man with a pleasantly cheerful personality, who
had finished Hebrew gymnasium before World War II, took me on long
walks around Riga, during which we spoke mostly Hebrew. These walks
greatly enhanced my Hebrew vocabulary. I still remember many words
that I heard from this marvelous man, above all naval terms, such as "shipyard" (*mispana*), "mast" (*toren*), and "to set sail" (*lehaflig*).

As I mentioned earlier, my paternal family had resided in Riga before
World War I. Grandma Zisl told me that they had lived there on Karlstraße.
The German-sounding name should not be surprising since Riga was
heavily Germanized at the time. After all, nearly half of its population were
Baltic Germans, and German was the city's official language until the early
1890s. By the time of my visit, in the summer of 1970, the city was heavily

---

42   *Oneg shabbat* is a celebratory gathering held following Shabbat services, often with food, singing, and socializing.

Russified and became (or at least so it appeared at the time) an integral part of the Soviet empire. No wonder, then, that when I inquired about Karlstraße, most people were baffled and some simply assumed that I was asking for Karl-Marx-straße. My Latvian-born friend, who knew the old Riga exceptionally well, helped me to find the neighborhood in which Karlstraße had been located at the turn of the twentieth century.

While I was on suspension, management was frantically looking for ways to get rid of me. To my bosses' painful misfortune, shortly before this rigmarole, I had been commended for my good performance. Finally, three months after the suspension, on January 29, 1971, the management, in consultation with their superiors and undoubtedly with the KGB, fired me because of the need for "staff reduction" (*po sokrashcheniiu shtatov*). Of course, I was the only one "reduced." It was a thinly disguised reprisal for my "bad behavior," but the semblance of legality was maintained.

My visa application predicament began a little bit earlier, in October 1970. At that point, my honchos refused to supply the required letter of reference, and OVIR refused to process my application without it, claiming that my dossier was otherwise incomplete. Only several months later, in February 1971, did I succeed at breaking this vicious circle and applying for an exit visa. At that time, OVIR agreed to my substituting a note from the Housing and Communal Services Office (ZhEK) for the work reference letter, since by then I was laid off and jobless. Upon completing my dossier and submitting all the necessary paperwork, I received a quick rejection of my visa application. Initially, my application was denied because of "bad behavior" and, among other things, for "being involved in demonstrations." After numerous appeals, I was given the "secrecy" reason—"For knowing the geography" was the way the OVIR officials put it. They further explained that while working within the Aviation Ministry system in my capacity as a chemical engineer, I visited numerous top-secret industrial plants and hence was familiar with their locations. When I countered that the locations of these plants could be easily detected by space reconnaissance satellites and were certainly known in the West, they only grinned. Of course, they knew all that but simply used this as an excuse to deny me an exit visa.

Some of my American friends ask me why the Soviet government did not allow for the free emigration of Jews. In response, I tell them a contemporary anecdote. Leonid Brezhnev, general secretary of the Communist Party, asked Alexei Kosygin, his prime minister:

> "How many Jews do we have in the country?"
> "About three million," Kosygin replied.
> "And how many of them would leave if we permit free emigration?" Brezhnev further queried.
> "Over fifty million."

The anecdote aptly illustrated a well-justified concern of the regime that if the Jews were allowed to emigrate, it would embolden many other Soviet citizens to leave and would eventually tear the Iron Curtain down. And over the course of time that is precisely what did happen!

When I was sacked from my deeply dissatisfying job, I found myself in a predicament artificially created by the Soviet regime. I was on the government's pitch-black list, and the authorities were determined to make my life utterly miserable. The establishment was carefully watching my every step, monitoring how long I would be out of work. Being unemployed for four months or more would let the regime label me a "parasite" (*tuneiadets*) and would land me in prison or a labor camp for up to two years. Job hunting was a true challenge. Seeking a position matching my education was out of the question. I could not expect any favorable references in support of my application since the administration of my last workplace would use a system of secret codes and arcane paragraphs to inform a prospective employer of the reasons for my dismissal. Finding a menial job, on the other hand, was equally if not more difficult because my Moscow University diploma would definitely raise many suspicious eyebrows. Fortunately, the Soviet system was far from "criminal-proof" and therefore had its gaps and loopholes. So in late April 1971, I found a temporary summer position as a telegram deliverer. The post office needed temps like me to fill in for regular workers going on vacation. As soon as I became familiar with the route, I started enjoying my walking job a great deal. Furthermore, my friends often popped by and accompanied me during the shifts. In addition, my Hebrew students visited and practiced the language with me on the go. I remember one telegram that contained congratulations for an upcoming wedding and, judging by the names, was addressed to the Jewish bride and groom. In my Zionist enthusiasm, I thought it would please the recipient of this telegram, presumably the mother of the bride, if I greeted her in Hebrew. My salutation, as I could tell by the expression on the woman's face, scared the living daylights out of her. I learned my lesson and never did it again.

One day, when I was out on a delivery, I ran into a former co-worker, an ethnic Ukrainian with another Chekhovian surname—Kovalenko.[43] He greeted me warmly and, upon learning about my situation, prophetically uttered: "I'm sorry to see you in this wretched position but sooner or later you'll leave for Israel." And then he added grimly: "But what's left for me to do? What options do I have to get out of this horrible country?" All I could suggest was either to find himself a Jewish wife, which, according to the witticism of the time, was "not a luxury but rather a means of transportation" (*ne roskosh', a sredstvo peredvizheniia*), or to find Ukrainian relatives in Canada or the United States and ask them for an affidavit of support.

By the end of the summer, when my telegram-delivery career was over, I once again faced the ominous prospect of being branded a parasite and therefore had to resume job hunting. For a brief spell, I worked as a night guard at the Donskoy Monastery, which was founded in the late sixteenth century. Shortly after seizing power, the Bolsheviks duly shut down the monastery. The Soviet authorities initially turned part of its facilities into a penal colony for children and later converted it into the so-called Museum of Russian Architecture, since it housed remnants of numerous demolished churches and cathedrals. In fact, it was not so much a museum as a gruesome cemetery of architecture. As a night guard, I was supposed to walk periodically around the site, spending the rest of the time in the guardhouse and desperately trying not to fall asleep. I still remember the eerie feeling I had when touring the premises in the wee hours, particularly the monastery's ancient graveyard. Little did I know that in the late 1930s and early 1940s the Stalin regime had used the graveyard as a dumping ground for the cremated ashes of executed political prisoners.

---

43 Kovalenko is the family name of two characters, brother and sister, who appear in Chekhov's story "The Man in a Case."

After quitting that spine-chilling job, I had to resume my job search. Among other things, I looked for work in the already familiar postal service system. Several weeks into unsuccessful job hunting, I chanced upon a regional communication center (*uzel sviazi*), hoping for some good fortune therein. Here is a bizarre exchange I had with its manager, Mr. Kolin, who naturally was wary of me. He carefully examined my papers, and the following conversation ensued:

> "Tell me, please, why you, a graduate of the highly prestigious Moscow University Chemistry Department, are seeking a menial poorly paid job?"
> "I became disillusioned with chemistry [which was true] and am interested in other things."
> "What interests you now?"
> "Eastern languages."
> "What kind of Eastern: Near Eastern, Middle Eastern, or Far Eastern?"

And before I had a chance to respond, Mr. Kolin shouted:

> "Don't you try to hoodwink me, buster! I've heard about you on the Voice of Israel."

He then called in his deputy, and they began to speak Yiddish. Just in case, Mr. Kolin asked me whether I spoke Yiddish ("*Redstu yidish?*"), to which I responded in the negative. I added, however, that I did speak Hebrew, which, as I could see, immensely impressed them both.

After the deputy had left, Mr. Kolin told me that he would give me a job, but under one condition. Before I began wondering what this possibly unsavory condition might be, he said, "As I understand it, you've been a refusenik for quite some time and know all the ropes.[44] My son has received an invitation from my cousin in Haifa. He wants to apply for an exit visa but doesn't know how to go about it. Would you be willing to guide him

---

44 At the time, "refuseniks"—the locution that derived from the verb "refuse"—was an unofficial term for individuals whom the Soviet authorities denied permission to immigrate to Israel. Nowadays, the term has entered colloquial English and refers to any person who refuses to do something, especially by way of protest. I recall a bizarre encounter I had with a Cornell Jewish student. When I mentioned to him that I had been a refusenik in the Soviet Union in the early 1970s, he told me, to my sheer bewilderment, that his younger brother was also a refusenik. It turned out that the student's family had immigrated to Israel, and his brother refused conscription to the Israel Defense Forces. Not my kind of refusenik, buddy!

through the process?" I told Mr. Kolin that even if he did not give me a job I would still help his son. And so I did, and his son, Izia, received an exit visa in no time and even had to ask OVIR for an extension. I was immensely grateful to Mr. Kolin. This job gave me some breathing space. I worked at the post office as a manual laborer until facing new challenges that resulted in my arrest and subsequent imprisonment.

With fellow refuseniks Nina and Moisei Bel'for, and Mark Nashpitz. Moscow, 1971.

By the fall of 1971, I indeed became a seasoned refusenik. The regime repeatedly turned down my visa application, and I was fighting back: signing letters of protest, conveying data to foreign journalists, receiving calls from abroad, and keeping my interlocutors abreast of the Soviet Jewry struggle for emigration. Our residence was regularly used as a center for dissemination of such news. Calls were coming in from all over the world, and knowledge of languages was much in demand. I conducted conversations in English and Hebrew, and Boris Kogan, a gifted linguist, handled those in French, Italian, and Spanish. For a while, the KGB let us maintain this venue. But then its operatives presumably got tired of dealing with multilingual translations of our missives. Although these missives did not include any information about our future plans, they did contain information about the regime's hounding and human rights violations against Jewish activists. KGB operatives, without a doubt, found it harmful to the image of their organization and of the entire Soviet establishment and disconnected our phone.

The regime, of course, did not reveal the true reason for this disruption and claimed that there was a severe breakdown in our phone system, which could not be easily rectified. After numerous inquiries, my father wrote a letter addressed to Boris Beshchev, minister of transportation and communication. In this letter, Father suggested that since Soviet technology admittedly was not up to snuff for the task, perhaps some American telephone company should be entrusted with the repair. The letter was broadcast by all Western radio stations and by the Voice of Israel. It drew attention to the plight and persecution of the Soviet Jews wanting to emigrate and evoked a sympathetic chuckle among the fellow refuseniks, but it changed nothing. The telephone remained disconnected.

Besides disconnecting our apartment phone, the KGB demonstratively shadowed me up until my very departure. It was more psychological harassment than spying. Once, just for the heck of it, I decided to turn the tables on a KGB agent. This minuscule, inconspicuously looking blondish man popped up wherever I went: on the subway, in the street, at the library. As I entered a bookstore, he stopped at the corner, lit a cigarette, and pretended to read a newspaper posted on the wall of a nearby building. As I exited the bookstore and caught sight of my "travel buddy," I started walking briskly toward him. When the sleuth realized that, in violation of the familiar script, he was the pursued rather the pursuer, he became fretful and frightened, yelped, and ran away.

As members of the Jewish movement, we knew that our apartments were bugged. This surveillance made it impossible to conduct any sensitive conversations even in a whisper, let alone out loud. We overcame this challenge by corresponding on a roll of toilet paper, frequently in Hebrew, just for fun, and by passing it from person to person. When the conversation was over, the whole communication was literally flushed down the toilet.

This way, we safely planned demonstrations, letters of protest, and simply shared news.

After countless visits to the Moscow OVIR and its as numerous refusals to grant me an exit visa, I at long last managed to schedule an appointment with Colonel Smirnov, its director, whose conduct was known to alternate drastically between curt and courteous. The meeting went amazingly well. The colonel was polite, promised me a definite response, hinting that it may very well be a positive one, and suggested I call him the next day. I returned home in the state of elation. To my skeptical mother I guilelessly exclaimed, "But Colonel Smirnov promised!" The next day, with my heart in my mouth, I phoned the colonel. Alas, he refused me an exit visa once again. No, he did not deny making nebulous promises but rather philosophically declared, "Yesterday was yesterday, and today is today—dialectics." Needless to say, my naive exclamation and Colonel Smirnov's brilliant adage, sophisticatedly steeped in Hegelian philosophical precepts, were added to the golden fund of our family proverbs.

In September 1971, if my memory serves me right, the Soviet regime agreed to meet with several representatives of the Jewish movement. This way, the regime in effect acknowledged that Jewish immigration to Israel was a serious widespread problem that should be addressed. The establishment designated Al´bert Ivanov to meet with us Jewish activists. A member of the Central Committee of the Communist Party, Al´bert Ivanov, among other things, oversaw the emigration process. On our side, five individuals were selected for the meeting: Boris Orlov, Vladimir Rozenblium, Viktor Pol´sky, Pavel Gol´dshtein, and I. For the Soviet regime, the Jewish movement was a novelty, so the establishment wanted to feel out its mindset in order to decide how to deal with this pain in the neck. For us, on the other hand, it was an opportunity to make it clear to the regime that our intent was serious and to call upon the authorities to work out a comprehensive solution. We also conveyed to Ivanov that the regime had to devise unambiguous rules and regulations and stick to them, but he affirmed that the administration would continue to tackle emigration on a case-to-case basis. The meaning of Ivanov's rejoinder was clear: *we the establishment* are running the show and calling the shots around here, and *we* decide who leaves and when, if ever. This was an early round of the confrontation between the Jewish movement and the Soviet regime that would last for two more decades. The outcome: the Soviet regime collapsed and is no more, and the Jews in the end won the struggle, albeit at a heavy price of many adversely affected lives—long-term refuseniks, divided families, and Prisoners of Zion.[45]

At the time of the meeting, Ivanov impressed me as a rather intelligent and well-spoken bureaucrat. Of course, he was in no position to make decisions but rather served as a go-between. While working on this book, I learned of Ivanov's inglorious end about nine years after our encounter. Ivanov had an argument with his wife, became quite depressed, and went alone to their summer cottage. He phoned and asked her to come over. When she refused, he got drunk and reportedly committed suicide by shooting himself in the head with the revolver that he received as a present from Afghani president Hafizullah Amin. Amin, oddly enough, had also come to an ignominious end a few months earlier, when he was assassinated in December 1979 by his Soviet patrons on the heels of their ill-fated invasion of Afghanistan.

Although I was chosen to participate in this pivotal meeting, I did not belong to any specific group or circle within the Jewish movement. While I took part in the actions that I deemed of major importance, I spent most of my time studying and teaching Hebrew. I had several groups, each consisting of approximately five students. Since, as I mentioned earlier, Hebrew was the forbidden language in the Soviet Union, for the reasons of safety we used to meet at random in the residence of one of the students. For my instruction, I adopted *Elef Milim*, the primer that I employed in my own initial studies of the tongue. I much favored this

---

[45] "Prisoners of Zion" was the term for Jews, such as Natan Sharansky, Iosif Begun, and Ida Nudel', who were incarcerated, sent to labor camps, or exiled to Siberia for their Zionist activities. For books chronicling the lives and struggles of some of the most prominent refuseniks and Prisoners of Zion, see, for example, Natan Sharansky, *Fear No Evil: The Classic Memoir of One Man's Triumph over a Police State* (New York: Random House, 1988); Chaim Potok, *Gates of November: Chronicles of the Slepak Family* (New York: Random House, 1997); Yosef Mendelevich, *Unbroken Spirit: A Heroic Story of Faith, Courage and Survival* (Jerusalem: Gefen, 2012).

textbook because it was based on the principle of not involving any other language.

The authorities were none too pleased with me. Every now and then, I was called in for conversations with KGB operatives, who, like a broken record, kept admonishing me for my "anti-Soviet Zionist activities." They kept demanding that I stop these activities, otherwise threatening, "to send me packing to the Far East instead of the Near East" (*vyslat′ na Dal′nii Vostok vmesto Blizhnego*). My adversaries were a couple of humorless chaps. They introduced themselves as Kotov and Karpov—"Mr. Cat" and "Mr. Carp"—and when I inquired if their partnership could be detrimental to Mr. Carp, my quip did not bring even a semblance of a smile to their mask-like, determinedly glum faces. Curiously, from what I gathered during the meetings with this sour-faced duo, what disconcerted the Soviet establishment the most was my teaching Hebrew, which they dubbed the "ancient Jewish tongue," or *drevneevreiskii iazyk* in Russian. Apparently, the regime viewed studying and teaching the language as a highly subversive activity. The regime's concern was well justified. For my part, I believed then as I do now that Hebrew is not only the most essential and efficient means of preparing people for the immigration but also the most powerful bonding tool between Diaspora Jews and Israel and among individual Jews all over the world.

Speaking of the "ancient Jewish tongue." In the early 1970s, when a growing number of Jews considered leaving for Israel, the Soviet authorities decided to take appropriate measures in dissuading them from making Aliyah ("repatriation," or, literally, "ascent" in Hebrew). They chose to conduct propaganda sessions with potential émigrés. The success of these sessions is reflected in the following story. A Communist Party instructor meets with Jews and tries to discourage them from going to Israel. He explains to them that "these retrograde Zionists" require all newcomers, even little children, to study Hebrew, that outmoded "ancient Jewish tongue," the language of "the Decrepit Testament" (*Vetkhii Zavet*), as the Old Testament is disdainfully referred to in Russian. The instructor also informs the Jews that the weather in Israel is horrific. There are merely two seasons in the country: a long torrid summer and a relatively brief yet cold and rainy winter. As the instructor continues his speech, he notices a little old Jew in the front row repeatedly flip-flopping his right hand. Finally, the irritated instructor could hold his cool no longer:

> "Comrade Rabinovich! What are you doing? Why are you moving your hand from side to side?"
> "Well," 'Comrade' Rabinovich replied, "I am trying to decide whether to take an umbrella, or not to take an umbrella; to take an umbrella, or not to take an umbrella ..."

The outlook of many Soviet Jews was succinctly and most expressively summed up by the distinguished Yiddish poet Iosif Kerler, who after many years of struggle for an exit visa finally left for Israel in 1971. Before his emigration, Soviet officials decided to have a "heart-to-heart" talk with him in the hope of grasping his motives as well as the mood on the Jewish street, and maybe even—a slim chance but who knows!—of persuading him to change his mind. One official began by describing the wonderful life the Kerlers were having in the Land of the Soviets: his poems were being published, his wife worked as a registered nurse, his son attended a good school, and they all lived in a nice apartment. Finally, another official asked: "Iosif Borisovich, aren't you happy with us?" "No," responded Kerler, "I am happy *with your us*, but I want *with our us*" (*Iosif Borisovich! Chto Vam u nas plokho?—Net, mne **u vas** khorosho, no ia khochu **u nas**.*) (The Soviet official's question implies that, as a Jew, Kerler is an outsider. Therefore, Kerler's response emphasizes that he does not want to be "with your us," a guest in the country to which he does not belong, but rather "with our us," that is, in his own country, Israel, where he will be accepted and treated as equal.)

Months later, I was summoned for a similar "heart-to-heart" and was asked in like fashion what motivated my decision to apply for an exit visa to Israel. After all, my parents have well-paying jobs, I graduated from Moscow University, we live in a nice apartment of our own, and have a car. My response was a bit different: "You see," I said, "I am a redhead. As you know, redheads habitually have color pigment deficiency that makes their eyes extremely sensitive and prone to irritation. So I find it hard to live in the country in which I encounter the red color no matter where I look. It is hard on my eyes. Therefore I want to move to Israel where blue and white will be not only easy on, but even soothing to my eyes."

Having occasional fun like this was the only way to survive in this gloomy and precarious atmosphere when the regime watched my every step. As if this were not hard enough, life occasionally threw additional challenges my way. Mother kept some dissident materials in our apartment at the behest of one of her colleagues, Leonard Ternovsky (1933–2006), a radiologist and distinguished human rights activist. Had the apartment been searched, it would have had severe implications for me. When I warned my mother about it, she naively said that she would take the blame, not realizing that this would arm the regime with an excuse to persecute and prosecute me, not her. One day, in September 1972, there was a close call. While I was walking through a vacant lot between our apartment building and the subway station to which I was heading, I suddenly discerned a car that looked suspicious to my expert eye. As I was about to cross the street, the car suddenly pulled up and plainclothesmen jumped out and grabbed me. My heart sank. If the KGB agents take me back to the apartment for a house search, I shall get a minimum of ten years for storing dissident or, as the regime labeled it, "anti-Soviet" literature.

When I realized that the car was moving in a different direction, I breathed a sigh of relief. The KGB agents drove me to a police station, where many Jews had already been rounded up, and loaded us all onto a truck. I remember Volodia Lerner, the son of a prominent cybernetics expert, Alexander Yakovlevich Lerner, saying to discharge the tension: "If you call yourself a Jew, get into the bed of a truck" (*Nazvalsia evreem, polezai v kuzov*), which was a witty paraphrase of the Russian proverb: "If you call yourself a milk-cap, get into the basket" (*Nazvalsia gruzdem, polezai v kuzov*), equivalent to the English saying, "If you pledge, do not hedge," that is, "once you're in, you can't back out."[46] The truck took us to a train station, from which we were transported to Volokolamsk, a town approximately eighty miles from Moscow. We then were incarcerated in the local jail without being charged, were kept there for three days, and thereupon were released and returned to Moscow with no explanations given. This was typical of the Soviet criminal justice system.

---

46 Volodia's witticism was based on the homonymic wordplay: *kuzov* means both a "basket," in which one gathers mushrooms and berries, and a "bed of a truck."

Of course, it was highly frustrating to be treated so unceremoniously. Yet we Jewish activists made the best of those three days. We sang Hebrew songs and practiced Hebrew among ourselves, being well aware all the while that the cell was most likely bugged and we ought to exercise caution in choosing topics of conversation. Only upon returning to Moscow did we find out that it was a so-called preemptive arrest. The authorities were apprehensive that we would hold demonstrations and disrupt the work of the Supreme Soviet and, without hesitation, detained us for the duration of its sessions. When we discovered the reason for our sudden capture and imprisonment, we found great solace in realizing that the authorities were worried about our actions, which would bring them bad publicity in the West. This awareness gave us extra strength and further motivation to continue our struggle.

The Jews who wished to emigrate habitually gathered near the synagogue on festive occasions, above all on Simchat Torah. This was the place where one could run into a fellow refusenik and exchange news, or meet a Jew from overseas, especially from Israel. Even though there were no diplomatic relations between the Soviet Union and the State of Israel, Israelis were coming to Moscow and other cities in the early 1970s to participate in a variety of international conventions. In the fall of 1971, shortly before the Feast of Tabernacles (Sukkot), I was listening to the Voice of Israel in Hebrew and learned that Michael Sela, a renowned Israeli immunologist from the Weizmann Institute, would be visiting Moscow within the coming week. I went to the Moscow Choral Synagogue on the eve of Simchat Torah and caught a glimpse of a man who, I had a hunch, was Michael Sela. I had the audacity to approach the man and greet him in Hebrew: "Shalom, Professor Sela!" He was evidently taken aback and rather worried, in all likelihood suspecting me of being a KGB agent. He looked visibly relieved when I introduced myself and told him how I learned about his visit to Moscow. I asked him to convey my best regards to Alex, whom he knew very well. When I came to Israel and Alex returned from her sabbatical leave, she told me how impressed Sela was with my Hebrew and my zeal for Israel.

In addition to Michael Sela, I met other Israelis who came to Moscow for various symposia, from surgeons to beekeepers. Most colorful among them was a young sabra kibbutznik, Yair Barzilai.[47] Dark-haired and well-tanned, Yair was powerfully built, free-spoken, loud and emotional, and stood in stark contrast to his fellow beekeeper Tzvi Hameiri. Romanian-born mild-mannered Hameiri, who was versed in more than half a dozen languages, was noticeably older and much more reserved. While doing research for this book, I learned that Tzvi (1926–98) went through the hell of the Holocaust (Auschwitz) and was detained in Cyprus by the British Mandate administration before immigrating to Israel. Meeting these Israelis of different personal, cultural, and professional backgrounds greatly enhanced my perception of the country.

Aside from frequent gatherings near the synagogue, we Jewish activists also occasionally had our indoor parties and outdoor picnics. We ate, drank, dreamed about going to Israel, and sang songs in Hebrew and Russian. Some songs were solemn, some jocular. Among the solemn songs, I specifically remember the one that we were all singing in both Russian and Hebrew with great gusto because it deeply resonated in our hearts. Chanting it together, in unison, we felt that we were one entity, the Jewish people (*Am Israel*):

> To pharaoh I say: Let my people go!
> To pharaoh I say: Let my people go!
> Let the Jewish people go to its homeland!
> Let the Jewish people go to its homeland!
>
> (*Faraonu govoriu: otpusti narod moi!*
> *Faraonu govoriu: otpusti narod moi!*
> *Otpusti narod evreiskii na rodinu svoiu!*
> *Otpusti narod evreiskii na rodinu svoiu!*)
>
> (*Lefar'o ani omer: shalach et ami!*
> *Lefar'o ani omer: shalach et ami!*
> *Shalach et haam hayehudi lemoladeto!*
> *Shalach et haam hayehudi lemoladeto!*)

Another song, this time a funny one, which was popular among Moscow Jews, emulated and mocked anti-Semitic slurs and accusations:

---

47 *Sabra* or *tzabar* refers to a native-born Israeli Jew. This nickname was given by way of comparison to the cactus pear, prickly on the outside but sweet on the inside.

If there is no water in the faucet, Yids drank all the water!
If the creek dried up, a Jew is to blame.
If rains are pouring, Yids are at fault.
Jews, Jews, nothing but Jews all around!

(*Esli v krane net vody, vodu vypili zhidy!*
Esli peresokh ruchei, v etom vinovat evrei.
Esli zalili dozhdi, vinovaty v tom zhidy.
Evrei, evrei, krugom odni evrei!)

The words of this facetious song may sound somewhat far-fetched to a Western ear. Regrettably, its content was not that remote from Soviet reality, riddled with out-and-out anti-Semitism.

This prejudice, so rampant in the street, was encouraged by the government. It escalated in the late 1960s and continued unabated for at least another twenty years. Among the Soviet rulers, the dubious palm of supremacy in promoting hatred of Jews belonged to Grigory Romanov. The Leningrad Communist Party boss between 1970 and 1983, Romanov had become one of the top figures in the Soviet Politburo. His obsessive animosity toward Jews is reflected in the following anecdote. A high-ranking Chinese delegation has arrived in the Soviet Union. The Soviet hosts, headed by Romanov, meet the foreign dignitaries for a red-carpet ceremony at the Moscow Vnukovo airport. As the members of the Chinese delegation are descending the gangway, Romanov greets them: "Hey kikes! Why have you squinted your eyes?" (*Chto, zhidy, soshchurilis´?*).

This acute Judeophobia at the top was readily emulated by the general populace. One could often hear in the overcrowded buses and streetcars or in long lines for groceries and merchandise: "Hey kikes! Shove off to Israel!" (*Ei, zhidy! Ubiraites´ v Izrail´!*). Some sharp-tongued Jews would respond to this aspiration of anti-Semites with an aspiration of their own: "From your mouth to God's Ears!" (*Vashi by rechi da Bogu v ushi!*). When in the course of an exceptionally protracted heat wave in the summer of 1972 the woods around Moscow were burning, filling the air with a bitter smoky smell, it was rumored that Jews set them on fire. As I learned at the time, Jews indeed had something to do with this matter but not in the way this libelous hearsay claimed. The chief forester, who was reportedly

Jewish, forewarned the authorities about the incoming dry spell and suggested measures for allaying its consequences. Of course, the featherbrained bureaucrats did nothing and, to avert the blame, were spreading these slanderous accusations. I personally recall an instance of that kind of vilifying and rabble-rousing anti-Semitism shortly before my departure from the Land of the Soviets. I stood in a long line to buy potatoes. The scorching heat that summer, with triple-digit temperatures for well over a month, caused a terrible drought that had a detrimental effect on the crop, including potatoes. The blame for the shortage of this vegetable, so essential to the Russian diet, was leveled at Jews (just as in the song). "Do you know why there are no potatoes in the city?" asked a corpulent middle-aged Russian woman, holding a string shopping bag colloquially known as *avos'ka* (from the Russian *avos'* meaning "perhaps," "maybe"). She immediately proffered the answer: "'Cause Yids ate all the potatoes!" (*Potomu chto zhidy s''eli vsiu kartoshku!*).

CHAPTER 5

ARREST, IMPRISONMENT, TRIAL, AND AFTERMATH

> When on May 6, 1972, Comrade Mukharinov from the recruitment office personally arrived to hand the call-up notice to Shapiro, the defendant declined to accept it and declared that he did not wish to serve in the Soviet Army since he considered himself a citizen of Israel.
> —From the trial verdict

But I am getting ahead of myself. Let me backtrack a little. By May 1972, I had been fighting for my exit visa for more than a year and a half. That month, President Nixon was scheduled to visit Moscow for the summit talks. This would be the first time since 1945, when Franklin Delano Roosevelt had taken part in the Yalta Conference, that a U.S. president set foot in the Soviet Union. To the dismay of the Soviet regime, a dozen or so Jewish activists, myself included, signed a petition requesting a meeting with the U.S. president. In response to this and other similar petitions, the KGB decided to cleanse the capital of Jewish dissenters by summoning the younger among us for military reserve service. Officially, the regime had the right to draft at any point, but the timing of this call-up made it clear that it was a political ploy. Besides, this call-up was a much more sinister move than it appeared: this recruitment would have armed the Soviet authorities with an additional excuse for refusing exit visas to the Jewish draftees on account of their putative familiarity with military secrets. My situation was unique in that about a year prior to the call-up I renounced my Soviet citizenship and was granted Israeli citizenship in absentia.

How did it happen? What did this citizenship in absentia signify? In early May 1971, I learned from a Hebrew broadcast on the Voice of Israel that the Knesset had adopted an amendment to the citizenship law, named after its chief proponent, Dr. Iosef Burg, the then Israeli interior minister. Until that time, Jews received Israeli citizenship only upon entering the country. The Iosef Burg amendment authorized the Ministry of the Interior to bestow Israeli citizenship upon overseas Jews who were prevented from coming to Israel. This move was conceived primarily with Soviet Jewry in mind. Supporters of the amendment trusted that if these Jews were recognized by Israel as citizens they might find it easier to obtain visas. Jumping ahead, I must say that the in absentia Israeli citizenship helped me a great deal. It provided me with the necessary legal basis for countering the draft evasion charges at my trial.

The instant I heard about the amendment resolution, I telephoned Alex in Jerusalem and asked her to submit an application for citizenship on my behalf. As I later found out, she did so at once. It is quite possible that I was among the very first Soviet Jews to ask for and receive citizenship in accordance with the Iosef Burg amendment. The in absentia citizenship was granted to me expeditiously—on May 31, 1971—but it took almost six months, until November 9, before I obtained the actual document, that is, the notification of received citizenship. As I learned upon my arrival in Israel, this uncharted territory led to a somewhat protracted correspondence between Alex and numerous officials of the Interior and Foreign ministries and caused a significant delay in the actual issuance of the document. Strange as it may sound, bearing in mind that the Soviet regime used to intercept any undesirable correspondence, especially when it came from Israel, the package arrived by regular mail. Upon receiving the notification, I immediately sent a letter to the Supreme Soviet, informing the regime of the change in my citizenship status:

> On April 7, 1971, I submitted an application for the renouncement of my Soviet citizenship to Nikolai Podgornyi, the President of the Supreme Soviet. In addition, I hereby inform you that on May 31, 1971, Dr. Iosef Burg, Interior Minister of the State of Israel, granted me an Israeli citizenship in absentia. Pursuant to this change and based on

article 15 of the United Nations Declaration of Human Rights, which proclaims that "no one shall be arbitrarily deprived of his nationality nor denied the right to change his nationality," I respectfully request an immediate answer to my earlier application for the renouncement of Soviet citizenship.

I kept the Israeli citizenship notification on me at all times and regarded it as a letter of safe-conduct, which to an extent it indeed turned out to be. When on May 5, 1972, I was summoned to the regional army recruitment office, I told its director, Colonel Lazarev, that I would not be able to serve in the Soviet military. I further explained to the colonel that I did not consider myself a Soviet citizen but rather an Israeli citizen held in the Soviet Union against my will. Apparently, my statement caught Lazarev completely off guard because he did not arrest me right on the spot. When the next day he sent his deputy, Captain Mukharinov, to hand-deliver the call-up notice, I refused to accept it. Once again, the officer left without arresting me since he presumably received no such orders. When the following day Captain Mukharinov was finally instructed to fetch me, I had already gone into hiding, staying with several friends for the extent of President Nixon's visit and beyond. The KGB waged a psychological war against my family. Its agents relentlessly harassed my parents and my sister by showing up at the apartment in the middle of the night and pretending to look for me, knowing full well that I was not to be found there.

While underground, I learned great news: my eighteen-year-old sister, Luba, received an exit visa to Israel. On June 2, on the eve of her departure, she was clandestinely brought to my hiding place to say good-bye. I had mixed feelings about this news. On the one hand, I was extremely happy for my teenage sister, for I was well aware that she had no future in the Soviet Union. On the other hand, I knew that it would not be easy for her to start a new life in Israel on her own, even with the assistance of our local relatives. Furthermore, I felt apprehensive since I had no idea when I would be able to see her again. Luba immigrated on June 5, 1972, and was the first member of our immediate family to arrive in Israel. (Grandma Zisl, aged ninety-three, her daughter, and my aunt, Niuta, and Niuta's third and penultimate husband, Grisha, left for Israel in February of that year. Grandma died five months later, on the eve of

Tisha B'Av, three and a half months before my immigration.)[48] Soon afterward, when I reemerged from hiding, I did not have the slightest shred of doubt that my arrest was imminent.

On June 12, I went to the Sheremetevo Airport to bid farewell to a friend who was leaving for Israel. As I was riding in a cab, I detected a couple of cars that looked suspicious to my well-trained eye. When I shared this observation with my buddy and fellow passenger, he poked fun at my paranoia. Upon seeing off the Israel-bound friend, I went to a taxi stand to take a cab back to the city.

Surrounded by other Jews, who were also waiting for a cab and who like me were fighting for their immigration to Israel, I was suddenly (no matter how mentally well prepared one is, these things always happen suddenly) approached by a police officer, who called me aside. "Are you citizen Dombrovsky?" was his question. I realized of course that it was a ploy but out of curiosity decided to stick to the proffered scenario. "No, I am not," I replied. At first, I was surprised by the choice of such an unusual name. Yaroslav Dombrovsky (more accurately Jarosław Dąbrowski, 1836–71), was an ethnically Polish military officer, initially in the service of the tsarist army. Dombrovsky became involved in the preparation of the 1863 Polish uprising and was arrested and exiled to Siberia. In 1865, he managed to escape to France and settled in Paris. In 1871, Dombrovsky took part in the so-called Paris Commune uprising. He served as the Commune military commander, died on its barricades, and was officially glorified by the Soviet propaganda. It later occurred to me that the name choice was not so haphazard after all: evidently, in the minds of the Soviet leaders, a non-Russian Dombrovsky, regardless of any formal glorification, was a rebel and a dissenter. The police officer asked for my passport, checked it against my appearance, and commented that I looked like the serial killer who had plagued Moscow with a string of brutal murders. Little did I know that there was another Dombrovsky, Yuri (1909–78), the author of *The Keeper of Antiquities* (*Khranitel' drevnostei*, 1964), a dissident writer and a "serial killer" of Soviet shams.

---

48 A day of mourning, Tisha B'Av commemorates many tragedies that occurred throughout the history of the Jewish people on that day, primarily the destruction of the First and the Second Temples.

In a deliberately loud voice, the officer suggested we go to the airport police station to verify my identity. Instead, he escorted me to one of the cars that I had spotted en route to the airport and handed me over to plainclothesmen. The detectives immediately drove me back to the city, to my neighborhood police station. There, a uniformed KGB officer, a fellow Moscow University graduate, judging by a golden-blue rhombic badge on his lapel, was already waiting for me. He politely asked me to empty my pockets. One item attracted his undivided attention: my in absentia Israeli citizenship notification. Upon my explanation of its contents, the officer left the room, doubtless to consult his superiors. Presumably, he received instructions to proceed as planned. The KGB man confiscated all my belongings and instructed one of his subordinates to place me in a chamber of preliminary confinement (*kamera predvaritel'nogo zakliucheniia*, or KPZ for short), where I spent four nights in the drunk tank. Apparently, the authorities wanted me to sober up, to stop being inebriated with the idea of going to Israel. The cell was clean, but I was left to sleep there on a hardwood platform with no bedding.

Incidentally, this was not the first time that I, a teetotaler, paradoxically, stayed in a drunk tank. On March 19, 1971, thirty-nine Jews, myself included, came to the General Prosecutor's Office and demanded a meeting with its chief, Roman Rudenko. It was the very same Rudenko who in the summer of 1953 masterminded the clampdown on the Gulag uprising in the Vorkuta coalmines, turning it into a bloodbath. Rudenko was reportedly rewarded for this "glorious deed" with the lucrative high-office appointment. Obviously, we did not expect Rudenko and his ilk to change their spots, but these were somewhat different times. The Soviet Union was in dire economic straits and badly needed U.S. assistance by way of so-called détente. In return, the regime, fearful of any negative international publicity that might jeopardize being granted the Most-Favored-Nation status, on occasion pretended to be on its, if not good, at least better behavior toward its own citizens, specifically Jews. For the most part, however, as the unfolding events clearly demonstrate, the regime kept showing its beastly, predatory grin.

Although we knew all that and were well aware that Rudenko was nothing but a faithful watchdog of the regime, we wished to discuss with him—and through him with the establishment, mainly for publicity purposes—our previously submitted letter. In this letter, we and two hundred additional signatories insisted on the release of Jews arrested in Leningrad, Riga, Kishinev, Odessa, and other cities for merely wanting to go to Israel. We also called for freedom of immigration to our historical homeland and drew attention to the illegality of keeping us in the Soviet Union against our will.

We were promised an appointment with Rudenko at 3 p.m. that day and were asked to wait. While in the anteroom, we would remind the office rank and file from time to time about our appointment and would be told that the general prosecutor was still busy and will meet with us once his schedule allows. The Soviet regime could not be outdone in its sinister cynicism. At 5:30 p.m., the building doors were suddenly tightly shut, and we were all arrested on charges of violating the public order. It was abundantly clear that the use of the anteroom as a mousetrap was a premeditated, well-planned operation. We were all loaded onto waiting buses and were transported to the drunk tank number 9. This drunk tank had a dubious distinction: it was often used for detaining Jewish protesters and for that reason was dubbed "the Jewish sober-upper" (*evreiskii vytrezvitel'*). There, each of us was interrogated, and we were all charged with hooliganism. (Curiously, Major Zolotukhin, deputy director of Moscow OVIR, seconded this allegation when a couple of months later, after having been once again denied an exit visa, I slammed his office door with such force that its glass pane shattered.) The next day, after spending a night in the drunk tank, we were all brought before the judge, who imposed on us various sentences, ranging from a twenty-ruble fine to fifteen days in jail. As a first-time offender, I was sentenced to a mere twenty-ruble fine.

To return to the story of my arrest and imprisonment in June 1972. After spending four nights in the police station drunk tank, I was taken to the detention center, euphemistically called "an investigative isolation ward" (*sledstvennyi izoliator*). Curiously, the word *izoliator* denotes a remedial facility where patients with infectious diseases are held in quarantine. I suppose the name fitted me right because Zionism in Soviet Russia, from the regime's standpoint, indeed quickly became an infectious disease of epidemic proportions.

Intriguingly, the name of the jail to which I was sent has a historical medical association. The romantic-sounding Matrosskaia Tishina (literally, "Sailor's Quiet") has been all over the news in the last decade because of the lengthy incarceration there of the recently pardoned and released Mikhail Khodorkovsky.[49] The jail received its name after the street that was immortalized by Alexander Galich's eponymous play. Initially the area housed a sail factory founded by Peter the Great alongside a nearby settlement for sailors. Later, the factory was moved to another city, and its premises were converted into a nursing home for veteran and invalid sailors. By imperial decree, no carriages or other means of transportation were permitted there. And that is how the street, in which the retired sailors were able to live in peace and quiet, reportedly received its name.

The penitentiary facility in that location was built in 1775, in the reign of Catherine the Great. In the Soviet era, the jail was initially converted into a reform school for juvenile delinquents, but after World War II it was transformed back into a jail, which it remains to this very day. Contrary to the jail's enigmatic and serene-sounding name, as I quickly realized, there was nothing enigmatic or serene about it.

To say that I was not afraid to be the sole political prisoner among hard-core criminals, not to mention the only Jew, would certainly be an egregious lie. A remarkable thing happened, though, the night before I was taken from the police station to the jail: the Almighty's messenger and my namesake visited me in my dream. Archangel Gabriel calmed me and promised that not a single hair on my head would be touched. The next morning, I woke up in a jubilant mood, and until my release from jail, I had the physical sensation that the Almighty was holding His Palm over my head to protect me from any harm.

---

49 Mikhail Khodorkovsky was a Russian businessman, head of the oil company Yukos. He spent ten years in custody after being accused of tax evasion and fraud. It is widely believed that he was incarcerated on trumped-up charges for voicing his opposition to corruption in the higher echelons of power. In December 2013, Khodorkovsky was pardoned by President Putin and left for Germany. He now resides in Switzerland.

Upon my arrival at Matrosskaia Tishina, I was first placed for a couple of hours in a box, a dark rectangular cuboid, with little to no ventilation. I was unable to sit or squat but had to stand the entire time. After the box, I was subjected to a few formalities. First, my fingerprints were taken (in criminal argot, this procedure is called "to play the piano"), then my head and armpits were shaved, and I had a quick shower. After having been thus physically disinfected (the regime, of course, viewed my Zionist convictions far more seriously than they would a highly contagious disease), I was sent to a cell. On my way there, I noted a large slogan hung overhead that summed up the Soviet attitude toward the concept of presumed innocence: "Only by honest work and exemplary behavior you may atone for your guilt" (*Tol'ko chestnym trudom i primernym povedeniem ty mozhesh′ iskupit′ svoiu vinu*). Although formally charged, I was not found guilty of anything as of yet, but the slogan clearly insinuated otherwise.

The appearance of a new inmate is obviously a welcome break from the jail monotony, and I saw more than sixty pairs of eyes fixated upon me with vivid curiosity. Extremely large by American standards, each cell had its elder, usually the inmate with the most "respectable" crime record. Sasha certainly fit the bill. Before getting caught, he was the leader of a gang that for years robbed the residences of Soviet higher-ups and of foreign diplomats. Sasha impressed me as a quick-witted fellow. It seemed to me that he felt trapped and totally bored within the Soviet Union, that gigantic penal colony, and could not apply himself to anything else but crime. Under different circumstances, in a free country, he could have realized his potential by doing something valuable. At a later point, when I knew him better, I shared this thought with him and he tacitly agreed with my assessment.

Sasha and his retinue quizzed me on my "misdeed." I told them that I was arrested for refusing to be drafted into the army reserve. I also told them that I renounced my Soviet citizenship and was granted Israeli citizenship in absentia. They were astounded to see a political prisoner in their midst but acted well toward me because they hated the regime and viewed me as a dissenter. Philo-Semites they were definitely not, but treated me along the lines of my "being a good guy despite being Jewish."

I quickly found out that the sought-after bunks were the ones located away from the toilet and near the window, heavily barred, of course. Furthermore, the bottom bunks were much favored over the top ones. This is despite the fact that whenever a top-bunk inmate moved, dust and dirt rained down upon the bottom-bunk occupant. The main reason for such preference was the eye-piercing overhead light, which made it impossible to get a decent night's sleep. (Needless to say, eye masks and pillow mints were not provided.) Top bunk or bottom, sleep seldom lasted long anyway. It was disrupted when the cellmates were called out in the middle of the night for interrogation.

I, too, was summoned for such midnight rendezvous. My first interrogator was a rather young fellow, my age or even younger, who knew nothing about Jews or Jewish history. He was quickly replaced by a much older and more seasoned antagonist who introduced himself as Yuri Nikolaevich Gorbunov. I reminded Gorbunov that I renounced my Soviet citizenship, received Israeli citizenship in absentia, and therefore regarded myself as a foreign national, held in the Soviet Union by force. Gorbunov, who evidently was instructed by his superiors to dodge this politically sensitive subject, met my declaration with complete silence. Gorbunov asked me a lot of questions and insisted that I write down the answers and sign the protocol of the interrogation. I told him that I had no objections to doing all this but only in Hebrew. Of course, I knew full well that the regime would never agree to such a thing. My opponent argued, based on the Soviet Criminal Code, that since I was born and grew up in Moscow and was a graduate of Moscow University, Russian was my native language, and I must render my written answers thus. I countered that as a Jew, whose historical homeland is the Land of Israel, and as a citizen of Israel, I considered Hebrew to be my native language. I also referred him to the Soviet Constitution, which entitled individuals of various ethnicities to conduct legal proceedings in their own tongue. I suppose it all boiled down to the definition of the native language. My adversary used the concept in the literal sense, whereas I used it rather within the historical-cultural and political perspective. In any case, I neither filled out nor signed any protocol. However, as an angry young man, I superfluously shared with my inquisitor some of my views on the Soviet regime. I had yet to read Vladimir Nabokov's *Invitation to a Beheading* and was unaware that Cincinnatus C., the novel's protagonist, already tried that when he guilelessly shared his thoughts with M'sieur Pierre and the executioner's minions to his own detriment. When my father came to jail to bring me a warm black sweater in case I was deported to Siberia, Gorbunov revealed wistfully and nostalgically: "In the good old days [by which he undoubtedly had the Stalin era in mind], for just a small fraction of what your son had said, I could have shot him right on the spot." While taking the sweater, Gorbunov refused to accept the Hebrew Bible, poignantly remarking, "It's not a synagogue here."

The jail administration did its utmost to enlighten the inmates, in the faint hope that they would give up their illicit ways, by bombarding the cells with radio news, both domestic and international. The prisoners, who loathed the Soviet system, mockingly reacted to the accounts of splendid harvests, the world's highest yields of milk, the record steel production, and the characterization of the Soviet Union as the light unto the nations. "Sure, sure, Soviet watches are the fastest in the world," they scornfully remarked. It so happened that the radio at the time reported the air skirmishes between Israel and Egypt, for which the Soviet propaganda predictably held "the Israeli military machine" fully responsible. My cellmates asked me to comment on these events and laughed their heads off at my sarcastic interpretations. As I found out later, the Soviet media angrily reported this news because on June 13, 1972, Israeli pilots shot down two Egyptian MIGs in a dogfight over the Mediterranean Sea, thereby demonstrating once again the decisive superiority of the Israeli air force. On occasion, to break the tedium, we held improvised concerts. Some told funny stories, some sang folk songs or songs popular in the criminal world (*blatnye pesni*). For my part, I recited Russian poetry and sang Hebrew songs.

Each evening, all transgressors for the day were put on trial. These internal trials mocked and mimicked the Soviet legal system. An alternative criminal code was drafted to determine the sentence for each given wrongdoing. The prosecutor and the defense lawyer presented their cases and the judge announced the verdict. As under the Soviet judicial procedure, there was no jury. I must say in the defense of this jailhouse legal system that it was by far more honest than the external one it replicated and ridiculed. The verdict was decided through deliberation and was not rigged and handed down to the judge, as was generally the case in the outside world of the Soviet totalitarian regime. Little did I know that the prisoners (save the elder and his entourage) were forbidden to interfere with due process. This disparity between the elite and the ordinary inmates also mirrored the Soviet system, according to which the Party *nomenklatura* was above the law, thereby illustrating the famous Latin saying: "What is allowed to Jupiter is not allowed to a bull" (*Quod licet Iovi, non licet bovi*).[50] When, on my very first day, a cellmate was accused of noisy chattering (*baklanka*) in disturbance of his fellow inmates' afternoon rest, I intervened on his behalf and offered some mitigating circumstances. For my interference, I received, in line with the internal criminal code, three smacks of a shoe on my bottom. At the same time, the cell elder pointed out, and the judge seconded his opinion, that I had defended the accused much better than the acting defense attorney. As a result, I was selected to replace him. Presumably, the genes of my legally trained great-great-grandfather Yaakov Kontorer and of Grandpa Gavriel were making themselves felt.

Hierarchy in the cell, based on the seriousness of one's crime, was strictly observed. As I alluded to previously, the most "respectable" crime was that of the cell elder, a skilled burglar. Among the run-of-the-mill but still well regarded felons were a very tall and dour-faced man nicknamed Shakhta ("Coalmine"), good-natured middle-aged Viktor, and Sergei, a young and lanky blond. Shakhta, a coalmine bookkeeper, was arrested for embezzling its funds; Viktor was detained for stealing and selling lab equipment; and Sergei was taken into custody for being a foreign-currency dealer (*valiutchik*). Although currency exchange is not viewed as a criminal offense in any democratic country, it was regarded as a serious infraction in Soviet Russia. Sergei knew that and to dodge a long prison sentence decided to feign temporary insanity (*kosit'na Serbskogo*[51]). Sergei

---

50 *Nomenklatura* was a self-appointed group running the Soviet Union.
51 This odd-sounding Russian phrase refers to the Serbsky Institute, named after the psychiatrist Vladimir Serbsky (1852–1917). One of the main purposes of the institute was to provide forensic psychiatry for the criminal courts. In Soviet times, particularly between the late 1960s and the

was a remarkable fellow. His knowledge of automobiles was comprehensive. If one asked him about any car model, say, a 1932 Ford Victoria 2-door sedan, he could provide a description of it in exquisite detail. On the other hand, those who were there on a misdemeanor, for example, pilfering a coat from a school cloakroom or pinching car wiper blades (like that guy in our neighborhood who sold them back to my father), were treated by all inmates with contempt and were forced to serve as errand boys (*shesterka*). These wretched creatures were supposed to perform undesirable duties, such as cleaning the cell.

Strange as it may sound, the cell leadership viewed my anti-Soviet stance on a par with the most respectable crimes. My status was further enhanced by my service as the defense lawyer at the internal trials. Anyhow, the cell elder decided that I should eat at the dining table and not in my bunk, as did the vast majority of prisoners. It was supposed to be a sign of recognition since the table accommodated ten out of sixty or more inmates. Another mark of respect was my receiving one of the bunks, albeit a top one, that was located near the only window. If I remember correctly, there were only thirty-six bunks in all. The bunk shortage meant that many inmates had to sleep either under the bottom bunks or in the space between them.

Of course, regardless of the crime committed, all Russians are great experts on alcohol and anything that contains spirits. For most of my fellow prisoners, it was the sole manifestation of spirituality. I vividly remember a spontaneous and fervent conference of these spirituous specialists. I knew that heavy drinking was rampant in Russia, but it took this conference to open my eyes and to show me how comprehensive this boozing zeal was. Although it is most common among ethnic Russians, even Jews at times join these ranks. (Such Jews are scornfully referred to in Yiddish as *shiker*. Thus, my former co-worker and namesake, the diminutive Il´ia Shapiro, was once arrested for getting dead drunk and stopping heavy traffic on the multilane Garden Ring [*Sadovoe Kol´tso*] Avenue.)

---

early 1980s, the institute was also used for forcible evaluations of political dissenters and their involuntary treatment at special psychiatric hospitals. The institute doctors, in collaboration with the KGB, frequently came up with most bizarre diagnoses, such as an "elevated sense of justice" or a "heightened sensitivity toward truth."

At this impromptu convention, my cellmates discussed, with great gusto and incredible know-how, the ways to extract, distill, produce, and otherwise obtain alcohol from the most improbable sources, such as BF glue, which they lovingly dubbed "Boris Fedorovich." This conference was a clear reminder that I was a total misfit, a pariah in the country of dedicated dipsomaniacs. By contrast, Israel is a country where alcohol is consumed in great moderation, except perhaps by some recent émigrés from the former Soviet republics. In June 2013, I attended the circumcision (*brit milah*) of my niece's son in Jerusalem. After the ceremony, a celebratory meal was served. Upon each table, which seated eight, there was one bottle of red wine. None of these bottles was uncorked. The only opened bottle was the one used for the circumcision ceremony itself. On the other hand, at a comparable festivity in Russia, such as baptism, most men and some women would have been three sheets to the wind. The celebration, in all likelihood, would have ended up in a brawl, possibly with fatalities.

Our cell was badly overcrowded, and ventilation, with only one window, was very poor. The outside high temperature of about 100°F made the existence rather intolerable, even for the most robust prisoners. No wonder that such conditions were hazardous for inmates with poor health, particularly for those with heart problems. When one prisoner complained about chest pains, the others began banging on the door to get him medical attention. It took quite some time for a guard, and even much longer for a jail doctor (known in the Russian criminal slang as *lepila*) to show up.[52] The doctor examined the patient most cursorily and then pronounced an unforgettable phrase: "You need to eat better and to take more walks" (*Vam nuzhno luchshe pitat'sia i bol'she guliat'*), which was entirely irrelevant given the extreme heat and the jail conditions. When I told my family, above all my mother the physician, about this incident, the doctor's prescription was added to the golden fund of our family sayings.

Speaking of spending time in the fresh air, our daily stroll lasted for about an hour. It was held in a jail yard, reminiscent of a gigantic cauldron whose "lid" was made of barbed wire. Consequently, inmates could not see the sky free and intact but rather in a checkered pattern. There was a metal

---

52 The word literally means "the one who sticks things on," presumably referring to primitive treatments, such as the use of a mustard plaster.

walkway with a guard pacing along it, literally looking down upon us. I had the physical sensation that the guard was trampling on our heads with his heavy boots.

Jail food of course was atrocious: the cheapest of Cuban cane sugar, a heavy brick of damp, slack-baked black bread, coarse barley porridge, and murky dark brown tea. On Sundays, whoop-de-doo, we were served semirotten boiled potatoes with unbearably salty herring. Once every ten days, we were allowed to receive food parcels. Naturally, these had to be divided among fellow inmates and would disappear in the twinkling of an eye. It is no surprise that the very first word I uttered upon my return home from the jail was "Food!"

I was released from Matrosskaia Tishina on Friday, June 30, 1972, during the ongoing three-digit heat wave. As my mother told me afterward, that day she had an appointment with my defense lawyer. When she came to see the lawyer, she was told to go home because I had just been released. Mother could not grasp the message at first: "What do you mean? But I have an appointment with you!" It took her a moment to fathom this astonishing news.

I had a recognizable prison buzz haircut and was dressed too warmly, to put it mildly, wearing the black woolen sweater that my father had brought for me.

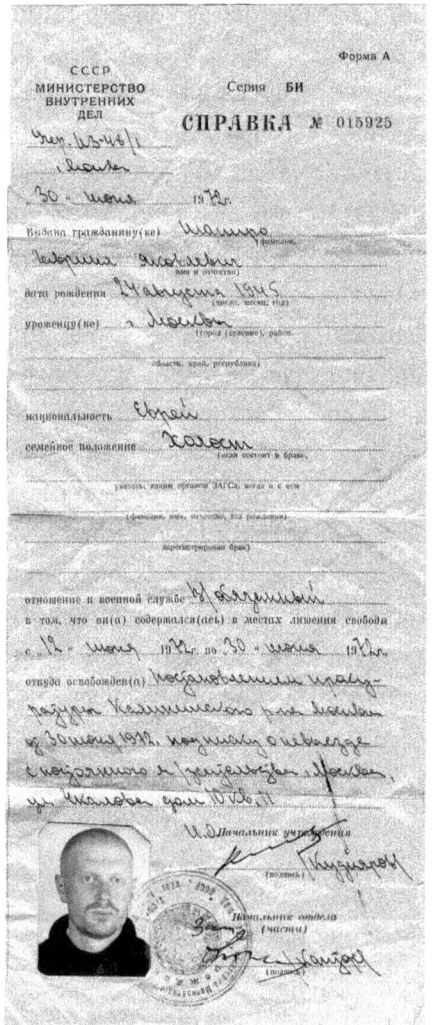

The prison release paper. Moscow, June 30, 1972.

(Throughout the years, I have kept this sweater in my closet as material evidence and a reminder—not that I need one—of my incarceration.) Before my release from jail, I obtained the pass that entitled me to a one-time subway trip. I walked the short distance between the facility and the Sokol´niki subway station, totally oblivious to my ghastly exterior. On my way, I saw an elderly woman carrying a heavy shopping bag and offered her my assistance. She responded to my well-meaning offer by fleeing as fast as she was able to, and I shall never forget the expression of horror on her face. When I boarded the train and sat down, all the passengers in the car took off in terror and in all directions as far away from me as they could. Only then did I realize what a grisly criminal appearance I must have had.

Soon after my discharge from Matrosskaia Tishina, several Jewish activists came over to hear about my jail experience. Not wishing to dwell on the dismal aspects of my incarceration, I cathartically tried to focus on its funny bits. One of the visitors, Sergei (Shmuel) Gurvitz, later a physics professor at the Weizmann Institute, presumably not comprehending my intent, remarked that, judging by my stories, it was not so bad in there after all. Upon hearing this comment, my mother gave the clueless fellow a stern glare and poignantly remarked: "Why don't you try it yourself some day!"

Sometime in early July, shortly after my release from Matrosskaia Tishina, I received an unusual visitor. One day, the bell rang in our apartment. Upon opening the door, I found a lanky KGB-looking man in his mid-forties, who introduced himself as an APN correspondent. APN, the Russian abbreviation for the Press Agency "News" (*Agentstvo pechati "Novosti"*), was the Soviet information, or rather disinformation agency, closely affiliated with the KGB. The correspondent explained his visit by saying that there were all kinds of contradictory rumors about me circulating in the Soviet Union and overseas. He came therefore to get the story firsthand and to set the record straight. The journalist asked me numerous questions about my family background and the reasons for my wishing to immigrate to Israel. My mother, who happened to be present at this impromptu interview, said that I and other young Jews like me had no future in the Soviet Union and told him about my postgraduation job-hunting saga. Finally, the journalist asked me a question that presumably was the main purpose of his visit. "You know," he said, "that the Soviet Union has military advisors in Egypt and Syria. Eventually you will leave for Israel, and since military service there is mandatory, you will be drafted into the Israeli army. What will you do if the war between Israel and its neighbors breaks out once again, you are sent, say, to the Syrian front, and see Soviet advisors across the border?" Without batting an eye and with no hesitation, I responded: "Soviet military advisors have no business being in Syria. But if, as an Israeli soldier, I see them in the war situation assisting the enemy, I will take my machine gun and start shooting." The correspondent diligently wrote down my answer. I suppose by asking this question the regime wanted to test the waters and learn not so much about my mindset as about the prevailing sentiment on the Jewish street.

Curiously, a similar question about such a prospective military confrontation was posed a year or so earlier to Iosif Kerler, as his son, Dov-Ber, recently told me. When Kerler was being expelled from the Union of Soviet Writers—this procedure was presided over by the infamous Sergei Mikhalkov—the Yiddish poet was asked what he would do if he was drafted into the Israeli army and was sent, say, to the Egyptian front. Kerler immediately retorted: "As I was fighting Nazi Germany during World War II, so I shall be fighting Nazi Egypt now." Mikhalkov was stupefied by Kerler's response and reminded him that President Gamal Abdel Nasser was awarded the title of Hero of the Soviet Union. To that Kerler rejoined, tongue in cheek, that when the Soviet authorities bestowed this great honor on Nasser, they were presumably oblivious to some crucial facts. It apparently escaped their notice that Nasser and his successor, Anwar Sadat, both collaborated with the Nazis. Kerler's opponents could not argue against these indisputable facts, of which, furthermore, they were completely ignorant.

Soon I found out that Soviet propaganda operatives, when mentioning my name in public, were, in their usual fashion, disseminating cock-and-bull stories. They were saying that I was a nice, goodhearted young man—it seems I am indebted to the APN correspondent for this compliment, quite dubious considering its source—but it was my mother, a staunch and seasoned Zionist, who led me astray. So much for the APN correspondent's declared intent to set the record straight! Nevertheless, this assertion gave us a hearty laugh. Every now and then, I would tease my mother about her swaying me off the right path by brainwashing me with her "despicable Zionist rhetoric."

Truth-bending for the sake of disinformation was a well-known Soviet specialty. Here is a political anecdote of the early 1960s that reflects this propensity and sinister ability of the regime. John F. Kennedy and Nikita Khrushchev took part in a two-man race. The younger and athletic Kennedy came in first, whereas the older and obese, huffing-and-puffing Khrushchev came in second. The next day, *Pravda*, the mouthpiece of the Soviet Communist Party, reported the event: "Yesterday, Nikita Sergeevich Khrushchev and President Kennedy took part in a race. Our Nikita Sergeevich came in a respectable second, whereas President Kennedy came in one before the last."

Ironically, of all of us in the family it was Mother who had qualms about emigration. She was born and raised in Moscow in a rather assimilated family and was deeply attached to Russian culture and nature. She loved her native city and refused to leave it in mid-October 1941 at a crucial time when the Nazis were only four or five miles from the capital. She also greatly enjoyed being part of the university hospital, where she worked for thirty years. There she treated patients who came to her from all over the country. She also taught students who loved and respected her. Even though Mother was always mindful of her Jewishness, like most assimilated Jews she was not religious, was ignorant of Judaism and Jewish history, spoke no Hebrew, and had only a smattering of Yiddish. It was hardly surprising that she had misgivings about immigrating to Israel, the country about which she knew very little and whose language and culture were unfamiliar to her. What changed her mind was a dream that she regarded as prophetic. It involved our downstairs neighbor, a certain Skoptsov, an alcoholic, ruffian, and rabid anti-Semite. Mother envisioned him climbing out of his window and breaking into our apartment with an ax in his hands. After this horrific nightmare, Mother made up her mind about the emigration. Yet during her first months in Israel, she felt an acute longing for Russia. To jog her memory and to relieve her from this anguish, my sister and I used to buy Soviet newspapers, most of all *Pravda*. These papers worked wonders as a powerful antidote to Mother's nostalgia.[53]

---

53 Speaking of Soviet newspapers, there is an anecdote that plays upon their titles. A man inquires in the kiosk, "Do you have *Pravda* (*Truth*)?"—"No." "What about *Sovetskaia Rossiia* (*Soviet Russia*)?"—"Sold out." "So what do you have?"—"*Trud* (*Labor*), 2 kopecks."

My trial was scheduled for July 26, 1972. My defense lawyer was the eminent Sofia Vasil´evna Kallistratova (1907–89), who frequently represented human rights activists and other opponents of the regime. Kallistratova defended some well-known dissidents, such as writers Vadim Delaunay and Natalia Gorbanevskaya, and General Petr Grigorenko. Later, upon her retirement, she openly joined the human rights movement. I felt extremely privileged to be represented by this remarkable woman. While pondering my line of conduct at the trial, I wished to create a precedent by giving my testimony in Hebrew. Sofia Vasil´evna strongly advised me against it, and I took her sagacious counsel to heart. Her exact words: "Do not corner the mad dogs!" (*Ne zagoniaite beshenykh sobak v ugol!*).

At the outset of the trial, I reminded the court that I had renounced my Soviet citizenship and had received Israeli citizenship in absentia. Therefore, for all intents and purposes, I considered myself an Israeli citizen who was held against his will in the Soviet Union and who by no means should be drafted into the Soviet army reserve. So I declared this a kangaroo court and refused to take any part in its procedure. My strategy, on which I consulted Sofia Vasil´evna, met with her full approval. She herself used a similar, albeit understandably, somewhat more dispassionate and balanced line of defense. Here is an excerpt from Sofia Vasil´evna's speech:

> Regardless of the factual evidence that forms the objective aspect of corpus delicti, the defense believes that the actions imputed to Shapiro are devoid of their subjective aspect and thus obviate the corpus delicti itself under Part 1 of Article 198-1 of the Criminal Code of the RSFSR. The subjective aspect of the given crime is characterized by *direct* intent, that is, when the defendant *is aware* that he violates the law [....] In this case, however, the defendant's actions could be qualified as an honest mistake that may attest to merely an *incautious* fault. Having the document on hand for his admission into the citizenship of the State of Israel and receiving no response to his letters to the Supreme Soviet of the USSR [regarding the renouncement of his Soviet citizenship], Shapiro had subjective grounds to view himself as a person with *dual* citizenship. The question of military service in the Soviet Army for individuals with dual citizenship (when the second citizenship is granted by a capitalist country) is not regulated by the Soviet law. By virtue of this, Shapiro inferred that, being a person with dual citizenship,

he *could not* serve in the Soviet Army. The foregoing provides the grounds for the defense to request the dismissal of the case against Shapiro owing to the absence of *direct* intent in committed actions, punishable by Part 1 of the article 198-1 of the Criminal Code of the RSFSR [italics in original].[54]

In spite of Sofia Vasil´evna's valid argument, it was abundantly clear that no matter what she said and how persuasive her defense was, the regime had already made up its so-called mind and had the sentence all typed up. The government's prosecutorial reasoning was plain and simple. No decision was reached on the renouncement of my Soviet citizenship. Furthermore, the court refused to admit as evidence the notification of my Israeli citizenship. Thus, in effect, I was a Soviet citizen and, as such, subject to a military reserve call-up. By refusing to serve in the Soviet army, therefore, I committed a felony punishable by law. Here is an excerpt from the verdict, which I render verbatim, preserving the clumsy Soviet bureaucratic lingo to the best of my ability:

> On July 26, 1972, the Kalinin regional people's court of the city of Moscow, under the chairmanship of people's judge Galkina, with participation of prosecutor Stepanov and defense lawyer Kallistratova, with secretary Paramonova, deliberated in the open court session on the case of Shapiro Gavriil Yakovlevich, born August 24, 1945, a native of Moscow, a Jew, with higher education. The defendant, a bachelor, non-Party member, with no prior convictions, residing at Lomonosov Prospect 18, apartment 271, is an ancillary worker at the Lenin regional communication center.
>
> The court has established that pursuant to Part 1 of the article 198-1 of the Criminal Code of the RSFSR, the article 60 of the Compulsory Military Service Law, and the directive of the General Staff of the Armed Forces of the USSR No. 315/0459 of May 5, 1972, Shapiro as an engineer lieutenant in the Soviet Army reserve was therefore liable for a call-up and was subject to the reserve duty draft for fifty-seven days. On May 5, 1972, Shapiro declined to accept the call-up notice from Comrade Lazarev, commander of the Kalinin regional army recruiting office, and categorically refused to report to his reserve duty. When on May 6, 1972, Comrade Mukharinov from the aforementioned office personally arrived to hand the call-up notice to Shapiro, the defendant

---

54 For the Russian text, see E. E. Pechuro, comp., *Zastupnitsa. Advokat S. V. Kallistratova, 1907–1989* [*The Protectress. Attorney S. V. Kallistratova, 1907–1989*] (Moscow: "Zven´ia," 1997), 60.

once again declined to accept it and declared that he did not wish to serve in the Soviet Army since he considered himself a citizen of Israel. Shapiro never reported to the reserve duty and disappeared from his residence. During both the interrogation and the legal proceedings, the defendant Shapiro declined to testify.

It is evident from the memorandum of the Department of Visas that as of June 21, 1972, the defendant is a citizen of the USSR, and no decision has been made regarding his application for the renouncement of the Soviet citizenship.

In finding Shapiro's guilt proven, the court holds that the defendant's actions were qualified correctly since he, being an officer of the Soviet Army reserve, deliberately evaded the call-up. Shapiro's actions were deliberate: he categorically refused to serve in the Soviet Army, to report to the reserve duty, and disappeared from his residence.

In determining the measure of his punishment, the court took into account that the defendant had no prior convictions and received positive references from his workplace.

Based on the aforesaid and being guided by the articles 303 and 315 of the Code of Criminal Procedure of the RSFSR, the court found Shapiro, Gavriil Yakovlevich, guilty as charged.

The court has ruled to subject the defendant to the penalty of one year of corrective labor at the discretion of the authorities responsible for its imposition, with the deduction of 20 percent from his wages payable to the state treasury.

The verdict may be appealed at the Moscow city court within a week from the day of its pronouncement.

"The open court session," referred to in the verdict, could be hardly classified as such. After all, neither my friends and fellow refuseniks nor foreign correspondents were permitted to enter the courthouse. With the exception of my father and several witnesses for the prosecution, the courtroom was jam-packed with plainclothesmen, who had absolutely nothing to do with the trial. They were brought into the courthouse by the KGB to fill up the room and to represent the Soviet people expressing their indignation at my wrongdoing. The appeal, predictably, brought about no changes in the verdict.

I realized, of course, that my sentence, which carried no further incarceration, was relatively lenient. Although at the time I did not know it for sure, I correctly attributed this to the actions of numerous Jewish organizations and individuals, world public opinion, media exposure, and to the pressure that the U.S. administration applied on the Soviet authorities. The latter was especially effective. According to Rabbi Marc H. Tanenbaum of the American Jewish Committee, this light sentence should be credited above all to the forceful intervention of the White House, the State

The court ruling on my appeal (front page). August 25, 1972.

Department, and the American Mission to the United Nations on behalf of my release.[55]

After having been sentenced to one year of "corrective labor," I was first dispatched to work as a manual laborer at the Moscow Brakes Plant. Ironically, the plant was located close by the notorious Butyrskaia Prison.[56] At the plant, I befriended another ancillary worker, an ethnic Tatar, who told me about the discrimination against Muslims, whereupon I told him about the persecution of Jews. Apparently, someone overheard our conversations and reported them to the management. As a result, my supervisor summoned me to his office and asked me to work on Saturday, knowing that it was against the Jewish religion. When I refused, the supervisor breathed a sigh of relief and sent me back to the Ministry of the Interior, which was in charge of placing me in a job. Its officials quickly found another workplace for me—the Kauchuk Rubber Factory. The factory administrators were astounded to see me, a Moscow University graduate, with mannerisms not in the least betraying any criminal past, assigned to them by the Ministry of the Interior as an unskilled worker. Naturally, they wanted to know what crime I committed. Upon my explaining that I was prosecuted for my desire to go to Israel, they freaked out, tried to shush me, and hastened to send me back to the Ministry. As at the Moscow Brakes Plant, they did not want to have a political dissenter in their midst. They were evidently worried that I might conduct anti-Soviet conversations with my co-workers and would get the factory management in big trouble.

After a few additional rounds that followed the same pattern and ended up in the same way, Ministry of the Interior executives began to suspect that something was going awry and caught up with the situation. One of them accused me of sabotaging the court verdict and threatened to send me to Siberia. Having learned a thing or two from human rights activists, I pulled

---

55　See *The Jewish Chronicle of Pittsburgh*, August 3, 1972, 5.
56　The first references to Butyrskaia Prison (commonly known as Butyrka) go back to the seventeenth century. Throughout the ages, the prison was known for its severe regimen. Its administration resorted to brutal violence every time the inmates attempted to stage a protest. After the Bolshevik takeover, Butyrka remained a place of confinement for many political prisoners and a Gulag transit station. During the Great Purge of the late 1930s, about twenty thousand inmates at a time were imprisoned there. Thousands of political prisoners were shot in its cellars after torturous interrogations.

out a pad and a pen and calmly asked the man for his given name, patronymic, and last name. The executive, utterly flummoxed, wondered why I needed this information. I replied, "Because tonight you will become a celebrity as your name will be broadcast all over Western radio stations." The man blanched, dashed out of the room, and ran to his superior's office. When he returned, his tone was conciliatory, bordering on the paternal. They decided to send me to one of the Ministry's construction sites, located in Tsaritsyno, then a southern suburb of Moscow, now part of the city.

Upon my arrival there on Monday, October 16, 1972, I got an inkling that my predicament might soon be over. When I told the major who was in charge of the site that I observed Jewish holidays, he did not yell at me as would be expected from someone in his position. Instead, he rather considerately, almost tenderly, suggested: "Why don't you hand me the list of all approaching holidays, and I'll give you the days off." Obviously, such humane behavior was uncharacteristic of the Soviet regime in general and for a Ministry of the Interior officer in particular. It was clear that the major had been ordered to be nice to me. The fellow workers, all petty criminals and winos, presumably having received no such orders, also treated me well. Prophetically, as it turned out, and most fittingly, they nicknamed me Foreigner. My work consisted of loading and unloading paint barrels, lumber, and other construction materials. Even though the work was physically demanding, I thoroughly enjoyed both the balmy golden autumn weather and the location. Although the place was renamed Lenino in 1918 and officially remained so until the collapse of the Soviet Union in 1991—the Soviet regime did its utmost to eradicate any memory of the imperial era—it was commonly known by its old name, Tsaritsyno, which stands for "Tsarina's," in reference to Catherine the Great.

The place has a captivating history. In 1775, Catherine the Great commissioned a distinguished architect, Vasily Bazhenov, to build a summer residence for her near the old capital. It took Bazhenov ten-odd years to carry out the project. He ran into debt and built the complex in part at his own expense. In 1785, upon visiting the just completed compound, the empress, for whatever reason, ordered the demolition of the main part of the palace and commissioned another well-known architect, Matvei Kazakov, to redesign the residence. Its construction continued for the next seven or eight years but was left unfinished because of budgetary problems caused by the war with the Ottoman Empire. The residence remained desolate after Catherine's death in 1796. In spite of its being incomplete and falling into disrepair, I was enthralled by its charm. At lunch hour, I would quickly eat my sandwich and would saunter around the palatial complex, looking at the arches, gates, and bridges, and stroll in the park full of flaming maples. Jumping a little bit ahead, shortly after my arrival in Israel, my parents conveyed to me greetings reminiscent of Tsaritsyno. Their first letter bore a stamp that depicted this imperial summer residence, which the Soviet postal service had issued several years prior in commemoration of this historical monument. Strange as it may sound, it was a pleasant reminder that brought with it a sense of closure. Despite being forced on me, Tsaritsyno was one of the last places that I fondly remembered after my departure from the city where I was born, grew up, and lived for more than twenty-seven years.

Indeed, my hunch turned out to be correct: my Tsaritsyno idyllic ordeal lasted all of one week. On Friday, October 20, 1972, I received a postcard summoning me to the Department of Visas on Monday, October 23. I did not know the reason for the call but certainly did not wish to get my hopes up. It happened many times before that I had been invited to the OVIR office, only to be denied an exit visa yet again. The strange thing about this invitation, however, was its timing. Why do the OVIR bureaucrats want to see me so soon when I have served merely two weeks of my year of "corrective labor" sentence? Could it be that they are unaware of the situation? Not uncommonly, in the Soviet Union the left hand did not know what the right hand was doing. It is easy to imagine how nerve-racking that weekend was for me: "Is it going to be another rejection, or perhaps . . . ?" I tried not to engage in speculations but rather to keep my mind off the subject as much as I could. It was easier said than done after two years of ups and downs, ups and downs—mostly downs.

When I arrived at the OVIR office that fateful Monday morning of October 23, 1972, General Shutov, to my great astonishment and delight, notified me that my application for the renouncement of the Soviet citizenship had been accepted and that concurrently permission for an exit visa

Arrest, Imprisonment, Trial, and Aftermath • CHAPTER 5

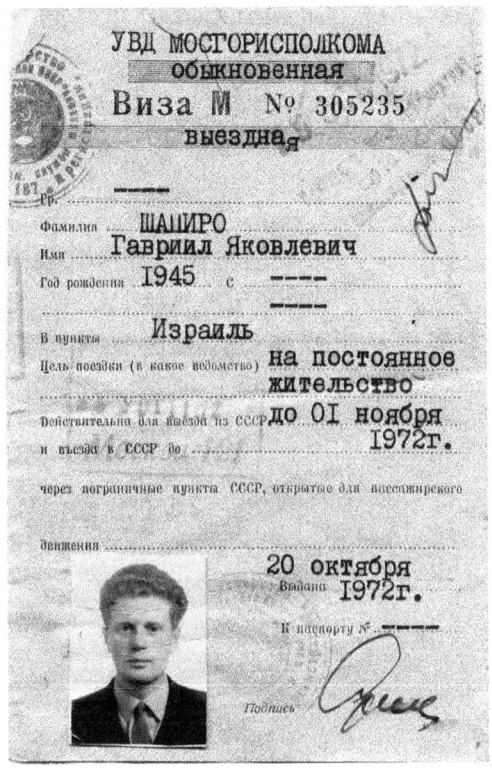

The exit visa. October 20, 1972.

had been granted.[57] Shutov also informed me that my education head-tax had been waived. This waiver meant that aside from 900 rubles for the exit visa and the citizenship renouncement (which in and of itself was a substantial amount of money equal to a six-month average earnings), I did not have to pay an additional exorbitant sum of 12,000 rubles for my university education. The de facto revocation of this draconian measure came on the heels of mass international protests that caused the Soviet regime to beat a hasty retreat. The regime rightly feared that its prospective trade agreement with the United States was in jeopardy. When I received the exit visa, this highly sought-after pinkish sheet of paper, for which I had struggled for two years, my hands trembled badly. A fellow Jew who happened to be in the OVIR office at the time helped me fold it into a small booklet.

Being given only a week to depart, I had to attend to numerous but nonetheless most pleasant chores. For starters, I had to visit the Dutch embassy to obtain an authorization to travel to Israel. This is because the Netherlands represented Israeli interests in the Soviet Union, whose government broke off diplomatic relations with the Jewish State in 1967

---

57 *Shut* (pronounced like "put") means a "buffoon" or "jester" in Russian. There is an appropriate Russian expression for this: "God brands the rogue" (*Bog shel' mu metit*).

in the wake of the Six-Day War. Then I had to visit the Austrian embassy since Vienna was the transit point on my way to Israel. I also had to notarize some important personal documents, such as a copy of my university diploma certificate, because the Soviet authorities did not let émigrés take any original papers out of the country. I also needed to acquire some convertible currency since rubles were not acceptable anywhere outside the Soviet Union. It is hard to believe, but the official and artificially overblown conversion rate at the time was approximately 83 rubles per US$100, the maximum amount an emigrant was permitted to exchange and to take along. Everyone understood that the rate was greatly exaggerated. In this regard, the relevant contemporary dialogue from the Armenian Radio series comes to mind. The Armenian Radio is asked: "What is the correlation between the pound, the ruble, and the dollar?" The Armenian Radio answers: "A pound of rubles is worth one dollar." (By comparison, the conversion rate nowadays is approximately 65 rubles per $1.00, that is, an eighty-fold increase over half as many years.) In addition, I had to pack up my belongings, and finally, of course, to buy an airline ticket.

My last battle with the regime, which I would lose, was to obtain a Western airline ticket for my flight to Vienna. At that time, the suburban Schönau Castle served as the way station for Soviet Jews immigrating to Israel. To fly on a Western airliner was not so much a matter of comfort as a matter of safety. An Aeroflot airliner, after all, was Soviet territory, and I heard of cases when a plane had been redirected, with Jewish émigrés being removed and their visas revoked. Nevertheless, I was told that on such short notice there were no tickets available to Vienna other than those on Aeroflot. So I had no choice but to stiffen my upper lip and to purchase a ticket for the Soviet passenger jet.

My plane was scheduled to take off from the Sheremetevo Airport on October 31 at 9 a.m. It was a heartrending experience to leave my parents behind. When would I see them again? For some time, while still in the airport, I literally experienced the physical separation from them, which was an agonizing first. I could see them only through a glass partition, and until I had to go farther and farther away, we stood and conversed in sign language, primarily sending air kisses back and forth. Before saying good-bye, my folks wanted me to have some Soviet currency, just in case. My first reaction: "What would I do with this wallpaper material?" They strongly urged me to accept the money. Thank goodness, I listened to my parents! For whatever reason, the flight was delayed from hour to hour—in the end, the plane took off only at 4 p.m.—and I became ravenous. With the cash my parents gave me I could buy food and beverages in the airport snack bar for myself and for a group of North American youngsters returning home. (I befriended some of them and we stayed in touch for many years to come.) Conversations with these youngsters staved off melancholy thoughts. Chatting with my new pals was therapeutic. It also gave me a chance to practice my English, which I knew would be helpful outside the Soviet Union, including Israel.

Although I was twenty-seven, I had never been apart from my parents for more than a month or two. When would I see them again? I was also apprehensive because as long as I was on the Soviet authorities' turf, they could change their mind at any time on a whim. So this seven-hour postponement was quite an excruciating experience. To top it off, there was an anxiety of the unknown, even though I was thrilled to go to Israel, the country about which I had dreamed all these years, and even though it appeared that the dream was coming true. I was also joyously looking forward to reuniting with Luba and to meeting our relatives. These and other conflicting notions were crossing my mind all through those protracted hours of waiting.

Before departing from the story of my life in Soviet Russia, I wish to thank those people outside my immediate family who exerted a lasting influence on me or touched my life in a significant way.

One such person was Solomon Matveevich Shur, my father's childhood friend. Salia, as we affectionately called him, was a talented architect. In the early 1930s, when he was a student, Salia was arrested on a trumped-up conspiracy charge of plotting with his fellow student, Vilensky, to gun down the entire Soviet leadership, standing atop Lenin's mausoleum, from the roof of the nearby department store GUM. After having been intensely interrogated in Butyrka, where he and Vilensky categorically denied all the charges, they were miraculously released. Apparently even the Soviet secret police recognized the lunacy of these accusations and realized that it carried things too far. Of course, this was before the mass purges of the late 1930s, which the British-American historian Robert Conquest fittingly dubbed the "Great Terror." During these purges, the secret police butchers and bone-crushers forced the most absurd confessions out of their victims.

In the summer of 1941, at the outbreak of the war against Nazi Germany, Salia was drafted into the Soviet army. He was sent to the front lines near Vyborg, situated on the Karelian isthmus, and was soon taken captive by the Finns. At first, Salia was dispatched to work for several farmers and, having a great knack for languages, quickly mastered Finnish. After a while, he was transferred to the transit labor camp in Naarajärvi and then to Loukolampi, a special labor camp for Jewish POWs. There Salia earned everyone's respect, from POWs and Finns alike, because of his outstanding leadership qualities, his exceptional fair-mindedness, and his extraordinary command of the language.[58] Unlike the Germans, Finns treated Jewish POWs fairly well and allowed them contact with the nearby Jewish community. The captives received additional food and clothing from the local Jews and were visited by the rabbi and members of the Jewish congregation. In September 1944, after Finland and the Soviet Union signed an armistice and before all POWs were handed over to Soviet Russia, the Jewish community offered Salia and other Jewish POWs assistance in immigrating to the Land of Israel. Salia was a resolute supporter of Jewish repatriation to the historical homeland. He liked to mention that among his maternal relatives there were prominent Zionists, such as Israel Elyashev (1873–1924), physician, translator, and literary critic, who wrote under the pen name Baal Machshoves (literally, Master of Thoughts), and Shmuel Eliashiv (1899–1955), translator, literary critic, and one of the first Israeli diplomats. As painful as it was, Salia declined the offer, knowing full well that had he gone, he would

---

58 See Shimon Yantovsky, "Sionist v plenu," in *Obrechennye pogibnut'. Sud'ba sovetskikh voenno-plennykh-evreev vo Vtoroi mirovoi voine: Vospominaniia i dokumenty* ["A Zionist in Captivity," in *Doomed to Perish. The Fate of Soviet Jewish POWs in World War II: Memoirs and Documents*], comp. P. Polian and A. Shneer (Moscow: Novoe izdatel'stvo, 2006), 536.

have never seen his beloved mother ever again. Little did he know that it was not going to happen anyway. Upon his return to the lion's den, Salia, like numerous other POWs, was put through a prolonged grilling security check and then was sent to work in a coalmine for two years without being permitted any contact with his loved ones. When Salia finally returned to Moscow in 1947, he learned, to his great sorrow, that his mother, Berta Solomonovna, died in 1945. Having not heard from her only child and therefore grief-stricken over Salia's presumed death, she passed away. Salia used to say that had he known ahead of time that he would never see his mother alive again, he would have moved to the Land of Israel in a heartbeat.

Salia's high proficiency in Finnish served as one of the main sources of his income. His Russian translations of numerous books and articles on construction, civil engineering, and architecture from this rare and difficult language were in high demand. Badly cut but strongly stitched together, Salia stood about five feet nine, had a high forehead, large straight nose, bushy eyebrows, and deeply set smallish gray-green eyes that sparkled with wit and humor. When I was a little boy, he always reminded me of a kindly elephant. Perhaps unbeknownst to him, Salia was my cultural mentor. He was well versed in Russian literature and, being endowed with a phenomenal memory, could recite Russian poetry for hours, usually from his favorites—Pushkin, Tiutchev, and Pasternak. To this day, his masterful declamations of Pushkin's "Exegi Monumentum," Tiutchev's "Silentium!," and Pasternak's "Hamlet" resonate in my ears. Married to an abysmal homemaker and with two children, one of whom was diagnosed with schizophrenia, Salia was not blessed with a happy family life. He visited us often, presumably enjoying the peace and stability that reigned in our home, which served as an outlet and antidote to the turmoil and unsteadiness of his own household. Salia used to bring with him a great deal of cultural news, openhandedly sharing with us *samizdat* materials, such as Osip Mandel´shtam's *Voronezh Notebooks*, or the recording of Dmitri Shostakovich's Thirteenth Symphony, which features five poems set to music based on lyrics by Evgeny Evtushenko. On my eighteenth birthday, Salia presented me with Zeev Jabotinsky's *Feuilletons*, a great rarity at the time, since Jabotinsky's works were banned in Soviet Russia. This book became extremely precious to me and was instrumental in shaping my Zionist convictions. When I was preparing to leave for Israel, Salia kissed me with fatherly tenderness and then burst into tears, evidently knowing deep down in his heart that we would never see each other again. Sadly, for a variety of reasons, Salia was unable to immigrate to Israel and died in Moscow in 1982 at the age of sixty-seven.

Whereas Salia, for the most part, was my Russian culture mentor, Father's other close friend and coeval, Saul Moiseevich Gorelik, helped to strengthen my Jewish awareness. Saul arrived in Moscow at the age of thirteen from a Belarusian *shtetl* and spoke Russian with a noticeable Yiddish accent. As a little boy, he studied in a *cheder* and as a result knew Hebrew and was well versed in Torah.[59] Like Salia, Saul was blessed with an incredibly sharp memory. Mother recalled that at their last Purim celebration in Moscow in the spring of 1973, shortly before her and Father's immigration to Israel, Saul had recited the entire Book of Esther (*Megilat Ester*) by heart. Living his entire adult life, until he immigrated to Israel, under the hammer and sickle, Saul was extremely cautious. If casually asked where he was going, Saul would say, "To one person on one business" (*K odnomu cheloveku po odnomu delu*). Having known my father since early teens, Saul would drop his conspiratorial air with us and would reveal himself as a man deeply grounded in the Jewish heritage and a stalwart Zionist. Saul was the one who introduced me to the ideas of Yehuda Leib Pinsker (1821–91). In his pamphlet *Auto-Emancipation* (1882), this Odessa lawyer and physician, more than a decade prior to Herzl, urged Jews to strive for their national consciousness and independence and to return to their homeland.

Saul's father-in-law, Aaron Isaakovich Elinson, received a rabbinical education and was ordained a rabbi prior to the Bolshevik usurpation of power. Aaron Isaakovich was a pious Jew who miraculously managed to keep kosher and to observe Shabbat in belligerently antitheistic Soviet Russia. He earned his bread as an inconspicuous accountant but spent all

---

59 *Cheder* was a traditional elementary school where boys studied the basics of Judaism and the Hebrew language.

his spare time studying the Holy Scriptures. When I turned twenty, Aaron Isaakovich helped my father to obtain for my birthday the much-coveted pre-Revolutionary *Jewish Encyclopedia* in Russian. The *Encyclopedia* was not only costly (120 rubles—an average monthly salary), but it was also extremely difficult to come by. It was a treasure trove of information on all matters Jewish. It was invaluable for someone like me who had been bereft of any Jewish education and was ignorant of Jewish history and culture. Aaron Isaakovich, who died in the late 1960s, did not live to see Israel. Saul, his wife, Chana, and their two sons, on the other hand, immigrated in the late 1970s and settled in Netanya.

When I was about fifteen, Father once brought home a colleague of his by the name of Vul´f Iosifovich Rishal´ (1904–89). A short but sturdily built man in his mid-fifties, Rishal´ was a proud Jew who knew his ancestral roots. He thought himself to be related to the famed sixteenth-century Rabbi Itzchak ben Shlomo Luria, the father of contemporary Kabbalah, and believed his surname to be an acronym of the Rabbi's name. In his younger days, Vul´f Iosifovich was a member of Hechalutz, an association of Jewish youth, whose aim was to train its members to settle in the Land of Israel. Vul´f Iosifovich was a courageous person: as a sixteen-year-old lad, he took part in the Jewish self-defense of Odessa when the local hoodlums attempted to instigate a pogrom in the city. An ardent Zionist, Vul´f Iosifovich aspired to immigrate to Israel. In 1948, on the assumption that this was possible in light of the Stalin government's support for Israel's establishment, Vul´f Iosifovich eagerly enlisted to fight for the nascent state, only to find himself and other volunteers like him sent to labor camps, where he spent more than five years. Vul´f Iosifovich offered to teach me Hebrew, but in order not to raise the suspicions of our daily housekeeper, Valentina Georgievna—as I have mentioned before, Hebrew was a taboo language in the Land of the Soviets—he pretended to tutor me in math.

Unfortunately, our lessons were rather short-lived as the circumstances were not auspicious for the task. I did not put my mind to it, not comprehending why I should be studying the language, and so my teacher grew impatient and irritable. He would get angry with me for not remembering the meanings of words and for mispronouncing them.

At any rate, Vul´f Iosifovich taught me Hebrew in the Ashkenazic pronunciation, the way he had learned it in his boyhood, instead of the Sephardic one that has been adopted in the present-day Israel. It did not help that the primer was an unappealing worn-out volume, published in 1902, with rather poor quality black-and-white illustrations. I still remember some words from that textbook, such as "stable" (*urva*), "cowshed" (*refet*), and "granary" (*asam*), quaint but worthless for a metropolitan resident like me. I also remember some of the book's phrases, such as "Gad climbed up on the roof" (*Gad ala al hagag*), or "Gad broke the jug" (*Gad shavar et hakad*). Moreover, it was not terribly helpful that the boy's name was Gad. As I found out later, it signifies "luck" or "success" in Hebrew and was given to one of Jacob's sons, but its Russian homonym literally means "reptile" and figuratively a "repulsive person," equivalent to a "rat" in American slang.[60] No wonder that as a fifteen-year-old youngster, I did not want to study the language, for which I felt no necessity, from an outdated, unappealing primer that contained the words and phrases absolutely useless for a city dweller, and whose protagonist's name was homonymous with "vermin."

Even though our lessons had ceased, Vul´f Iosifovich would frequently come to dine with us and even stay overnight when the KGB was breathing too heavily down his neck. Alas, the secret police arrested him once again in 1961. Vul´f Iosifovich later told me how his second arrest took place. He was aboard a train when a man quickly passed by and shoved a foreign magazine into his hands. At that moment, a bunch of plainclothesmen emerged out of the blue and arrested Vul´f Iosifovich on charges of possessing and disseminating anti-Soviet literature. Although this KGB operation was carried out clumsily, Vul´f Iosifovich was sentenced to seven years of prison and hard labor.

Vul´f Iosifovich was a fearless man. While he was in a labor camp, some criminal attempted to kill him. Providentially, Vul´f Iosifovich was forewarned. He pretended to be asleep, and when the offender crept up to

---

60 Similar homonyms, of course, exist between Hebrew and English. English-speaking Jews who study Hebrew facetiously point them out to suggest the "oddity" of Hebrew and employ their juxtaposition as a mnemonic device: "me" is "who," "who" is "he," "he" is "she," and "dog" is "fish."

him, Vul´f Iosifovich critically injured his assailant with a metal rod. Although Vul´f Iosifovich did two weeks in solitary for this, nobody dared to bother him ever again. I am much indebted to Vul´f Iosifovich for teaching me to be proud of my heritage, for enlightening me about Jewish modern history, and for greatly contributing to the awakening of my desire to go to Israel. Regrettably, Vul´f Iosifovich himself succeeded in doing so only with the best years behind him, but he nonetheless lived the remaining time in the country of his dreams.

In addition to those people who exerted a strong influence on my cultural development, national awareness, and Zionist convictions, there were also those whom I knew only slightly but who, all the same, touched my life in a profound way. I mentioned one such person earlier, the Yiddish poet Iosif Kerler (1918–2000). I grew up in a rather assimilated family and meeting a living Yiddish poet who spent more than five years in the Gulag for merely writing in Yiddish was in itself an enormous eye-opener. Kerler greatly impressed me by his devotion to Jewish tradition and culture and by his firm resolve to immigrate to Israel. He finally did so in 1971 after a prolonged struggle with the Soviet regime.

Meir Gel´fond was another individual who affected me deeply. Mother, who knew him as a colleague in Moscow, attests to his being a brilliant doctor. Meir was born and grew up in the Ukrainian town of Zhmerinka and became an ardent Zionist in his early youth. As a teenager, he was one of the organizers of the youth Zionist group *Eynikayt* ("Unity" in Yiddish). In 1945-46, the members of this group were striving for immigration to the Land of Israel, where they wished to take part in the struggle for creation of the Jewish State. The youngsters were disseminating flyers in Yiddish and Russian, in which they advocated Aliyah. In 1949, when Meir and his friends matriculated at various universities, they were all arrested for "nationalist propaganda" and sent to labor camps. Meir was released in 1954, successfully completed his medical education, and continued his active involvement in the Jewish national movement. Meir never abandoned his dream of immigration to Israel and revived it in earnest in the late 1960s.

I knew Meir only briefly during my struggle for an exit visa. He impressed me as a human being of great moral rectitude. He cared deeply for and about people. He was wise beyond his years, and his counsel therefore carried a great deal of weight. At the same time, there was something youthful, even boyish, about this extraordinary man. Meir was a born leader. Old and young alike were drawn to his outstanding personality worthy of emulation. After his repatriation to Israel in 1971, Meir continued his medical practice. He died in 1985 at the age of fifty-five. All who knew Meir were deeply saddened by his untimely passing. Meir Gel´fond worked at the Meir Hospital in Kfar Saba, named after Iosef Meir (1890–1955), the first director of the Israel Health Ministry.[61] Most fittingly, it appeared as though the hospital was also named after Meir Gel´fond. There is a plaque therein dedicated to his blessed memory.

Yet another person who had an intense effect on my life was Pavel Gol´dshtein (1917–82). Once again, I knew Pavel only slightly all through our struggle for the right of emigration and a little bit more in Jerusalem. The indescribable hardships notwithstanding—Pavel spent seventeen years in the Gulag—his heart did not become hardened or embittered. What struck me about Pavel was his inner goodness, his immense benevolence. Already as a young man, he was sensitive to injustice and was eager to come to the rescue of the wrongly accused. Pavel was arrested after writing a letter to Stalin in defense of Vsevolod Meyerhold and his theater. For me, a young man in my mid-twenties, it was an enlightening and instructive example of compassion and bravery. These sentiments were uncommon in Soviet Russia, where people were terrorized by the regime and learned not to stick their necks out for anybody.

Pavel harmoniously combined his devotion to Jewish heritage with his love for Russian culture, above all its literature. In the spring of 1971, when Pavel was working at the Moscow Literary Museum, he gave me a copy of the book that bore neither the author's name nor the title. It was, as Pavel told me upon my returning the book, *The Luzhin Defense*, an early masterpiece by Vladimir Nabokov, a name I heard for the first time. Since Nabokov's works were barred in the Soviet Union and reading or disseminating them was punishable by law, the writer's name and the book's title

---

61   Incidentally, my second cousin Tzofnat Ashbel recently sent me a letter dated December 14, 1938, in which Iosef Meir, the then director of the Sick Fund (*Kupat Cholim*), expressed his condolences to Tzofnat's grandfather, Dov Ashbel, on the passing of his father and her and my great-grandfather, Iosef Menachem Ashbel.

were removed for safety reasons. If arrested, I could claim in my defense (pun unintended) that I found the book on a subway train and had no idea of its authorship and contents. Reading the novel left me with two conflicting feelings: elation upon discovering this remarkable book by a great writer and fury at the Soviet regime for keeping it and his other works away from me all that time. Only upon my immigration to Israel a year and a half later was I able to read Nabokov's works freely. They started appearing in Soviet Russia after Nabokov's death, in the late 1980s, shortly before the collapse of the totalitarian empire. My reading *The Luzhin Defense* turned out to be fatidic: in later years, Nabokov's oeuvre would become the main source of my scholarly inspiration and personal delight.

While in Moscow, Pavel Gol´dshtein introduced me to Savely Grinberg (1914–2003). It appeared that we formed a kinship bond despite our wide age difference. I took pleasure in listening to Savely's poetry and learning about his eventful life, and he was presumably fond of my great interest in literature and my zeal for Israel and the Hebrew language. As a token of amity, Savely gave me a generous present, a Hebrew notebook from the 1930s. I greatly valued the gift because Savely preserved this precious memento through thick and thin for several decades after the time he spent in the Land of Israel. He told me about those days, remembering, among other things, rumblings of the 1935–36 Italo-Abyssinian War in contemporary Hebrew press. Then, inexplicably (I never dared to ask him for the reasons), Savely returned to the Soviet Union on the eve of the mass purges. Fortunately, he came out of this horrific meat grinder unscathed, at least physically. When I met him in 1971, Savely worked at the Vladimir Maiakovsky Museum. A couple of years later he immigrated to Israel. For thirty years, he resided in downtown Jerusalem, where I would meet him from time to time. Savely, or Shura, as he was known among friends, was an accomplished poet in his own right and a brilliant translator of Hebrew poetry, from the medieval (Ibn Gabirol) to the modern (Yehuda Amichai, David Avidan, and Yona Valakh). I thank fate for placing this highly refined and artistic human being in my path.

A person who contributed a great deal to my advancement in the study of the Hebrew language was Vadim Borshchevsky. When I was introduced to Vadim, he was by far more proficient in the language than

I. Vadim told me with great pride that he was related on his maternal side to the Levontin family: its prominent member, David Zalman, was among the earliest known pioneers to the Land of Israel in the 1880s. Vadim kindly agreed to tutor me. In the beginning, we customarily had our lessons at my family apartment. As time passed by and my vocabulary grew, we habitually walked around Moscow speaking the language. One day, as we rode a streetcar and conversed in Hebrew, I caught sight of a young Russian woman who stared at us throughout the trip and got off at the same stop we did. She approached us and asked me what language we were speaking. Obviously, I could not reveal that we were speaking the outlawed language. It just so happened that Vadim was a small man, with black curly hair and swarthy skin. Without missing a beat, I told her that I was a student at Moscow Institute of Foreign Languages, where I specialized in Turkic languages. Then, pointing at Vadim, I said that he was a Turkish student with whom I was practicing the tongues.

Although our lessons lasted for only a few months, I was grateful to Vadim for helping me break the conversation barrier after accumulating a relatively sizable vocabulary. Vadim, who had been fighting for his exit visa since early 1969, left for Israel in February 1971. I started receiving his letters written on Tel Aviv University Library stationery. Hebraizing his name to Dan Bar-Shai, Vadim worked in book cataloguing and took history courses at the university. By that time, Vadim, who was a couple of years my senior, had a family. While in Moscow, he married Rita, a Japanese language expert, a divorcee who had a son from her first marriage. Soon Vadim and Rita had a daughter together, born in Israel.

As is often the case in any country, even in Israel where the assistance to newcomers is substantial, Vadim and Rita's road was not covered with rose petals. Rita had problems finding work. At the time, Japanese was not among the most sought-after languages in Israel, and freelancing was not yet an option in that pre-Internet era. Meanwhile, Vadim's university studies were not going too well either. When I got together with them in the beginning of 1973—they came to Jerusalem to pick up the roller skates that Rita's parents asked me to bring for their older grandson—I discerned Vadim's sour attitude toward Israel. He painted everything in bleak colors, and his criticism was not sensible in the least. For instance, Vadim claimed that there was no culture in Israel. His assertion was all the more puzzling because he, unlike most greenhorns, could read Hebrew literature and attend theatrical productions. I pointed this out to him, but Vadim countered that there was no culture of the caliber of the Bolshoi Theater. I asked him, then, how many times he actually attended Bolshoi productions when residing in Moscow. He responded: "Admittedly none, but I always had an opportunity to do so."

As I realized later, there was an explanation for my quondam Hebrew teacher's U-turn toward Israel. While experiencing hard times, Vadim and Rita fell prey to Christian missionaries. The missionaries were offering them monetary support and relocation to Australia in exchange for the conversion. Regrettably, Vadim and Rita succumbed to the financial pressure, converted to Christianity, and moved Down Under. At first, upon hearing the news, I was shocked. But then I recalled Vadim telling me back in Moscow that he had thought of converting to Russian Orthodoxy and attending the Theological Academy to become a priest. This was not long before he decided to move to Israel, by which time he began keeping kosher and observing Shabbat.

Unbeknownst to the missionaries, they found just what they were looking for: a man without a backbone, uncertain about his belief system, and with no qualms about changing his convictions at the first appearance of hardships. Last thing I heard about Vadim and Rita was from a mutual acquaintance in Jerusalem some years ago. He told me that Rita, who was doing well in Australia, where the Japanese language was in high demand, had walked out on Vadim. He also told me that Vadim, a dispirited man, had lived in extreme poverty. I wished to get in touch with Vadim but had no idea of his whereabouts and turned for help to a local Chabad rabbi. The rabbi forwarded the information to Chabad emissaries in Australia and New Zealand, but to no avail. In all likelihood, Vadim changed his name once again after the conversion. I am writing these lines in the hope that he will somehow stumble upon this book and will get in touch with me.

Vadim's antipode to no small degree was Ernst Trakhtman, better known in the Moscow Zionist circles as Moshe Palchan (b. 1939). Moshe, whose legendary Hebrew gatherings I occasionally attended, made a strong impression on me. Quiet and modest, Moshe possessed a great deal of inner power. He was a man of deep Zionist convictions, which he imbibed from his parents, particularly from his mother, Leah. In 1922, at the age of nine, Leah emigrated with her family from Ukraine to the Land of Israel. In 1931, the British Mandate administration deported her, an eighteen-year-old girl, to the Soviet Union for her pro-communist leanings.[62] Moshe, who initially struck me as being reticent and taciturn, was in fact a deeply passionate individual and an ardent aficionado of Hebrew language and culture. He was a remarkable pedagogue and his distinguished role in dissemination of the language in the Soviet Union is hard to overestimate. Moshe left for Israel in the spring of 1971 and passed the baton to his numerous disciples, including his younger brother, Izrail´, who followed him after a short while. Since immigrating, both Moshe and Izrail´ continued their remarkable efforts to enlighten Russian-speaking Jews about the intricacies of the Hebrew language. Each wrote several textbooks that made their way to Soviet Russia, where they were used widely in language instruction despite most unfavorable conditions and circumstances.

The son of a Polish-born communist and Comintern lecturer, Mikhail Zand (b. 1927) was yet another person who left an indelible mark on me.[63] From his early childhood, Zand was exposed to a variety of Asian languages. Even though his father was arrested and perished during the Stalin purges of the late 1930s, Zand was admitted to the Institute of Oriental Studies. He studied Arabic, Hebrew, and Farsi, the last eventually becoming his main field of research. As an Orientalist, Zand was allowed to have books in Hebrew. As one might expect, he was very selective about loaning works of Hebrew literature, given its illegal status. Zand, however, was most generous in lending his Hebrew books to those who earned his trust. It is largely owing to him that I familiarized myself

---

62   See Leah Trakhtman-Palchan, *Vospominaniia. Iz malen′kogo Tel′-Aviva v Moskvu* [*Recollections: From Little Tel Aviv to Moscow*] (Moscow and Jerusalem: Mosty kul′tury/Gesharim, 2010).

63   Comintern, the abbreviation of the Communist International (1919–43), was an organization initiated in Moscow. Its declared goal was the creation of an international Soviet republic. In practice, it meant dissemination of communist ideas and Soviet domination by undermining the existent political systems all over the world.

with numerous works of Hebrew literature, both poetry and prose. Aside from being a talented linguist and a great connoisseur of Hebrew, Zand also served for us youngsters as a model of courage and fortitude. When he was detained in March 1971, he held a fifteen-day hunger strike in jail. Zand immigrated to Israel in June of that year and had a long and productive academic career. Shortly upon his arrival in the country, he was appointed professor at the Hebrew University of Jerusalem.

❋ ❋ ❋

I was leaving Moscow on October 31, Halloween Day, as I learned years later in the United States. Although Halloween has some eerie connotations in popular American culture, it has none for me. In fact, I consider that day to be my second birthday, the day when I was liberated from the Soviet oppression and reborn as a free human being. Each year, I mark this occasion, this personal Passover, with great jubilation and thank the Almighty for His unconditional love.

When I tell people about this special birthday of mine, many automatically ask me when I last visited Russia. They seem surprised when I tell them that I have not been back since I left more than two score years ago. Some wonder why I avoid the country of my birth, in which I spent the formative years of my life. Well, for one, I wish to remember things, both good and bad, the way they have been etched in my memory. Going there nowadays may distort or even destroy whatever old recollections I have by supplanting them with new impressions. As readers of this memoir have come to realize, I left the Soviet Union on less than amicable terms with the regime. Of course, it is true, the country has a new name, the Russian Federation (the Soviet Union is no more), and many things have changed over the last four decades. At the same time, while watching from afar what is going on in present-day Russia, I cannot help but think that much, in essence, has stayed the same there. The regime remains, if not totalitarian, authoritarian and kleptocratic. Furthermore, xenophobia of all kinds, including anti-Semitism, is even more rampant there than before, for the new relative freedom of expression enables many people to speak their spiteful heart. More than seventy-five years after Vladimir Nabokov composed *The Gift*, I can only repeat the most relevant rhetorical question of the novel's protagonist, which succinctly sums up the effects of Russia's Bolshevik and post-Bolshevik history: "Why had everything in Russia become so shoddy, so crabbed and gray, how could she have been so befooled and befuddled?"[64]

When the Aeroflot plane landed in Vienna that evening, the first things I saw were neon signs in German. As I was walking down the gangway, a wild thought, just for a split second, crossed my mind long before I read Vladimir Nabokov's phantasmagorical story "The Visit to the Museum." What if all these surroundings are a sham just to taunt me, and this is not Vienna at all but rather some distant corner in Siberia? A KGB officer will appear out of nowhere, snap his fingers, and the whole setting will turn in the twinkling of an eye into the all-too-familiar environs, with red banners and slogans inscribed in Soviet lingo. Luckily, this frisson of fear lasted but an instant and proved to be delusory, chimerical. In retrospect, I see this as an illustration of how the Soviet reality temporarily warped my psyche so that such a peculiar idea, to put it mildly, flashed through my mind.

I was warmly received by the Israeli officials in Schönau. In my state of exhilaration, I wished to speak Hebrew as pedantically as possible. In this regard, one funny episode comes to mind. When the Jewish Agency official suggested I put my suitcases in the trunk of his car, using for the latter the colloquial *bagazh* instead of the puristic *ta hamit'an*, I shouted at him, "Shame on you! Don't pollute the language!" (*Titbaesh lekha! Al tizahem et hasafa!*) and corrected his "contaminated" Hebrew. Unaccustomed to Hebrew fluency among new immigrants, the official was astounded by my proficiency and even more so by my zealous attitude. Despite my angry rejoinder, he rightly interpreted my reaction as a patriotic stance. The man hugged me and said, "Your words are balm to my soul!" (*Dvareikha heinam mazor lenafshi!*). Because of my so-called celebrity status, the Agency representatives told me that I could stay in Vienna as long as I felt like it. I appreciated their gracious offer but was eager to see

---

64 Vladimir Nabokov, *The Gift*, trans. Michael Scammell, with the collaboration of the author (New York: Vintage International, 1991), 175.

my sister, meet my relatives, and familiarize myself with the country of my dreams as soon as possible.

I left for Israel on the first available flight in the wee hours of Friday, November 3, 1972, and arrived at what was then called the Lod Airport (since 1973 the Ben Gurion International Airport) at daybreak. I was overwhelmed by emotions as the plane skirted the Mediterranean Sea at the crack of dawn while approaching Tel Aviv. I must admit that my heart beats faster each time I come back to Israel, which happens twice a year. But nothing could be compared to that heightened, most powerful feeling of elation and anticipation I experienced that day in late 1972.

CHAPTER 6

LIFE IN ISRAEL

> Because the country was given to our
> forefathers from time immemorial,
> we shall settle her with vigor.
> She is our heritage and our legacy,
> and we have no other land.
> —I. M. Ashbel, "The Situation"

> After the Land of Israel was recognized
> as the home of our nation,[65]
> her sons gazed and exclaimed:
> "Here is our homeland!"
> They began to stream into her bosom
> after she had long been barren and forsaken.
> —I. M. Ashbel, "Our People"

I set my foot on the Israeli soil for the very first time on Friday morning, November 3, 1972, the day after the fifty-fifth anniversary of the Balfour Declaration. Upon my arrival at Lod Airport, I was approached by members of the Hebrew and English media. Not realizing that many of the English-speaking journalists also represented the Israeli press, such as the *Jerusalem Post*, I said that because of the approaching Shabbat, I shall first answer questions in Hebrew. This rash statement produced an appreciative chuckle, but a chuckle nonetheless. Some of the journalists decided to stick around and ask me similar questions in English for

---

65 An allusion to the Balfour Declaration; see note 39.

the sake of accuracy. I can only say in my defense that I was unaware of the intricacies of the Israeli media at the time. Furthermore, I was sleep-deprived as a result of both the anxiety and the excitement prior to my departure from Soviet Russia and my stay over in Schönau, and was extremely tired from the flight to Israel in the middle of the night.

After the encounter with the press, I was met by my sister, Luba, and by my great-uncle Moshe and his wife, Shula. They graciously invited Luba and me to spend the weekend at their residence in Gat Rimon, a cooperative agricultural community (*moshav*) less than two miles from Petach Tikva. It was my first visit with family members and a welcome transition. While staying with Moshe and Shula, I met their daughter, Sarele, their son, Yossi, and his wife, Gina. At last, I had an unlimited opportunity to practice Hebrew because, except for my sister and Shula, who left Ukraine as a little girl, no one spoke Russian.

With Luba upon arrival in Israel. Gat Rimon, November 3, 1972.

Alas, the rustic restful atmosphere that reigned in Moshe and Shula's household was disrupted by a barrage from the Israeli media, the result of my fifteen-minutes-of-fame status, totally undeserved I might add. Moshe and Shula were courteous hosts—I visited them numerous times afterward. I would not be surprised if deep down they regretted inviting me that weekend because of this media blitz. Having been very private people, they were taken aback by all this hoopla. I, on the other hand, astonishingly, felt comfortable speaking Hebrew in front of the cameras, even though I was completely exhausted and it was my very first experience of this kind. The interview went quite well and was broadcast on TV. Dov-Ber Kerler recently shared with me that as a fourteen-year-old boy he watched the interview. He recalled a moment when, asked about my life as a Jew in Soviet Russia and about my decision to leave for Israel, I said that, "I had had it up to here!" (*Nishbar li!*). This Hebrew expression, even in its euphemistically truncated form, as Dov-Ber pointed out, had been deemed inappropriate at the time for public use, and certainly on TV. According to him, the interviewer's jaw dropped in disbelief, and there was an awkward moment of silence, of which I was presumably clueless. It appears, as Dov-Ber facetiously remarked, that I was the unwitting trailblazer, paving the way for a broad use of this dubious colloquialism.

A small country, Israel surprised me by its great range of microclimates. The weather forecasters habitually give numerous temperature readings, from the northernmost and periodically snow-covered Mount Hermon, to the southernmost and incessantly sun-drenched Eilat, from the Mediterranean Tel Aviv, with its steam-bath humidity in summer, to the no less hot but arid Jerusalem, perched at the edge of the Judean Desert. In winter, the City of David is every so often blanketed with snow, creating an even more divinely magnificent view of the ancient Jewish capital.

Israel also surprised me by its plethora of accents. Jews from all over the world, from America to Morocco, spoke Hebrew with their characteristic pronunciation (*mivta*). Their language patterns differed drastically from the Hebrew used by the Voice of Israel newscasters, to which I had become accustomed in Moscow. Most of my Israeli-born relatives spoke Hebrew with good articulation and clarity. I had no problems understanding journalists. But when I took a taxi and the Tunisian-born cabbie asked me for the destination, he had to repeat his question a couple of times before I figured out what he was asking. Uncle Aminadav's cook was an older Hungarian-born lady, and it took me quite some time to get used to her quaint enunciation. This was a riveting experience, to which I was rarely subjected in Moscow. There I encountered now and then, say, a Ukrainian or a Caucasian accent, but certainly not such a multitude of them, and not in my daily life, as I did in Israel.

A couple of weeks after my arrival in Israel, as I began to live in Jerusalem with my great-uncle Aminadav (see Chapter 1), his personal physician, Dr. Meir Sgan-Cohen, invited me to see Chanokh Levin's play *Chefetz*, which was being performed at the Jerusalem Theatre. I was familiar with more than 90 percent of the words and expressions, yet people in the audience were splitting their sides with laughter, and I only had a sorry smile on my face. Why? Because the play was replete with references and allusions to contemporary Israeli political and cultural life, of which I was totally ignorant. So I realized that language skill alone was not sufficient for discerning the culture of a country—one ought to obtain an intimate knowledge of its character and of its everyday life. I doubt I shall ever attain that level of understanding. Be that as it may, but when a few years later I saw *Krum*, another play by Levin, at the Haifa Municipal Theatre, I was heartily laughing with the rest of the audience.

When I immigrated to Israel at the age of twenty-seven, I was uncircumcised. At the time of my birth, in 1945, it was too risky to have *brit milah* in a communal apartment, and it was impossible to have it performed in a hospital. As I have pointed out often, the regime was fiercely antireligious, and any attempt to adhere to this important Jewish ritual would have had most hazardous repercussions for my family and everyone else involved. When I made up my mind about immigrating to Israel, I pledged to myself that I would undergo circumcision upon arriving in the country. *Brit milah*, the physical sign of the covenant with the Creator, has been performed by Jews from generation to generation for more than four millennia. The Almighty in His infinite wisdom and generosity protected me from harm and granted me my personal miracle by delivering me from the modern version of slavery in Egypt to the Promised Land "with a mighty hand

and an outstretched arm" (*beiad chazaka ubezroa netuia*).[66] It was high time for me to deliver on my pledge.

My great-uncle Aminadav had considerately put me in touch with his urologist, an observant English-born Jew, who kindheartedly offered to operate on me gratis. On the eve of the surgery, Rabbi Yaakov Rakovsky, the Hadassah Hospital chaplain, paid me a visit. To be sure of my Jewishness, which is determined by the traditional Jewish religious law (*halakha*) through maternal female predecessors, Rabbi Rakovsky inquired for the names of my mother and my maternal grandmother. The latter, Sara Zil'bershmidt, left some doubt in his mind. I presume this was because he perhaps imagined it could very well be the name of an ethnic German. Rabbi Rakovsky's doubts were evidently heightened because my grandmother hailed from southern Ukraine, where there were numerous settlements of ethnically German farmers in imperial times. He then asked me whether I, by any chance, knew the name of my maternal great-grandmother. I was glad I had listened attentively to Mother's accounts of her family. As it came to pass, it benefited me even then to know the family history and ancestry. When I blurted out "Enta-Reiza Kontorer," Rabbi Rakovsky's face lit up and he wished me a successful surgery. Curiously, Luba had a similar experience. A Jewish Agency official, who had some doubts about her Jewishness, was not satisfied with the names of our mother and grandmother. The official issued her an immigration document (*teudat oleh*) only after learning the name of our maternal great-grandmother.

In early December 1972, I was invited, among other newly arrived Aliyah activists, to celebrate Chanukah with members of the Israeli government. The celebration was held in Beit Elisheva, the women's training and cultural center in Jerusalem's Katamon neighborhood. It was raining like cats and dogs that night, and I brought an umbrella with me. Maybe it was that same umbrella that the Rabinovich of the Soviet anecdote was debating with himself whether to take to Israel or not. I could not help but notice a sign of the Israeli reality, unfamiliar to me from the then untroubled, terrorist-free Moscow: my umbrella was thoroughly checked by the security

---

66 Deuteronomy 26:8.

personnel. Upon entering the reception room, I was greeted by Golda Meir in Hebrew, but with her inimitable American accent: "Here comes our redhead!" (*Hinei ba hadzhindzhi shelanu!*). I was so staggered by Golda Meir's greeting that all I could do was to shake her extended hand in silence. To this very day, her words resonate in my head. I utterly regret not thanking Golda, as she was affectionately called by all in the country, for what she and her government had done on my behalf and on behalf of so many other refuseniks and Prisoners of Zion in Soviet Russia. I would like to do so here, belatedly. I also wish to express my gratitude to two remarkable individuals who most efficiently worked behind the scenes to bring Soviet Jews to Israel—Nechemiah Levanon and David Bartov.

Latvian-born, like my Grandpa Gavriel, and my father's exact coeval, Levanon (1915–2003) came to the Land of Israel in 1938 at the age of twenty-three. He joined the kibbutz Afikim and later became one of the founding members of the kibbutz Kfar Blum. In 1953, Levanon was appointed an emissary and many years later head of the agency codenamed Nativ ("Path" in Hebrew) but officially called Lishkat HaKesher (the Liaison Bureau). The agency maintained contacts with Soviet Jewry and encouraged immigration to Israel. Levanon's official position at the Israeli embassy in Moscow was the agricultural attaché. Levanon humorously remarked many years later that he was interested in raising Jews, but the Soviets thought that he was interested in raising potatoes.[67] In 1955, when Levanon was declared persona non grata for his contacts with Soviet Jewry, he had to leave the country.

Bartov was born in 1924 and grew up in the Polish town of Motal, the birthplace of Chaim Weizmann, the first president of Israel. In 1939, after the division of Poland in the wake of the Ribbentrop–Molotov Pact, the town became part of the Soviet Union. Prior to this, Bartov studied in the Hebrew gymnasium Tarbut ("Culture" in Hebrew) in nearby Pinsk. For belonging to a Zionist youth organization, Bartov was exiled to Siberia, where he did hard labor for five or six years. In the aftermath of World War II, he returned to Poland and immigrated to Israel in 1949.

---

67 See Peter Golden, *O Powerful Western Star: American Jews, Russian Jews, and the Final Battle of the Cold War* (New York: Gefen, 2012), 126.

Bartov received a legal education and became a career diplomat. He served in the Israeli embassy in Moscow until the Soviet Union broke off diplomatic relations with the Jewish State in 1967. Both Levanon and Bartov continued to work assiduously to disseminate knowledge about Israel behind the Iron Curtain and to stimulate the immigration of Soviet Jews to the country.

I found out that Alex had corresponded with Nechemiah, and he had done his utmost to accelerate the progress of my Israeli citizenship in absentia. I met Nechemiah a couple of times, and he impressed me as a man of uprightness and of firm Zionist convictions, as did Bartov. I became acquainted with Bartov and his wife, Ester, soon after my parents arrived in Israel in 1973, most fittingly on the eve of Passover. Since we had not yet settled as a family, Uncle Aminadav courteously invited the Bartovs and us to his home, where we all had a lovely evening. The last time I saw David was in 2000 in the Jerusalem Russian-language municipal library at the centennial commemoration of Tzvi Preigerzon. A man of letters and a staunch Zionist, Preigerzon was arrested in 1949 and spent seven years in the Gulag merely for writing in Hebrew. He was one of those outstanding individuals who kept the Hebrew language alive and aflame in Soviet Russia. Preigerzon, who died in 1969, did not live to see the country of his aspirations. In 1970, his remains were brought to Israel and were laid to rest at the kibbutz Shefayim cemetery.

Yet another person whom I would like to thank from the pages of this narrative is Sarah Frenkel, then an up-and-coming and now a highly accomplished veteran Israeli journalist. Sarah, who has specialized in Diaspora affairs, contributed a great deal to publicizing the plight of the Soviet Jewry and to circulating the news about its struggle for the freedom of emigration. I repeatedly spoke with Sarah on the phone while in Moscow, and she expeditiously broadcast the time-sensitive information. Like so many other refuseniks, I was grateful for her outstretched hand of support, thereby feeling reassured that I was not alone in my battle for exodus. Upon my first steps on the ground in Israel, Sarah's counsel was most beneficial. When my parents arrived, Sarah took it upon herself to make arrangements for renting an apartment for all four of us in downtown Jerusalem. This was far beyond the call of duty and a manifestation of her humane care, her willingness to help a family of new immigrants.

Parents on the eve of their immigration to Israel. Moscow, April 1973.

Our family reunited. Jerusalem, May 1973.

This downtown apartment was located on Pines Street, near the Mechanei Yehuda street market. The proximity was beneficial. Money was tight, and we saved a lot on transportation by walking. Shopping there was most economical toward the end of the day, when prices were substantially reduced, primarily on fruit and vegetables. We could not afford any meats and for months subsisted on stewing chicken wings that would otherwise be discarded by meat vendors. At the end of our ten-month contract, we received an apartment in the state-subsidized housing within the Kir'yat Menachem neighborhood in the southwestern part of Jerusalem. (It occurred to me at the time that our last Moscow residence was also in the southwestern part of the city.) Like us, our neighbors were predominantly recent émigrés from the Soviet Union. By that time, both of my parents found jobs in their respective fields, and our standard of living began to improve significantly. Over the years, my parents saved enough money to purchase a much more spacious three-bedroom apartment in the French Hill neighborhood, in which my family resides to this day.

The origin of the neighborhood's appellation is unclear. Some say that the area was named after John French, a British general, who reportedly had his headquarters on the Hill during World War I. This etymology appears to be erroneous—General French never served in this region. According to the renowned Israeli geographer Zev Vilnay, the neighborhood got

Parents in front of the Old City of Jerusalem.

With Father in front of the Western Wall.

its name because the land belonged to the Catholic Monastery of St. Anne, whose monks hailed mainly from France.⁶⁸ The official appellation of the neighborhood since its foundation in 1971, Shapira Hill, is a tribute to Chaim Moshe Shapira, a key Israeli politician and a signatory to the State's Declaration of Independence. The neighborhood's name, as can be imagined, has been the source of numerous jokes among our family and friends. The neighborhood is located on the northeastern side of Jerusalem, near the Hebrew University of Jerusalem campus on Mount Scopus. As the latter name suggests, it is one of the most breathtaking observation sites of Israel's Eternal Capital.

I greatly enjoyed living in Israel, especially in Jerusalem, my favorite city in the whole world. When I lived in Soviet Russia, I idealized the country, but once there, I quickly came to realize that it consisted of human beings, not angels. Oddly enough, native-born Israelis called me a "Russian" (*rusi*), thereby underscoring the country of my origin, whereas all I wanted was to blend in, to become an integral part of Israel. Moreover, it did not help that many Israelis had misconceptions about the living conditions in Soviet Russia. True, the average standard of living in the Soviet Union was inferior to that of Israel, but some people went way too far in their perception of Soviet backwardness. On several occasions, they asked me whether we had a refrigerator in our Moscow apartment or whether I knew how to operate an elevator. They were surprised to learn that my family had a car. Once I was even asked whether Moscow, a city of eight million at the time, had traffic lights. It appeared that my

---

68 See Zev Vilnay, *The Guide to Israel*, 24th rev. ed. (Jerusalem: Hamakor, 1984), 130.

interlocutor bought it when I pulled his leg: I told him about a special school in Moscow that trained bears to serve as traffic cops. I was greatly perturbed when shortly after my arrival I was watching a TV interview with high school students. In this interview, one of the students said, and others seconded his opinion, that they felt closer to Israeli Arabs than to the newly arrived Jews from Soviet Russia. Of course, this was the opinion of this specific group of teenagers, and I comforted myself by surmising that this sentiment was not endemic. (I trust that after the two intifadas these teenagers of four decades ago do not feel that way anymore.)

In 1976, when the time had come for me to be drafted into the Israel Defense Forces, I expressed my strong wish to join the Intelligence Corps. (After the injury sustained in basic training, which I describe later in this chapter, I could not serve in a combat unit because doctors deemed me unfit to be on the front lines.) I was terribly dismayed when an interviewer told me that I could not be recruited to an intelligence unit without someone from the country of my origin vouchsafing my loyalty to Israel. I found this precondition asinine. If newcomers are under suspicion, what recent immigrant could be trusted to guarantee another recent immigrant's loyalty to the country? From what I gathered when reading about spies, they routinely have a splendid, most believable legend fabricated for them by their superiors to establish their impeccable credentials. This exchange with the recruiter, who apparently was following protocol, did not make me feel good. I thought, "Am I not fully trusted in my own country, which I love with all my heart, simply because I happened to be born overseas?" Curiously, just three or so years prior to this ill-fated interview, the Israeli Security Agency, Shin Bet, uncovered a spy ring that passed classified information to Syria. Some of its participants, among them Ehud Adiv and Dan Vered, were Israeli-born Jews. And what about the infamous traitor Mordekhai Vanunu? Vanunu was born into an Orthodox Jewish family and immigrated to Israel at the age of nine, and yet it did not preclude him from disclosing top-secret information about the Israeli nuclear program. Surely he was well regarded and deemed trustworthy. Otherwise, he would not have passed the security clearance and been hired as technician at the Negev Nuclear Research Center. So much for being wary of tyros and for having unconditional confidence in natives and those who grew up in Israel!

There was another aspect of life in Israel that I found quite disconcerting. I am speaking about an animosity between Ashkenazic and Sephardic Jews. Fortunately, this problem seems to have abated significantly with time. Habitually, these were European Jews who looked down upon their North African brethren with contempt and an air of superiority. As greenhorns, we were not up to snuff on the nuances of Hebrew slang. In particular, we were completely ignorant about those reprehensible racial manifestations of disdain and superciliousness that were nothing but supersilliness. Here is a funny and at the same time sad and instructive story to exemplify this point. When my mother began working at the Rokach Pulmonary Center, one of her co-workers, while referring to a third party, kept calling her son-in-law *frenk*, a disparaging reference to Sephardic Jews. Mother was oblivious to this and simply presumed that it was the young man's last name. After all, a similarly sounding surname, Frank, is rather common among European Jews and may be found even in Russia. So when this son-in-law showed up at the center one day, Mother unsuspectingly greeted him with "Shalom, Mr. Frenk!" Mother's innocuous greeting caused a scandal. It exposed and put to shame the racist co-worker, who, one would hope, learned her lesson.

In addition to the animosity between Ashkenazic and Sephardic Jews, there existed enmity among Jews from different European countries. I experienced it firsthand. When I served in the army, I woke up one morning feeling very ill. In such cases, a soldier must be evaluated by a military doctor who decides whether or not sick leave is warranted. In Jerusalem, such a place at the time was the Schneller Camp. While riding a bus to the Schneller, I was coughing badly, had difficulty breathing, and in general felt extremely fatigued. The military doctor who was assigned to examine me there happened to be from Romania. Upon hearing my Russian accent, he treated me with utmost hostility. When the nurse took my vitals, the thermometer for whatever reason showed a normal body temperature. The doctor chose to ignore all other major symptoms: severe mucus-producing cough, shortness of breath, and excessive sweating. Not bothering to give me even a cursory medical examination, he accused me of playing sick, "as you Russians always do," and ordered me to report to my unit. Deeply insulted by this unprovoked hatred and in a daze, I left the doctor's office. On my way back to the bus, I decided to stop by at the Rokach Pulmonary

Center, where my mother worked. It took me more than half an hour to reach Rokach from Schneller, even though the distance between them was less than half a mile. I was walking like a drunkard, clinging for support to each tree and electric pole on the way. Mother was horrified by my appearance, and being a superb pulmonologist, immediately realized that I had a case of acute pneumonia. She telephoned the Schneller, spoke with the physician in charge, and accompanied me back to the camp. I was admitted at once to its infirmary, where I stayed for two weeks. Mother filed a grievance report about the doctor's deliberate mistreatment based on my being an immigrant from Soviet Russia. A month later, she received an official response that the doctor had been reprimanded.

When I arrived in Israel, I did not have a clear idea what I wanted to do. All I knew was that I wished to quit chemistry and to embark on a new career in the humanities, leaning toward the study of literature. Since I arrived too late for the 1972–73 university enrollment, I had ample time to sort things out. I could not consult my parents, who were still in Moscow and at any rate were unfamiliar with Israeli realities. Luba was too young to give sound advice, and she herself was going through a rough patch. Members of my extended Israeli family tried to talk some sense into me and to persuade me against quitting chemistry. They argued that chemistry would guarantee me a career, but literary studies would be a waste of time because such a degree would almost certainly leave me without work. "And why study something altogether different and new, with bleak employment prospects, if you already have a master's degree in a solid discipline?" they asked rhetorically. They pointed out that both my parents had practical professions that would enable them to find jobs with ease as soon as they immigrate and acquire the necessary proficiency in Hebrew. They also appealed to my sense of family pride and tradition, reminding me of their own occupations in the natural sciences, from botany to meteorology, from agriculture to biochemistry. They forgot that their own father, Iosef Menachem, though he showed interest in nature, had received a rabbinical education. He was a prominent Hebrew teacher and an amateur poet at the turn of the twentieth century. They had no way of knowing, of course, that my maternal great-great-grandfather Yaakov Kontorer and grandfather Gavriel both had received a humanistic, legal education. Most important, they did not know that our parents always

With parents and Luba in the company of (from left) Uncles Moshe, Dov, and Aminadav. Jerusalem, fall 1973.

At a family picnic. (Sitting): Yossi and Gina with their daughters, Anat and Irit, and Luba; (front row): Niuta, Shula, Moshe, Rivka, Alex, and Mother; (back row): Israel Mayber. Jerusalem, fall 1975.

taught my sister and me to follow our hearts and not to be swayed by pragmatic or opportunistic considerations.

Of all the relatives, Aunt Rivka was the most energetic. She convinced me to take advantage of the time I had before the 1973–74 university academic year. I had nothing to lose and agreed to try. Aunt Rivka suggested I should pursue a doctoral degree in chemistry. It was easier said than done. I knew no one in the field in Israel and had no contacts at the Hebrew University of Jerusalem. "Leave this to me" (*Taniach li*), said Aunt Rivka and at once set the process in motion. She made a round of phone calls and, in particular, contacted Gabriel Stein, a distinguished Budapest-born Israeli chemist, and arranged for me to meet with him. Stein was a charming European man, broadly educated, and we spent little time discussing chemistry but instead mostly literature and history. In 1976, I was deeply saddened to learn of his premature death at the age of fifty-six.

Stein put me in touch with and warmly recommended me to Assa Lifshitz, a younger colleague of his in the Department of Physical Chemistry. A native of Tel Aviv, Assa, a highly intelligent and dedicated scholar and a most likable person, accepted me for a one-month probation. He watched me closely, and we had several conversations. At the end of the trial period, Assa concluded that I had a good head on my shoulders but was better suited for the humanities than for chemistry. I breathed a sigh of relief: Assa's evaluation corroborated what I knew deep down in my heart.

I then enrolled in the Department of Russian Studies at the Hebrew University of Jerusalem. In the interim, I decided to find a job in order to save up some money toward the arrival of my parents and our subsequent family reunion. (For some mysterious reason, I was certain that they would arrive shortly.) So I found a job as technician at a pharmaceutical factory. Most workers there were, like me, recent Jewish immigrants from various countries, from Romania to Morocco. One of my co-workers, though, named Daud, was an Arab man in his mid-forties. Prior to the Six-Day War, he was a tour guide in Jordan. When Daud lamented his fate, I asked him why he did not apply for an Israeli license. He responded that had he done so, his fellow Arabs would have considered it an act of treason and would have killed him and his family as collaborators.

One day, I visited Aunt Rivka right after a work shift, wearing my tall rubber boots and a sweater with sulfuric acid burn holes. She was visibly repulsed by my hideous appearance and asked me if I was enjoying my work at the factory. I told her that I was not enjoying it at all but was rather doing it to set aside some money for a refrigerator and a stove in anticipation of my parents' immigration. She then suggested I look for a more satisfying job. She pointed out a few alternatives and, among other things, asked me whether I would like to work for the Voice of Israel. I was certainly thrilled at the prospect but had not the slightest idea how to go about it. Once again, I heard her famous "Leave this to me." Without further ado, while I was present in her apartment, Aunt Rivka made another round of phone calls. She quickly arranged an appointment with Eliyahu Jonas, head of the Russian Broadcast Division. After a brief interview and upon checking my proficiency in Hebrew and English, Jonas asked me to assume the duties of a news editor right on the spot.

I was well aware that Hebrew pronunciation could be tricky for all greenhorns, including native speakers of Russian. For instance, the Hebrew equivalent for "worried" (*mud'ag*), if not articulated properly, may sound like *mudak*, which means an "asshole" in Russian. The following story illustrates how tricky an incorrect enunciation could become. An employee of the Voice of Israel's Russian Division, a Moscow-born lady of most ample proportions, had a dispute with the management over her salary. And so she went to the director of overseas broadcasting, who spoke no Russian, to clear up the matter. In the course of their conversation, the lady tried to point out that the director was familiar with her contract. In accordance with the Muscovite "brogue," the lady pronounced the unstressed "o" as "a." Thus, the intended phrase "but you saw my contract" (*aval ata raita et hachoze sheli*) sounded like *aval ata raita et hachaze sheli*, which means "but you saw my chest." The poor director blushed profusely in his chair. He did not know which way to look since the prominence of the lady's bosom made it impossible not to have it in his direct field of vision.

My immediate supervisor, Yuri Grauze, senior editor of the news sector, was the most intriguing person in the Russian Division. Yuri was a lanky, silver-haired middle-aged man, with sad-gazing dark eyes behind gold-rimmed eyeglasses. Yuri grew up in Harbin, China. He was taken there as an infant from Petrograd by his Jewish mother and Baltic German father across the country torn by the civil war. In 1939, Yuri graduated from the Department of Oriental Studies and Commerce of St. Vladimir Institute, where he majored in ancient Chinese literature. Grauze immigrated to Israel from the People's Republic of China in the late 1950s and, aside from working on the radio, taught Chinese at the Hebrew University of Jerusalem. His impeccable Russian was of the unmistakably recognizable and refined pre-Soviet brand. Yuri's high intelligence and wide erudition, combined with his rich, mellow baritone, made him an exceptional choice for political commentary and cultural analysis of the events of the day. I remember listening to and greatly enjoying Yuri's programs in Moscow on those infrequent and therefore cherished occasions when the Voice of Israel's Russian-language broadcasts were not jammed. On his rare breaks, Yuri would sit behind his desk and habitually scribble something in outsized Chinese characters that none of us in the news sector could understand. With his characteristic melancholy humor, Yuri liked to say that he was ready for any geopolitical eventuality, thereby alluding to either a Soviet or a Chinese world takeover.

Grauze was more of an exception, though. The news sector consisted primarily of young men my age, in their mid- to late twenties. The sliding work schedule provided a high degree of leeway, and most of the editors, including me, viewed this job as temporary while acquiring a university education. The only two youngsters I can think of who launched a lifetime career in the radio were the Moscow-born Yuri Vasserman and the Vilnius-born Shmuel Ben Zvi. Vasserman came to work at the Russian news sector in 1974. Before long, he moved to the Hebrew Division and became its news editor, the position he held until 2003. This was quite a landmark. To the best of my knowledge, Vasserman was the first Russian-born radio journalist from the 1970s wave of immigration to accomplish this feat. Ben Zvi began working in the Russian Division in 1972. He gradually rose through the ranks and eventually attained the position of director of overseas broadcasting, which he held until the end of 2011.

Two other people in the news sector who deserve a special mention are Vladimir Fromer and Mark Zaichik. When I met Fromer, he was a short stocky man in his early thirties. Aside from being a news editor at the radio, Fromer co-edited *Ami* (*My People*), the first, albeit short-lived, Israeli Russian-language literary magazine, which had the distinction of publishing Venedikt Erofeev's postmodernist prose poem *Moscow–Petushki* (also known as *Moscow to the End of the Line*). I have been reading and enjoying Fromer's essays all these years. In the last decade or so, Fromer has acquired for himself the title of the "Israeli Plutarch" after publishing a collection of chronicles that contains historical-biographical essays about the country's most outstanding personalities.

Mark Zaichik immigrated to Israel in 1973 from what was then called Leningrad, now again St. Petersburg. When Zaichik joined the sector, he was a tall, athletic young man in his mid-twenties. Back in Russia, he played soccer and hockey and was well versed in boxing. Although we were on amicable terms, Mark carefully guarded his inner world behind the façade of a sarcastic skirt-chasing boozehound. Unlike with Fromer, I had no idea at the time that Zaichik tried his hand at writing fiction, but I was not surprised when I later read his captivating short stories. Already then, Mark distinguished himself by his keen capacity for observation and an attentive attitude toward language. Zaichik is one of the best Israeli storytellers writing in Russian today.

Between 1973 and 1976, I had the opportunity to study Russian literature and history at the Hebrew University of Jerusalem. Unlike in Soviet Russia in general and at Moscow University in particular, where the entire curriculum was mandatory and exactly the same for every student, the Hebrew University of Jerusalem allowed for a great deal of flexibility. Thus, I took a course in comparative literature with Heda Stein and a couple of courses in classical studies (in translation) from both Barukh Lifshitz and Lisa Ullmann. Incidentally, Mrs. Ullmann, at the age of eighty-seven, recently published a Hebrew translation of *The Jewish War* by Flavius Josephus, on which she had worked for ten years. I attended Mrs. Ullmann's classes together with my sister, Luba, who by that time had been married and had assumed her husband's last name. Since we were the only students, Mrs. Ullmann held the meetings at her elegant apartment in the Rechaviah neighborhood. Both Luba and I much liked the course but never divulged to our teacher that we were siblings.

Originally, the Hebrew University of Jerusalem was built on Mount Scopus and opened in 1925. In the aftermath of the War of Independence, Jerusalem was divided, and the university campus was relocated to Giv'at Ram. This new campus was completed in 1958, and since 1960 has also housed the National Library of Israel. After Jerusalem was reunified in 1967 and construction work on the original campus was finished in 1981, the university was able to return to Mount Scopus. In the 1970s, when I studied there, I attended classes in Giv'at Ram. At present, in addition to the National Library of Israel, the Giv'at Ram campus houses several research institutions, from the Albert Einstein Mathematics Institute to

With parents and Luba at our double Hebrew University of Jerusalem commencement. Giv'at Ram, 1977.

the Alexander Silberman Institute of Life Sciences. There is a shuttle bus connecting the two campuses.

I warmly remember many of my university teachers, most of all Ada Steinberg, and Edith and Jonathan Frankel. The Odessa-born and Kishinev-raised Ada Steinberg was a native speaker of Russian. She initially worked as a secretary for the legendary Israeli poet Leah Goldberg, who had founded and headed the Department of Comparative Literature at the Hebrew University of Jerusalem and who had also founded its Department of Russian and Slavic Studies. Steinberg was an insightful student of nineteenth- and early twentieth-century Russian literature. She made a name for herself by her nuanced analysis of Andrei Bely's works in their relation to music. She taught me to read primary texts closely and to recognize the place of Russian literature within a Western context. She also taught me to view literature as an integral part of the sister arts. Edith Frankel, a native of the United States and a graduate of Cornell and Columbia, amplified my fascination with Russian literature of the 1920s and 1930s, such as the works of Isaac Babel, Mikhail Bulgakov, Yuri Olesha, and Mikhail Zoshchenko. Above all, it was her propitious hand and sound advice that helped me get my scholarly career off the ground. Several years ago, at the memorial for her husband, Jonathan, I had an opportunity to give credit where credit was long overdue and to thank her for putting me on a successful academic track. The English-born and Cambridge-educated Jonathan Frankel inculcated in me a fascination with history, mainly with that of Russian Jewry—the overarching subject of my present book.

As with every Israeli citizen, it was my duty and privilege to serve in the Israel Defense Forces (the IDF). At the outbreak of the Yom Kippur War (October 1973), I was not drafted since I was attached to the Voice of Israel's Russian Division. Like all my colleagues, I worked round the clock as information was pouring in from the theater of the war. Upon the conclusion of the war and with the beginning of my Hebrew University of Jerusalem studies, I was given a choice: to fulfill my tour of active duty first, or to earn a B.A. degree and then serve in the army. I chose the second option, even though it somewhat extended my military service. While at the university, I was supposed to join the academic reserve, and after the first year of studies, to undergo two months of basic training that would not count toward my eighteen-month active duty. I trusted that as a university graduate I would be of more use to the army in my future military service.

In the summer of 1974, I began my basic training with fellow students from the academic reserve. Like me, most of them were new immigrants from different countries, primarily from the Soviet Union but also from Romania, France, Argentina, and Chile. The only difference between them and me was age: most of the students were in their late teens or early twenties, whereas I was twenty-nine. As a result, many fellow recruits looked up to me and viewed me as their older brother. What also propelled me into that role was my relatively high language aptitude. (For the most part, my fellow trainees were still learning Hebrew.) Foolishly, I liked to show it off. When our Israeli-born drill sergeant made a common grammatical mistake, I did not hold my tongue. It would have been silly enough had I corrected his Hebrew in private, but I did so in front of the entire detachment. Fortunately, the sergeant, a kibbutznik who presumably did not receive much of a formal education, was far smarter than I. He simply countered my pedantic cavil by acknowledging, with disarming self-deprecation, that he "never excelled in grammar" (*Af paam lo hitztaianti badikduk*).

My fairly good command of the language made me stand out and serve as the spokesman for the group. One incident confirmed me in that role. Regular military personnel and trainees ate in separate dining rooms. Once we were served curdled chocolate milk for breakfast. Such things, of course, could happen in the scorching Israeli summer weather. What outraged us was that the spoiled chocolate milk had first arrived at the military personnel's mess hall. When realizing that it could not be served there, the cook, without a second's hesitation, dumped it on us trainees. We found this treatment insulting and decided to protest. I was asked to air our grievances to the officer on duty. Upon hearing the case, he was visibly perturbed and promised that such a demeaning attitude would never happen again.

Another incident, which took place soon afterward, was of a more significant and complex nature. One night, around 3 a.m., we were ordered to fall out and then were told to board a bus. We all assumed that we were being taken out for a field exercise, but we were dead wrong. Instead, we were instructed to contain settlers in order to prevent them from descending upon the area.[69] This was Elon Moreh, a village mentioned in Genesis (12:6–7), which the settlement movement wished to reestablish. I was shocked. I saw many fine patriotic people, among them familiar Russian Jews, who recognized me and invited me to join their ranks. Wearing the IDF uniform, I obviously could not cross over. But as a Zionist, I could not and did not want to engage in a struggle with fellow Jews whose cause I fervently supported. The next night, I already knew what to expect and categorically refused to go. I explained to my commanding officer that I had not immigrated to Israel to prevent Jews from settling in their historical homeland. He threatened to throw me into the stockade. I responded that I had been incarcerated in Soviet jail for Zionism, and this detention in the Israeli military prison and, ironically, for the same cause, would give me an opportunity to compare the conditions. Staggered by my reply, the officer went to his superior for instructions. He then offered me a compromise: I will go with the rest of the unit but will take no part in the operation. I was to stay near the bus to keep an eye on the equipment. I accepted this compromise but was dismayed by the entire affair, and after my return to the base went to see its commander. The commander's aide would not give me the time of day and refused to schedule an appointment. I insisted. To make a point, the aide referred to the disparity in rank: "*You* want to see *him*?" I countered: "Yes. Even though he is a colonel and I am a trainee, we are both Jews and therefore equal before the Almighty." The aide looked at me as though I completely lost my mind but in the end, miraculously, granted me an appointment with his superior.

When I met the commander, I told him that as a Zionist I found this whole business of the Israeli army engaging in political maneuvering against settlers utterly abhorrent and wanted no part of it. "I don't blame you," he muttered under his breath, but then, suddenly realizing that he should not have said this in his official capacity, added, "I have my orders."

---

69 I am referring here to those highly patriotic individuals and families who have built civilian communities in Judea, Samaria, and near Jerusalem. Although in the early and mid-1970s the Labor government tried to put obstacles in their way, they eventually prevailed. These people are true Zionists. They populate and cultivate the lands that have belonged to Jews from time immemorial by virtue of God's covenant with Abraham. This bond has also been corroborated and reinforced over and over again by innumerable archeological excavations.

After this meeting, however, I was released for good from this shameful action. Incidentally, I was not the only recruit who vehemently opposed this policy. There was a religious youngster from Strasbourg, France, who himself happened to be a member of the settler movement. His response to this myopic strategy of pitting the army against the settlers was much more drastic: he chained himself to the barracks in protest. It is to the IDF's credit that we were treated with respect and consideration. I have a hard time imagining anything like this being tolerated in the Soviet army, where I would have been court-martialed and sentenced to a long prison term. In Stalin's time, I would have been instantly executed.

Toward the end of my basic training, I had a bad accident. One day, during a field exercise, a drill sergeant threw a training grenade (*chaziz*) to test our startle responses. The grenade was supposed to explode ten yards from us, but instead it struck me directly on my left arm and blew up. I was immediately evacuated to the Hadassah Ein Kerem Hospital. Aside from the bleeding arm, my beard was singed, but worst of all, as the tests indicated, I had an internal bleeding in one ear and a ruptured eardrum in the other. Because of this accident, I suffered a substantial loss of hearing and my military profile dropped precipitously. Even now, more than forty years later, I occasionally experience zooming in my ears and my hearing has remained deficient.

So when I completed my course of studies in 1976 and was up for active military service, I was not sent to the front lines. I was assigned instead to serve in RAM-2, an office at the Assaf HaRofeh Medical Center in Tzrifin, whose purpose was to attend to the needs of sick and wounded military personnel. For the most part, I lived at home and traveled daily between Tzrifin and Jerusalem—about an hour-long bus ride each way. The head of this RAM-2 office was Master Sergeant Yaki, three years my junior. Yaki's father had died when he was a little boy, and he was brought up by his mother. Yaki was badly wounded in the Six-Day War, in which he served as a paratrooper. As a result of this injury, Yaki developed a heart condition. In spite of this and against doctors' stern warnings, he was a chain smoker, going through two packs of cigarettes a day. For some reason, Yaki did not feel too comfortable speaking with doctors and therefore habitually sent me to discuss patients with them.

Serving in the
IDF. 1977.

I enjoyed attending to the needs of convalescing soldiers. One day, however, I ran into a serious problem when a high-ranking officer was admitted to the hospital after a minor car accident. He had an attached chauffeur, whom he treated as an errand boy. When the officer attempted to address me in his typical haughty manner, I told him that unless he changes his deportment and speaks to me politely and with respect, he leaves me no choice but to ignore his requests. The officer, unaccustomed to such insubordination (I was only a private), could not believe his ears and immediately sent for Yaki. When I told Yaki what had happened, he turned white as a sheet. As a cadre military man, he did not relish being called on the carpet by a high-ranking officer on account of his underling. Nonetheless, Yaki acquitted himself of the task admirably. As Yaki told me later, he explained to the officer that I was not a run-of-the-mill soldier. Yaki told him about my struggle with the Soviet regime and about my two university degrees. Apparently, this made an impression on the officer. To his credit, from that point on, the officer changed his demeanor. He spoke to me amicably and politely, and even on one occasion introduced me to his daughter, who visited him in the hospital. After having been released from Assaf HaRofeh, the officer always asked Yaki to convey to me his best regards whenever they ran into each other at military functions.

Overall, the army service was an important landmark in my life in Israel. I learned a great deal about the country by interacting with members of various strata of the Israeli population, and not just with my academic family, professors, and fellow students. Especially crucial was my work in RAM-2, where I met people from all walks of life. I also witnessed first-hand how liberal and democratic the IDF was, thereby making it one of the best armies in the world. My military service helped me to forge a powerful everlasting bond with the country.

While serving in the IDF, I applied to several Slavic graduate programs in the United States. In those days, there was no full-fledged Slavic doctoral program in Israel that could offer a five-year support package, as has been the case in the United States. By the time I finished my military duty I was thirty-three. Had I stayed in Israel, I would have had to get a job to support myself and that would not have allowed me to study full time. Consequently, it would have taken me at least ten more years instead of the usual five to complete the process. For this and other reasons, my Hebrew University of Jerusalem teachers, most of all Edith Frankel, strongly encouraged me to continue my education in the United States. Edith recommended that I apply to the Slavic program at the University of Illinois and wrote a favorable reference letter to Maurice Friedberg, head of the department, who happened to be her fellow Columbian. In the spring of 1978, I received a letter of admission. I was delighted to learn that as part of the graduate program package I was to be given a teaching assistantship, with all the trimmings—a stipend, dorm accommodations, a meal plan, and a tuition and fee waiver. In return, I was expected to teach one section of the Beginning Russian. I found these conditions most advantageous and gratefully accepted the offer.

Shortly afterward, a couple of my former Hebrew University of Jerusalem teachers spoiled the joy. They told me that when I go to the University of Illinois I should transfer to a more reputable school as quickly as possible. Otherwise, so they claimed, if I do not find a job back in Israel as I planned, all I could hope for upon graduating would be a small Midwestern college in the middle of nowhere. Of course, after hearing such a grim forecast, I became quite apprehensive. Jumping ahead, I have to say that I took their advice to heart and after my first semester at the University of Illinois went to visit the University of California at Berkeley. Since the University of California was on the quarter system at the time, it was in session in early January 1979, when the University of Illinois was on its winter recess. I did not regret the visit in the least. I had a chance to attend the classes of Simon Karlinsky and Czesław Miłosz. I had a lovely conversation with Gleb Struve and discussed my transfer prospects with Olga Raevsky Hughes, the department's director of graduate studies. After our talk, Raevsky Hughes told me that they would be glad to admit me into their Slavic program. However, I would receive no credit for my year at the University of Illinois and would be obliged to start the graduate program from scratch. Upon thinking it over, I decided to place my fate in the hands of the Almighty and to stay at the University of Illinois. I am very glad I did.

CHAPTER 7

GRADUATE STUDIES IN THE UNITED STATES

> To stay in these two professors' good graces, a student had to perform a balancing act by taking an equal number of their courses in any given semester.

In late July 1978, shortly after concluding my eighteen-month military service, I left for Chicago. Upon connecting from O'Hare Airport to the Amtrak Union Station, I took a two-and-a-half-hour train ride from Chicago to Urbana–Champaign. Although I had toured the United States from coast to coast by Greyhound three years earlier, my familiarity with the country in general and with its rural Midwest in particular was quite limited. The first surprise was my cabbie, a local resident, originally from the Deep South, who spoke rather decent Hebrew. I was astounded to find a Hebrew speaker in this cornfield town. When I asked him for the reason of his interest in Hebrew, he told me that as a devout Christian he had studied the language to be able to read the Old Testament in the original. Unbeknownst to me, I encountered a veritable representative of the Bible Belt.

Speaking of the Bible Belt. Soon afterward, I experienced its different, less attractive facet. I was homesick, and as time allowed, visited the periodicals reading room to browse the latest Hebrew newspapers. One day, when I was leafing through *Maariv*, I became aware of a pretty, blue-eyed, buxom blonde sitting at the other end of the room and staring at me. There was no one else there at the time, and we struck up a conversation that began, as is often the case, with an exchange of pleasantries and meaningless remarks. The girl, an Alabama native, behaved quite coquettishly toward me and, upon hearing my distinct accent, naturally asked me where I was from. To keep up with the flirtation game, I suggested she take a guess. "Sweden," was her hasty reply. She then came up to me, and I advised her to look not at me but rather at the newspaper I was reading. Oddly, not distinguishing between Hebrew and Roman letters, or perhaps displaying wishful thinking, the girl blurted out: "Norway." Just as I was about to tell her that I came from Israel, there appeared Larry F., a Jewish fellow from Milwaukee. Larry studied architecture and lived in the same graduate dorm as I did—Sherman Hall. The dorm was usually referred to by its occupants as Vermin Hall, among other things, due to its less than meticulous kitchenette. Leaning unceremoniously over the paper, Larry exclaimed, "Ah, you are reading the Israeli *New York Times* again!" The moment the girl heard "Israel," her facial expression instantaneously changed from playful to horrified. In terror, she ran back to her distant seat as fast as she could, snatched up her belongings, and dashed out of the room. The girl, unsurprisingly, was at sixes and sevens because my physical appearance contradicted the image that some people comfortably reserve for Jews. No wonder the poor thing became panic-stricken!

The most pleasant surprise, as far as the University of Illinois goes, was its library, above all its vast Slavic collection. This collection was amassed owing to the keen vision of Ralph Fisher, professor of Russian history and the founder and longtime director of the Russian and East European Center. In the golden 1960s, when money was no object, the federal government gave it out quite liberally. It was particularly generous in allotting funds for the development of Russian studies at the peak of the Cold War and the race for outer space. At that time, Fisher astutely decided to invest in the library. As he told me one day, "Faculty come and go but books always stay." Because of Fisher's foresight, the Slavic Collection at the University of Illinois became one of the best in the country. In addition, the library could boast of the most qualified Slavic reference experts on its staff, such as Laurence Miller, Marianna Tax Choldin, Robert Burger, and Mary Stuart.

Fisher, who took pride in being a descendant of the *Mayflower* pilgrims, had a strong passion for maps, which he used extensively in his teaching. Aside from presumably inheriting this passion from his progenitors who traveled centuries ago across the Atlantic, Fisher acquired an additional predilection for maps during World War II, in which he had served as a military cartographer. Having a minor in Russian history and Fisher on my dissertation committee, I took a couple of his courses in which his wide use of maps was both helpful and refreshing.

Fisher had three children, two sons and one daughter. The younger son earned his Ph.D. in math and went for a post doc to the Hebrew University of Jerusalem. While in Israel, the young man befriended an Arab girl. When Fisher visited his son in Jerusalem, they were invited over by the girl's family. Later Fisher told me how shocked he was to see a map hanging in their hosts' living room, on which the entire Land of Israel was presented as the Palestinian State. Fisher was not pro-Israel in the least, liked to emphasize that he had no connection or relation to the ethnically Jewish journalist and Russian historian Louis Fischer, and made it clear that he was "Fisher—not Jewish." At the same time, being a fair-minded individual, like most Americans, Fisher, who remained an avid cartographer at heart, found this map's misrepresentation appalling and as a historian was perfectly aware of its devious political ramifications. Although not a prolific scholar, Fisher deserves credit for his prudence and organizational talents that turned the University of Illinois into a supreme center of Slavic studies.

I was fond of the man, and he seemed to reciprocate the sentiment. On one occasion, Fisher pleasantly surprised me: on a bet with a colleague, Fisher, when he was already in his early sixties, memorized Pushkin's *Eugene Onegin* in the original and recited it canto after canto. Conversely, Fisher once shocked me by the deafness of his heart: in the summer of 1990, a year after my father's tragic death, I ran into Fisher and his wife, Ruth, at an international Slavic congress in Harrogate, England. I told him about my devastating loss, but he was in a hurry to some prior engagement and did not muster even the most trivial words of sympathy. It was especially astounding and traumatic because on his visit to Israel, Fisher met my father, who took him out one day on a drive around

Jerusalem. Even after Ruth tried to draw his attention to the matter, assuming that he did not hear me right, Ralph did not shift his focus and kept insisting that they should be going. I was stunned and deeply hurt by this insensitivity. A couple of months later, Fisher sent me a condolence card, but the irreparable harm was done, and I could no longer find in me the warmth I previously felt for the man.

The Slavic Department at the University of Illinois consisted of language instructors, linguists, and literary scholars. As a teaching assistant, I taught a section of Russian, for which I used the first volume of *Modern Russian*. Clayton Dawson, a Russian language professor, taught one section and supervised the rest (there were four or five sections at the time). The textbook, which Dawson co-authored, was richly illustrated with black-and-white photographs of scenes from everyday life in Moscow of the early 1960s. To my great astonishment, I recognized myself in one of them, entitled "A Chemistry Lecture at Moscow University."[70] The photograph provided a partial view of a lecture in the Department of Chemistry main auditorium. I am sitting way in the back, at the far right, with one foot out in the aisle, as if ready to leave at any moment. As it later turned out, I was ready to leave not only the auditorium but also chemistry and the country of my childhood and youth altogether. Upon examining the photograph and recognizing many of my classmates, I felt as though a space-time machine transported me back fifteen years across the Atlantic.

The linguistic division in the department was represented by Steven P. Hill, Frank Y. Gladney, and Rasio Dunatov. I met Hill on the day of my arrival at the university. It was late July and most faculty members were away. Hill, however, was in his office. I knocked on the door to introduce myself. At that time, I had not yet shed some vestiges of my Russian superstitions. When Hill opened the door and offered to shake my hand over the threshold—and shaking hands over a threshold is perceived as a bad omen in Russia—I clasped his and yanked the diminutive fellow through the doorway into the corridor. Poor Hill! He probably thought to

---

70 See Clayton L. Dawson, Charles E. Bildwell, and Assya Humesky, *Modern Russian I* (New York: Harcourt, Brace & World, 1964), 82.

himself, and not entirely without foundation, "What a nut we must have let into our program!" It was no doubt an amusing scene but, luckily, there was no one in the department to see it. In spite of that inauspicious beginning, Hill was always cordial toward me. I never took his classes, though. Perhaps Hill's cordiality was his way of expressing gratitude for my steering clear of his classroom. From my occasional conversations with Hill, I got the impression that he was fully immersed in Russian culture: he spoke Russian with near-native fluency and was intimately familiar with the Russian and Soviet cinema. One of Hill's idiosyncrasies was calling people in the department, students and faculty alike, by name and patronymic, Russian style. I recall how a very Anglo-Saxon Dawson, whose first and middle names were Clayton Leroy, cringed each time Hill addressed him as "Nikolai Lavrent´evich."

Unlike the miniature Hill, Gladney, an expert in Polish linguistics, was tall, athletically built, and dapper looking, always wearing a bow tie. I never took classes with him either, but once we had a conflict. For my dissertation on Gogol and the Baroque, I submitted an application for the Foreign Language and Area Studies (FLAS) fellowship that would support my studies of the Polish language. I maintained that the role of Ukrainian Baroque, which exerted an extensive influence on Gogol, could not be fully understood without taking into account how it in turn was influenced by Polish Baroque, above all its literature. At the time, Gladney served as the department's acting chair while Friedberg was on sabbatical leave. Gladney turned down my application and justified his resolution by claiming that there was no connection between Polish and Ukrainian cultures. I appealed this decision and in the end received the fellowship. I studied Polish with Friedberg. After a brief survey of the grammar, we began reading and discussing Polish Baroque literature, which I found most enjoyable, even if quite challenging. (Later, many native speakers of Polish were flabbergasted when I would quote passages from Samuel Twardowski, Jan Andrzej Morsztyn, or from his cousin Zbigniew Morsztyn. Most of them never even heard of these poets.) Despite this conflict, Gladney harbored no ill feelings. In fact, years later I had rather amicable encounters and friendly chats with him at various professional gatherings. At one such meeting, Gladney shared with me the results of a comprehensive evaluation of the department's doctoral program. According to Gladney, the evaluation determined that producing several first-rate Slavists constituted the program's raison d'être.

The Dalmatian-born Dunatov grew up on one of the numerous islands scattered along the eastern shores of the Adriatic Sea. His father was a commercial fisherman, and fishing, for which Rasio felt genuine passion, was in his blood. Dunatov spent summers trawling in the Pacific off the coast of Seattle, and upon his return to Urbana–Champaign, would throw bountiful salmon parties. Dunatov was a likable, easygoing human being, and a lenient grader. I took his year-long course in Serbo-Croatian, as it was called then, which I needed to fulfill my Ph.D. language requirements. Now, more than thirty years later, I still remember "Good day! How are you? Very well, thanks!" (*Dobar dan! Kako ste? Vrlo dobro, hvala!*), which comes handy when I greet my Serbian-born primary care physician.

Maurice Friedberg, the department head, although imperious, was an equitable individual. When a student, lazy and anti-Semitic, griped about my being too demanding an instructor, Friedberg said to her, "Had you told me that Shapiro was incompetent or a bad teacher, I would have investigated the matter, and if proven accurate, would have dismissed him. But you're claiming that Shapiro demands a lot from his students, and that's how it should be. Only then will the students be able to learn such a difficult language as Russian. Go and work harder." Friedberg ruled the department with an iron fist, which in this case was a blessing—otherwise the unit would have turned into an endless combat zone.

Both inside and outside the classroom, Friedberg liked to pepper his speech with funny stories, which he told masterfully. I remember one of them. Between 1966 and 1975, Friedberg taught in the Slavic Department at Indiana University. That year, he was offered and accepted the position of head of the Slavic Department at the University of Illinois. While traveling from Bloomington, Indiana, to Urbana–Champaign, Illinois, and upon crossing the border between the two states, Friedberg stopped for gas. After a little chitchat, the gas station attendant, mystified by Friedberg's accent, said, "You talk kinda funny. Where're ya from?" "Indiana," was Friedberg's reply, which left the poor attendant totally stumped. Many years later, I somewhat replicated the joke. While passing through a small sleepy town in upstate New York, I stopped at its farmers market. A vendor, puzzled by my accent, asked me where I was from. When I told him that I was from Illinois, he responded, "I never knew it for sure but always suspected that people in the Midwest talk funny!" Although Friedberg spoke English with a perceptible accent, his knack for languages—he knew more than half a dozen of them—was considerable. His Russian was of a near-native quality. Only occasionally did he stress the wrong syllable in a word, and his pronunciation at times betrayed his Polish-language origins.

In 1964, Friedberg, then a faculty member at Hunter College, was set up as the fall guy by one of his erstwhile Columbia professors, who used him to attack Vladimir Nabokov's translation of *Eugene Onegin*. Friedberg's review, which he without a doubt lived to regret, appeared in *Novyi Zhurnal* (*New Review*), a reputable Russian-language periodical. When commenting on this incident, Friedberg would remark, self-deprecatingly, that the review earned him a footnote in the history of Russian literature. In his own writings, Friedberg approached literature largely from a sociopolitical vantage point. He relished the negative reputation he earned among Soviet Cold War hack journalists, such as Yuri Zhukov and Al′bert Beliaev, and enjoyed being called every now and then to Washington, D.C., for consultations on Soviet affairs.

Unlike lean and lanky Fisher, Friedberg was short in stature and roly-poly. I always surmised that this excess weight was a result of the deep trauma caused by the terrible food deprivation that Maurice had endured in his formative years during World War II. Fortunately for him, and unlike the vast majority of Polish Jewry, he and his family were expelled by the Nazis to the Soviet Union at the outbreak of the war and thus survived.[71]

On one occasion, Friedberg also showed me how highly sensitive and emotionally vulnerable he could be. In 1987, before leaving northern Illinois for upstate New York, I spent some time doing research in my

---

71 See an interview with Friedberg at http://collections.ushmm.org/search/catalog/irn38082.

alma mater's magnificent library. There I ran into Friedberg, who was warm and pleasant and who graciously invited me to dine with him and his wife, Barbara, at their residence. Before we parted, he asked me about changes in my life. I told him about my divorce from Jennifer (whom I shall introduce shortly) and about my assuming a tenure-track assistant professorship at Cornell. Upon hearing the latter, his demeanor all of a sudden drastically changed. He muttered something about the need to call off the dinner invitation and abruptly left. I was perplexed by his mood swing and felt that perhaps I committed some gaffe that hurt his feelings. Barbara, who happened to be present and witnessed this sharp reversal, solved the riddle. She explained that about twenty-five years earlier Maurice interviewed for a position at Cornell but did not get it. Although powerful head of the reputable department, Friedberg evidently remembered this rejection of long ago and was still so much upset by it that he vented out his frustration in such clumsy and discourteous manner.

I saw Friedberg for the last time in 2006 at a Slavic annual convention in Washington, D.C. By then seventy-seven years old, he had been suffering from severe diabetes and had become almost completely blind. It was highly upsetting to watch Maurice helplessly standing there as younger conference participants were darting in and out of the elevators and brushing up against him. I came up to Maurice and offered help. He recognized me by my voice and was grateful for my escorting him to his hotel room.

Other literature professors in the Slavic Department at the University of Illinois included Evelyn Bristol and Temira Pachmuss. There was no love lost between these two at the time. (I recently learned that they eventually mended fences and even developed amicable relations toward the end of their lives.) In fact, to stay in their good graces, a student had to perform a balancing act by taking an equal number of their courses in any given semester. The atmosphere was reminiscent of the one brilliantly depicted by Mikhail Bulgakov in his *Theatrical Novel* (*Teatral'nyi roman*). The novel exposed the paralyzing effects of the feud between Konstantin Stanislavsky and Vladimir Nemirovich-Danchenko, the two famed directors, on the functioning of the Moscow Art Theater. I had a better rapport with Pachmuss and decided to choose her as my advisor. Luckily, she gave me almost an entirely free hand, herself conceding at one point that she had no clue about the subject of my dissertation.

Although Pachmuss never made any derogatory remarks to me personally, her behavior on at least a couple of occasions demonstrated her prejudice against Jews. I was in the final throes of writing my dissertation and brought a chapter for her to read. Before I left her home that afternoon, Pachmuss wished to show me some valuable items that had originally belonged to the famous émigré writing couple, Zinaida Hippius and Dmitri Merezhkovsky, and had come into her possession. (Hippius was the focus of Pachmuss's scholarship.) These valuables included an icon. With a wry smile on her face, Temira Andreevna all of a sudden thrust it up to my lips for kissing. She got a kick out of the expression of horror on my face as I sprang back from the icon. Some years later, at a conference, I overheard her conversation with another Russian expatriate Slavist, in which they both lamented the preponderance of Jews in the field.

Pachmuss was known for her eccentricities. She was convinced that squirrels were capable of undermining trees, perhaps confusing them with wild boars. She engaged graduate students in the task of catching the rodents and transporting them in cages from her lawn to remote parks and groves. (Thankfully, I was not one of them, for I did not know how to drive at the time.) Although squirrels could possibly cause damage to trees by stripping bark, removing the critters was not a solution. At the end of the day, new ones replaced those sent into exile, thereby turning this banishment into a futile never-ending practice. Another ritual, which demonstrated Pachmuss's self-centeredness, had to do with her out-of-town traveling. Whenever she needed to get to or from the Urbana–Champaign Willard Airport, she would ask several people, usually colleagues, sometimes also graduate students, to help her out. More than a few cars would show up for her transportation. Pachmuss would then select one of the vehicles without blinking an eye and without apologizing to the rest of the people for the inconvenience she had caused. She once explained that she did so to be absolutely sure that she would not be left without a ride. Apparently, it never entered her head to call a cab.

Even though Pachmuss always gave me very high marks for my term papers, she did not seem to acknowledge my scholarly potential. After my first article was published while I was still an M.A. student, Pachmuss remarked on how everything in it fell into place so nicely. Her backhanded compliment implied that the article miraculously came together all on its own, with little to no effort on my part. All the same, I was grateful to her for not interfering with my research. In due time, I also learned to appreciate her insistence on my translating the original Gogol quotations into English, just as I was grateful to Fisher for being resolute about my writing the dissertation in English. Although this presented me with a daunting task, it forced me to work hard on my language proficiency and served me in good stead when I was reworking the dissertation into my first book.

After the doctoral graduation. University of Illinois, Urbana–Champaign. May 1984.

Gradually my scholarly interests crystallized. In exploring works of literature, I have focused my attention on their close reading, all the while viewing them in the broad context of cultural history. In addition, being an aficionado of the fine arts and of art history, I have been enthralled by the interaction of word and image. In light of these interests, I chose for my dissertation the works of Nikolai Gogol (1809–52), whom I have always considered Russia's greatest prose writer. Furthermore, for my doctoral thesis I decided to explore the role of the Baroque cultural heritage in forming and framing Gogol's worldview. Gogol grew up in Ukraine. As a cultural phenomenon, the Baroque was prevalent there throughout the eighteenth century, which drew to a close only a decade before the writer's birth. Moreover, one of the main strands of the Baroque was an interaction between the verbal and the visual. This interaction was most congenial to Gogol, an amateur painter, whose writings are suffused with picturesque colorfulness and visual imagery. This subject matter had not been studied systematically or in depth before then, and I intended to fill this serious gap, at least in part.

Among my fellow graduate students, there were some peculiar characters. One of them, a Moscow native who struggled with the English language, sincerely believed that all Americans actually knew how to speak Russian and feigned ignorance just to tick him off. He repeatedly conducted an experiment to check the validity of his hypothesis by suddenly accosting American-born people and speaking Russian to them. In spite of being taken by surprise, they responded in English every single time. These failed attempts did not dissuade my fellow student from clinging to this language conspiracy theory for a long while. Many years later, when I bumped into him at the Frick Collection in New York City, he spoke rather decent English. By that time, he was married to an American woman, who was present with him at the exhibit. He never completed his Ph.D., withdrew from the program, and opted instead for a library science degree. Subsequently, he found employment in some small-town public library in the Big Apple area that definitely required a certain level of English language proficiency.

While at the University of Illinois, I became acquainted with Amir T., a Tel Aviv native, two years my junior. Feeling homesick, we discussed Israeli news, talked about girls, and attended concerts of classical music together. One day, Amir told me that he had gone to a Jewish singles party where he had met a nice-looking young woman, named Jennifer. His description of the woman piqued my curiosity. Amir saw her once more but after that had no success in setting up another date. It was only a matter of time before Jennifer turned him down. When it happened, I asked Amir for her phone number. He did not seem to mind and proffered it to me. Before contacting her, I realized that I was facing an uphill battle. Sure enough, when I called Jennifer and told her that I obtained her phone number from Amir, she did not wish to talk to me at all, let alone see me. Being Amir's friend did not work in my favor—Jennifer had found him frightfully boring. All I could say in response was to ask her to give me a chance and to hear me out. We talked for over two hours, and Jennifer agreed to meet me. The encounter took place at the end of November 1980. Eventually, Jennifer and I fell in love and got married approximately six months later.

Jennifer was a teacher. Fortunately, she found a position in one of the nearby schools. Jennifer was greatly devoted to her work and used to share with me stories about her pupils. From what I gathered, on at least one occasion she probably saved a child's life. Jennifer told me that the school had admitted a new student, whose scholastic aptitude was ostensibly poor, so much so that he was pronounced mentally challenged. Yet Jennifer figured out in no time that the school administrators screwed up. The boy simply spoke little to no English as his family had emigrated from Hungary a short time before. It was unfathomable how and why the administrators did not take this serious matter into account. Jennifer tirelessly worked with the pupil, first through an interpreter and later one on one when he became more proficient in English. She told me with great joy how bright the boy was and how eager to learn.

I much respected Jennifer for her professional dedication, but our marriage did not stand the test of time and began coming apart at the seams. I think that after a while the exotic allure of her being married to a Russian-Israeli novice in America and for me of being married to a Jewish-American woman gradually wore off. Most important, our upbringing was very dissimilar: I came from a scholarly family, whereas Jennifer came from a business background. In my family, money was of minor importance, while in hers it was the principal measure of success. A distinct disparity between our outlooks soon emerged. The first indication of this disparity came when her older brother, Stewart, whom Jennifer admired and viewed as a role model, told me that his primary goal in life was to become a millionaire by the age of thirty-five. Jennifer herself was rather unhappy with my meager assistant professor salary. To rectify this "deficiency," she suggested I should not waste time writing scholarly monographs that rarely make money. Jennifer advised me instead to compile textbooks or anthologies on Soviet civilization that would be widely adopted, thereby guaranteeing most handsome royalties. From a business standpoint, it was a valid suggestion, but I was not the least bit interested in moneymaking as the motivation behind my scholarship. It got us embroiled in our first serious argument when I told Jennifer that I earned a Ph.D. not to sell myself out but rather to embark on a productive scholarly career.

I knew that Jennifer had dabbled in composing fiction since her early teens. I saw some of her writing, believed it to be rather good, and encouraged her to continue. One day, though, when I chanced upon Jennifer in the catalogue room of the university library, I became dismayed by her attitude toward the creative process. When I asked Jennifer what she was researching, she told me in all seriousness that she was attempting to crack the bestseller formula. I reasoned with her that looking for such a formula would be tantamount to seeking the philosopher's stone. I tried to impress upon her that a writer must rather draw on unique personal experience and only then, given the talent, could meet with success. I doubted Jennifer found my arguments persuasive. At that time, I began to have deep concerns over the widening differences in our worldviews.

CHAPTER 8

LIVING, TEACHING, AND WRITING IN AMERICA

> When I dwell in Nabokov's world, I feel like I am breathing a pure, rarified air of mountain meadows.

In the summer of 1983, as my work on the doctoral dissertation was nearing completion, I received a call from the Foreign Languages Department at Illinois State University. After a brief telephone interview, its chair, Louis Olivier, offered me a lectureship for the upcoming 1983–84 academic year. Initially, I was concerned that a heavy teaching load would get in the way of my finishing the dissertation. On second thought, I decided to take up the job because the teaching experience could give me an edge in my prospective job hunting. Olivier promised that the lectureship would convert into an assistant professorship as soon as I defended the thesis. He also told me that there was a good chance this assistant professorship would be upgraded to a tenure-track position the following year. Subsequently, Jennifer and I moved to Bloomington–Normal, located about fifty miles northwest of Urbana–Champaign. The teaching load was indeed heavy—four courses per semester. Furthermore, I had to sit on all kinds of committees to represent the language since I was the only one in the department teaching Russian. Still, I managed to make significant progress on my dissertation and was scheduled to defend it on Friday, November 18, 1983. That same morning, Friedberg told me that a Hebrew University of Jerusalem professor, Il´ia Zakharovich Serman, was in town and would be present at my defense. Serman was among the best and most reputable Slavists in the world, and I was understandably worried. Serman asked me a pertinent question about the impact on Gogol of the writings of Grigory Skovoroda, an eighteenth-century philosopher, nicknamed the Ukrainian Socrates. I seemed to have acquitted myself rather well and even dared to argue with Serman. Later, on my visits to Jerusalem, Il´ia Zakharovich would speak of this episode with humor. As Serman told me then, he got a real kick out of my debating with him at the defense. Serman, who had a most distinguished and prolific scholarly career both in Soviet Russia and in Israel, died several years ago in Jerusalem at the age of ninety-seven.

Earlier that fall, I attended an Illinois State reception to which both the well established and the newly hired faculty were invited. There I was approached by an old-timer. He sounded amicable and attentive and asked many questions about my background and field of study. I was quite pleased and flattered by his interest. "What a nice school," I mused, "where new faculty members are so welcome and are made to feel so much at home!" When the man asked me about my rank, and I told him that I was a lecturer, he cringed and bluntly inquired whether I had a Ph.D. When I replied that I did not have it just yet, intending to go on about my forthcoming defense, he abruptly spun on his heel and strode away. This respectable professor did not wish to waste his valuable time on chatting with a lowly ABD.[72] Surely, had he known this ahead of time, he would not have graced me with his company. After all, I was in my late thirties and could very well have been his peer. This was a clear oversight on the part of the event organizers. They should have distributed name tags indicating each participant's academic degree and rank to avoid the sort of unpleasantness to which they unwittingly subjected this esteemed educator. In all seriousness, it has been my observation that academia is riddled with arrogance and snobbery. The haughtier the individual is, the more chances are that he is a puffed-up mediocrity. I remember a snooty

---

72 This abbreviation stands for "all but dissertation."

Illinois State University colleague whose only claim to fame was his Ph.D. from Stanford. He liked to mention this fact season in and season out, even though as a scholar, at least when I met him, he was an underachiever, to put it mildly. He spent most of his office time scissoring paper birds and indeed excelled at this unquestionably meticulous and demanding task.

It appeared that the populace of Bloomington–Normal at the time was for the most part unaccustomed to Jews and Jewish names. Here is an anecdote to illustrate this point. One day, as I was out teaching, I received a parcel notification slip. I called the post office to ask for the parcel's redelivery. "What is your name?" the postmaster inquired. "Shapiro," I answered. "And what is your last name?" the postmaster further queried.

The frame of mind at Illinois State during my brief tenure there was distressingly Judeophobic and anti-Israeli. The campus teemed with pugnacious Palestinian supporters. Even back then, these Islamic radicals were both Holocaust deniers and Nazi sympathizers who welcomed the "Final Solution." This Jew-hatred reached its culmination when the office door of a faculty member, a Romanian-born chemistry professor and a Holocaust survivor, was spray-painted with a swastika. I was furious and wished to contact the Anti-Defamation League, but the members of the local Jewish community were so terrified that they implored me not to do it. They promised to deal with the problem in their own way, quietly, but of course did absolutely nothing. Their behavior brought to mind Elie Wiesel's *The Jews of Silence*, which this recognized humanitarian, himself a Holocaust survivor, wrote about Soviet Jewry. Anti-Semitism in the late twentieth-century United States was news to me. All the more amazing was the hush-hush attitude to this malodorous malice on the part of American Jews. One could certainly identify with the fear of Soviet Jews under the totalitarian regime. But even they, according to Wiesel, were overcoming their fright. They were hungry for any information about the Western world, specifically about their brethren living in Western Europe, the United States, and most of all Israel. Wiesel's account was based on his impressions from the mid-1960s. A few years later, Soviet Jewry acquired its loud and clear voice and began its triumphant struggle against the despotic establishment. That is why it was baffling to see such a timid reaction in the United States, the bastion of democracy, in the 1980s.

Perhaps the sheepish response to this abhorrent phenomenon, as I experienced it at Illinois State, was in part responsible for its ever-present nature. I recall Jennifer telling me that when her family lived in a small town, she, a little girl, was called on by her teacher in the following fashion: "Hey, Jew! Go to the blackboard!" To the best of my knowledge, Jennifer's parents did not protest, and the family soon left the town and moved back to their original residence.

Obviously, racism in general and anti-Semitism in particular are not limited to provincial regions. The importance of not letting bigots get away with their hatemongering but rather confronting them and fighting back became painfully apparent to me when I myself had fallen victim to anti-Semitism, in Manhattan of all places. I came to New York City in late December 2002 to attend the annual Slavic convention (AATSEEL) and stayed at the Hotel Newton. The next day, the hotel boiler broke down. As a result, there was no hot water and, furthermore, there was no heating in the entire building. I inquired of the hotel front desk administrator, Mr. Khan, as to when the heating would be restored, and in the interim requested a small electric heating coil to be able to warm up at least a small amount of water and to wash up. Under the circumstances, all I could hope for was a birdbath, if that. Both my inquiry and request did not elicit a favorable response from Mr. Khan. Moreover, he indulged in an anti-Semitic rant that I quote here verbatim: "You belong to the Shapiro family. I know your kind! You're always complaining! If you don't like it here, get out!" I was shocked by this unprovoked outburst of hostility and decided to call a nearby police precinct. Soon, two police officers, a man and a woman, arrived in the hotel lobby, and I recounted the whole incident to them. After hearing my side of the story, the police officers approached Mr. Khan for an explanation. His lame excuse was that shortly before my arrival, there stayed in the hotel a Shapiro family from Chile. According to Mr. Khan, the family gave him a hard time by constantly carping about the conditions. He assumed that I was a relative of theirs but then realized his mistake. Maybe because the police officers happened to be Hispanics, they did not appreciate Mr. Khan's singling out a South

American family for scorn. They reminded Mr. Khan that this was not the first time the Hotel Newton mistreated guests based on their ethnic origin. They warned him that if it happened again, there would be heavy fallout for him and for the entire establishment. They also insisted on his giving me at least two nights on the house for the inconvenience and distress to which the hotel administration had subjected me. Mr. Khan readily accepted this ruling, no doubt realizing that he got off quite lightly. Furthermore, to improve his image in the eyes of the police officers, he instantaneously provided me with an electric heating coil and apologized profusely for the trouble the boiler breakdown had caused.

While teaching at Illinois State University, I was applying for various job openings, but no suitable positions turned up. In the meantime, my employment situation was far from satisfactory. After I earned my doctoral degree, the lectureship was not converted into an assistant professorship as promised. The department administration was now saying that it would be done at the beginning of the next academic year. No less disappointing was the news that the position would remain temporary for the time being. One Monday morning in late April 1984, Olivier called me in and offered to renew the job for just one year. The offer included the long-deserved assistant professorship and a small pay hike. For some strange reason, I asked for a week to think it over, even though I did not have any other prospects in the offing. Yet the very next day I received a phone call from the Foreign Languages Department at Northern Illinois University, to which I had applied the previous fall. Its chair, Francis Valette, inquired if I was still interested in the job. Compared to Illinois State University, it was a win-win situation: a better school, a tenure-track position, and slightly higher pay. Of course, I responded in the affirmative, and an on-campus interview was scheduled for the coming Friday. The interview went well. In fact, as I learned later, I was not placed on the department's short list only because George Gutsche, the faculty member who taught Russian there, specialized in the nineteenth century (Pushkin), and since I wrote my dissertation on Gogol, the department was hesitant to hire another nineteenth-century specialist, preferring instead a twentieth-century expert. Although all signs pointed to the department's readiness to hire me, I was not offered the job right away. Valette and other members of the search committee probably wished to observe protocol, perhaps they also wanted to think it over, and promised to contact me the following Monday morning. Indeed, on Monday morning I received a phone call from DeKalb with the job offer and gladly accepted it. All I had to do was to go back to Olivier and to inform him of my imminent departure.

DeKalb, Illinois, is conveniently situated forty-five minutes from the O'Hare Airport and an hour and fifteen minutes from downtown Chicago, in particular from the Civic Opera House. DeKalb's location was no doubt instrumental in bringing many international and Chicago-based students to the university. At the same time and for the same reason, DeKalb would turn into a ghost town on weekends and extended holidays as students and faculty would leave it in droves.

At the time of my arrival, in the mid-1980s, DeKalb had a sizable Lebanese Christian community. Being clan-oriented, Lebanese expatriates would come to the town to join their extended family members. The first among them arrived in the early 1970s as the fighting began to rage between the Christian Phalange militia and the Black September.[73] The war broke out in 1971 after King Hussein of Jordan, rightly fearing for his rule over the country and for his own life, expelled Palestinian terrorists to Lebanon. Before long, the terrorists started causing trouble for the local population and turned the Pearl of the Middle East, as Lebanon was known then, into a continuous battlefield. The subsequent wave of Lebanese refugees came to DeKalb in the early and mid-1980s during the next outburst of hostilities in the region. I vividly remember one Maronite Catholic couple from Beirut, Maria and George, whose eldest son was killed by Palestinian terrorists in the sectarian struggle.[74] Although grief-stricken, Maria and George showed great resilience and resourcefulness when, speaking little English, they settled in the new country and opened a restaurant. I frequented the restaurant and became good friends with

---

73 The Black September was a Palestinian terrorist organization founded in 1970. It was responsible for the kidnapping and murder of eleven Israeli athletes at the 1972 Summer Olympics in Munich. The Phalange is a Lebanese Christian political party founded as early as 1936.

74 The Maronite Church is an Eastern rite Catholic Church that functions in close association with the Holy See of Rome. It traces its heritage back to the community founded by Maroun, a fourth-century monk venerated as a saint.

them. On one occasion, I even allowed myself to give them advice. They were clearly unfamiliar with the concept of a menu price list. So when local customers wished to pay for their meals and asked Maria and George how much they owed, the couple would counter: "And how much would you give us?" The question resulted in a great deal of discomfort and consternation for the customers. I told Maria and George that people in the United States were unaccustomed to this in restaurants and strongly suggested they establish fixed prices. I warned Maria and George that otherwise they could be in danger of losing their enterprise. The couple heeded my advice, set up the price list, and their business flourished. As a show of their appreciation, Maria and George invited me to have coffee and baklava with them on the house. I habitually prefer tea to coffee. However, since I lived in and regularly visit Jerusalem and am familiar with Arabic customs, I knew that my declining to join Maria and George would be misperceived and taken as an insult. Well, the coffee was splendid. I much liked their delicious baklava, which I used to get from them henceforth by the cookie sheet, even though it was not the least bit beneficial to my waistline. I complimented Maria and George on their coffee and their baklava and asked Maria how she made the pastry so mouth-watering. Mistaking my praise for a recipe request, Maria responded: "You know, Gavriel, I can't give you the recipe because our business depends on it, but this much I can tell you: the main thing is not to be stingy on honey and walnuts." Maria's reply echoed my father's explanation for making delicious cream of wheat porridge, and both signify a splendid metaphor for life that should be savored and lived to its fullest.

Northern Illinois University has had an outstanding Southeast Asian Studies program, second only to Cornell. No wonder the town boasted a high-quality Thai restaurant, fittingly called "The King and I." The cuisine reportedly was quite authentic, but the understanding of what food should be considered spicy hot and what mild differed at times between the patrons and the proprietors. I remember one evening, in the beginning of my tenure at Northern Illinois, when I came to have dinner at the restaurant for the first time. I repeatedly asked the waitress to make my dish as mild as possible. She assured me that that would be the case. When the food arrived and I took the first bite, I thought I came there to die, not to dine. I felt as if I swallowed a flame and needed a large pitcher of cold water to extinguish the fire. I discussed the problem with the owners, and we resolved our palate differences. The waitress served me a new, this time indeed mild dish, and I remained the restaurant's faithful and happy customer for the extent of my stay in DeKalb.

I was glad to move to a better school and to gain stability. As is often the case in such wall-to-wall departments, there were all sorts of factions and fractions, but I decided to stay away from them. I was on good terms with all my peers but more so with George Gutsche, my only fellow Slavist, and with Jack Weiner, an expert on the Spanish Golden Age, who also had a keen interest in Russian literature. Jack was genial and meant well when he expressed his wish that I would remain there "forever." Nevertheless, when I heard that "forever" wish of his, my heart, to use James Joyce's neologism, quopped (that is, quivered and flopped at the same time), because I eventually hoped to move to a better school.

Here is one poignant and instructive episode related to the contemporary mindset of some faculty members. The department was steadily growing and was hiring additional instructors each year. As a junior faculty, I was not privy to the departmental hiring process. One year, the deliberations, usually ending in spring, spilled over into summer, which I regularly spent in Jerusalem. Upon my return, I inquired of a senior faculty member as to whom the department had hired to teach German language and literature. He responded, "We hired a young woman, a Brown University graduate with superb credentials, but there is one serious problem: she is ugly and obese." I was shocked by this callous remark and felt compelled to respond. So I said to the colleague, "You are a good-looking guy and I am not too shabby myself. Why don't we take a couple of rifles and gun down all ugly and obese people in the area." My colleague froze for a moment, had a horrified expression on his face, but got the message. Incidentally, this "ugly and obese" instructor was a sweet woman and a first-rate teacher. Students and faculty alike loved and respected her.

In the spring of 1985, Northern Illinois hosted a Soviet delegation of graduate students led by a man who looked like and certainly was a KGB functionary. One not terribly bright member of that delegation could not grasp why I spoke Russian so well until I told her that I too was a Moscow native and a graduate of Moscow University and that I had left the country in 1972. She looked at me with terror in her eyes and asked, "You are *not* an anti-Soviet, are you?" To which I sarcastically rejoined: "Anti-Soviet? What are you talking about? How could *anyone* be anti-Soviet?" The poor girl did not catch my derisive drift.

The interactive agenda between the Soviet delegation and the Northern Illinois University students and faculty consisted of a Q&A session followed by lunch. Since Soviet Russia was in the midst of its invasion of Afghanistan, there were numerous questions on the subject. Although these questions differed from one another, all Soviet students responded in the same robotic fashion: "The Soviet Union has extended its helping hand to the people of Afghanistan." Apparently, those who coached them for this event and sent them overseas did not realize how embarrassing this parroting would sound. The Soviet delegation, together with a Northern Illinois Russian historian who mediated this Q&A session, was sitting at a table facing the audience. The KGB man positioned himself in the front row, opposite his countrymen, and was glaring at them the whole time. He carefully watched each student's "performance" and took elaborate notes, presumably for a report to his superiors. At lunch, the Soviet students were interspersed with the Northern Illinois faculty and students and were not as tense and mannequin-like as before. I was seated next to a Moscow University doctoral student who specialized in American literature. Looking around carefully to be sure that no one, most of all the KGB man, was eavesdropping, the student leaned toward me and sotto voce apologized for the coached performance. He expressed his disgust with the system that coerced people into telling such blatant lies and spoke wistfully about the dream of continuing his education in the United States. In a roundabout way, he was trying to let me know that the prospect for his post doc in the United States hinged squarely upon his spurious answers at the Q&A session. I felt sorry for the wretched fellow and, with all my heart, wished him the best in fulfilling his dream. Not that the thought needed any affirmation, but I once again expressed my deep gratitude to the Almighty for liberating me from the Soviet totalitarian yoke.

Although the overall conditions at Northern Illinois were by far better than at Illinois State—a smaller teaching load, full-fledged B.A. program, better library, and last but not least, a close-knit Jewish congregation into which Jennifer and I were warmly welcomed—I was not quite professionally satisfied. Having been spoiled by the marvelous library collection and the scholarly atmosphere at the University of Illinois, I yearned for a similar school. Therefore, while securing a solid base, I started looking right away for a research institution. As a result, by late 1984, I had several job interviews at conferences, including one with the University of Michigan. At that interview, I was asked, among other things: "Whom do you view as a scholarly model worthy of emulation?" When I mentioned Victor Terras and Robert Louis Jackson, the names of these eminent Slavists met with the interviewers' visible approval. But when I brought up the name of Carl Proffer, an expert on Gogol and Nabokov (who were to become my two main specialties) and their former colleague, who had died three months earlier, some of the interviewers inexplicably frowned. At this instant, I realized that after mentioning Proffer I did not stand a chance of getting the job. Nevertheless, I was glad to name the scholar whom I have always held in high regard.

While looking for a satisfying job in the United States, I still very much wanted to return to Israel and to teach at one of the universities there, above all at my alma mater—the Hebrew University of Jerusalem. My wish to return to Israel created another stumbling block between me and Jennifer who did not want to live there. Our views on the Arab–Israeli conflict were not in sync either, to put it mildly. Jennifer argued, with baffling ignorance and bias, that Israel should relinquish the West Bank, as she dubbed Judea and Samaria, to "its indigenous people, the Palestinians." Jennifer's stance was incomprehensible. A political science major, she of all people should have known that Jews have been living there since time immemorial, long before the appearance of any Arabs, let alone of so-called Palestinians. To remind her of this, I told her an anecdote. Menachem Begin and Yasser Arafat were about to start negotiations. Prior to the discussions, Begin told a story. Moses led the Jewish people from Egypt by way of the Sinai Desert to the Promised Land. It was swelteringly hot in the desert, everyone was dirty and exhausted from the journey, and Moses decided that it was time to wash. He struck a rock with his rod, and the desolate and parched terrain transformed into a small lake. Moses removed his clothes, put them aside, and entered the water. When he came back to the shore, he realized that his clothes had vanished. "Damned Palestinians!" Moses exclaimed. "They stole my clothes!" "What are you talking about?" the indignant Arafat shouted. "There were no Palestinians at the time." Begin smiled and rejoined: "And now that we have made that clear, let us proceed with our negotiations." Jennifer did not seem to appreciate the anecdote. In fact, I began to realize with ever-growing clarity that our worldviews were so manifestly incompatible that no marriage counselor would be able to help us resolve our differences. It was a very traumatic move, but I knew I had to initiate the divorce. Fortunately, we had no children, and after a year of separation, the dissolution of our marriage resulted in a clean break.

Although I did my utmost to find an academic position in Israel and to resettle there, this wish of mine, regrettably, never materialized. Incidentally, in January 2012, at the family reunion in Jerusalem, one of my relatives asked me why I did not live and work in Israel. In response, I told him a story. Many years ago, at a social function, an Israeli official reportedly asked Anna Kerler, the wife of the well-known Yiddish poet, why her son, Dov-Ber, then a budding Yiddish scholar at Oxford and now a distinguished professor at Indiana University, did not live in Israel. Anna, a real firecracker who was never at a loss for words, riposted: "You are asking *me* why my son does not live in Israel? I should be asking *you* why my son does not live in Israel!," thereby referring to the inadequate employment of academics, especially humanists, in the country. The poor official no doubt regretted pushing Mrs. Kerler's buttons.

I do not know and cannot speak for Dov-Ber's postgraduate experience with Israeli academia, but I can certainly speak about mine. While in the United States, I kept abreast of the job situation in Israel, first and foremost at the Slavic Department of the Hebrew University of Jerusalem. In the early fall of 1985, I received an official invitation from the department to apply for an opening. Needless to say, I was elated and immediately submitted an application. A couple of months later, the department chair, Theodore Friedgut, telephoned to let me know that I made the cut and was among the finalists. I kept inquiring about the timeline of the selection process and was informed that the decision would be reached in late May. In mid-April 1986, shortly before the end of my school year at Northern Illinois, as I was planning my family visit to Israel, I contacted the Slavic Department at the Hebrew University of Jerusalem and requested an interview with the search committee, giving the date of my arrival in Jerusalem—May 8. I thought it was only fair. The search committee was apprised of the internal candidate's qualifications but knew me only on paper. Upon my arrival in Jerusalem, I went straight to the department office, only to be told that Friedgut had a toothache and would be unavailable for a few days. I found this tooth-nursing maneuver highly suspicious. When Friedgut finally emerged from his putative dental challenge, he imparted to me that the decision had been already made and that I did not get the job. When I inquired into the reasons, he responded: "You don't have as much teaching experience as the other candidate," which, even if true, was known from the very start. When I went to see Yochanan Friedmann, dean of humanities at the time, and protested the unfair treatment by the department that did not even have the decency to grant me an interview, he also told me that it was too late because the decision had already been made. I became extremely vexed by the situation, lost my temper, and in frustration raised my voice at Dean Friedmann. Later on, it was reported to me that he had remarked: "Shapiro is a hooligan but what fabulous Hebrew!" (Of course, my Hebrew has markedly dwindled since then from lack of steady practice.) In retrospect, I realized that it was a classic case of double-dealing, in which the job was all sewn up before I even applied. (Curiously, Hebrew has a similar expression for this, known as *esek tafur*, literally, a "sewn business.") It appeared that the department had never seriously considered me for the job but rather used me to create the impression of a kosher search, all the while safeguarding the position for the internal candidate.

Incidentally, the Russian-born internal candidate who did get the job proved to be nothing but an embarrassment to the department and the university. His research was subpar, and he never bothered to learn

Hebrew, or English for that matter. So when his turn had come to chair the department and to attend the chairs' meetings, he always had to bring along a departmental secretary to take notes and to interpret the deliberations for him. Consequently, he could not represent the department in any adequate way. As a teacher, he was pedestrian, and, in any case, because of his practically nonexistent Hebrew, he was unable to communicate with the majority of the university's student population. Following twenty years of such sorry service, he retired after merely attaining the rank of senior lecturer.

While I was being (or so I was led to believe) considered for the position at the Hebrew University of Jerusalem, I kept one foot in the door of the North American academic system, just in case. Thus, I was granted a job interview at the Slavic annual convention, albeit not by a research institution, as I desired, but with Vanderbilt University in Nashville, Tennessee. Upon entering an interview room, I found two gentlemen, already a touch tipsy, who immediately offered me a glass of wine. I politely declined and told my interviewers that I did not drink alcohol. This statement, as I could see, did not please them in the least as they exchanged the most eloquent of glances. In the spirit of southern hospitality, these two gentlemen then offered me some hors d'oeuvres. When I asked them about the appetizers' fillings, they countered: "Why do you ask? Are you sick?" My response, "No, I am not sick—I am Jewish," prompted another exchange of expressive glances. Finally, we proceeded to the interview itself. Among other things, they asked me, "What would you be checking out if invited for an on-campus interview?" I mentioned the department, the library, Nashville's cultural life—and the Jewish life in the city. When my response triggered a third exchange of glances, I realized that I flunked out. My hunch proved to be accurate. Bumping into me the next day, one of my interviewers revealed, in total violation of protocol, that although they were impressed with me and my résumé, they reckoned that, as he put it, "You wouldn't be happy with us."

Yet another interview, this time on campus, at Dartmouth, once again not a research-oriented institution, took place in mid-January 1986. The department faculty included well-known Slavists, such as Barry Scherr (who served as department chair), Lev Losev, and Walter Arndt. Just as impressive, considering the size of the college, was its library. When I arrived, the campus, located in Hanover, New Hampshire, though small, was very picturesque: it was under a blanket of virgin snow. Apparently, there had been a blizzard shortly before my arrival. I imagined it would look highly attractive to a winter sports enthusiast. As part of my visit, I conducted a language class and presented a literary paper. My performance was well received by faculty and students alike, which made me think that I had a rather decent chance of getting the job. This hope evaporated the moment I told Barry that I was being considered for an opening at the Hebrew University of Jerusalem, which was my highest priority. Of course, this candid declaration sealed my fate at Dartmouth. Little did I know that the Hebrew University of Jerusalem never had the least intention of offering me the position. But then again, when one door closes another door frequently opens.

This truism proved itself during the final chapter of my job-hunting saga. In late December 1986, I was being interviewed at the AATSEEL convention in New York City for a tenure-track assistant professorship at Cornell University. The interview went well, and I had every reason to think that I made the cut for the next crucial stage—an on-campus interview. Yet January came and went, followed by February and March, and I heard nothing from the school. Just when I abandoned all hopes of being short-listed, William Kennedy, who chaired the department at the time, contacted me in early April and invited me to come to campus as soon as possible. We scheduled my arrival for April 21. I knew that Bill was a Renaissance expert, and to make it interesting for him, I chose for my presentation a talk (accompanied by visual imagery) about the emblem and its reflection in Gogol's writings, with references to the *Emblematum Liber*, a book of emblems by Andrea Alciato, a sixteenth-century jurist and writer. My rather innovative and lively lecture was well received. Furthermore, the entire visit, consisting of a series of personal interviews along with lunches and dinners—which were obviously nothing but the continuation of interviews in a more informal setting—appeared to be successful. I returned to DeKalb with high expectations that I would be offered the job. Apart from the feeling of great anticipation, however, I had some misgivings about this crucial move in my life and career and was seeking heavenly guidance.

Back when I still lived in Russia, I realized how important it was to detect divine signs in order to reach the right decision. The tale I am about to tell here drives this point home. Once upon a time, there was a man who lived along the coast. One day, as he was watching TV, a hurricane alert came on, warning everybody to evacuate. The man thinks about it for a moment: "I don't need to worry. God will save me." Sure enough, the storm surge starts flooding the man's street. A National Guard truck stops to pick him up, but the man refuses help: "Don't worry! God will save me." The water continues to rise faster than before, and the man must climb out onto the roof. A rescue boat shows up. The crew tells the man to get into the boat, but he responds, "Don't worry! God will save me." As the water rises even higher, the man scales the roof antenna, clutching it for dear life. Just then, a rescue helicopter appears, but he gestures it away and shouts, "Don't worry! God will save me." Soon the storm water engulfs the house and the man drowns. When he arrives in Heaven, he says to God, irately, "I can't believe you forsook me in my hour of need! Why didn't you save me?" The Almighty replies, "And who sent you the truck, the boat, and the helicopter?"

I was mindful of this tale when debating with myself whether or not, if offered, I should take up the position at Cornell. There were a few reasons for my hesitation. I had a secure job at Northern Illinois, where, unlike at Cornell, a published book was not required for tenure. In early 1987, two-odd years after my appointment, I was well on the way to receiving tenure with just a score of articles. I had fears of failure and disgrace if I did not succeed in meeting the tenure conditions at Cornell in a timely fashion. Another and more objective reason was the library. I became accustomed to the magnificent Slavic collection at the University of Illinois, to which I had easy access through the statewide university library consortium. The University of Illinois library catalogue was already fully digitized, whereas Cornell's Olin Library, which contained most of the books in the humanities, had an old-fashioned card catalogue. Yet another reason was the presumably discordant atmosphere in the Department of Russian at Cornell. There seemed to be something wrong with it if the dean appointed Bill Kennedy, an outside faculty member, to serve as its chair. The situation was reminiscent of the apocryphal story from early Russian history, according to which the Eastern Slavic tribes, incapable of self-governing, invited the Varangian Prince Rurik and his kinfolk to rule over them.

I was well aware that university departments rarely exude harmony and brotherly or sisterly love, but the situation in the department at Cornell sounded exceedingly alarming and did not bode well for a newcomer. Of course, there were clear advantages. At Cornell, I would be joining an Ivy League research institution that boasted its Department of Russian Literature, with a Ph.D. program, whereas at Northern Illinois I was a member of the conglomerate called the Department of Foreign Languages and Literatures. The department had merely two Russian positions and planned to upgrade its Russian program to the master's level only in some foreseeable future.

As I was having these misgivings, I received three signs of divine guidance. At that time, in the spring of 1987, after a year of separation, I was in the process of divorce from Jennifer. We owned two cars, and in line with the settlement, I kept the older one, a secondhand 1982 Honda Civic hatchback. As I obtained a new Illinois license plate for the car, I noticed that its alphanumeric combination began with IVY—a clear allusion to the Ivy League Cornell. On my way from the on-campus interview back to DeKalb, I was sitting next to a woman. We struck up a conversation, and I shared with her my worries about assuming the Cornell position. The woman asked me point-blank if I was hungry. I began pondering her question and realized that I was indeed far too ambitious to remain at Northern Illinois. Finally, long before my divorce was settled out of court, I made arrangements to go for the first time to Italy. It so happened—with incredibly perfect timing!—that the divorce was finalized on May 5, 1987, and I was scheduled to leave for Italy on May 7. When discussing my summer plans with Bill Kennedy, I told him about my itinerary and the length of stay in each of the four major Italian cities and suggested he communicate with me via poste restante. I also mentioned that after Italy I would be spending time with my family in Israel and, just in case, gave him the Jerusalem address. As I was traveling in Italy, I diligently checked my mail at the main post offices in Rome, Florence, Milan, and Venice, but there was no letter from Cornell.

Here I have to interrupt my career-related narrative and recount a rather unpleasant, possibly even life-threatening experience I had in the Italian capital. One day, while meandering around Rome, I was approached by a man who initiated a friendly conversation with me. Unsuspectingly, I answered some questions that tourists are commonly asked: where I was from, what I did for a living, and so on. Thus far, it sounded like a harmless chitchat. However, when the man invited me to a restaurant "with good food and drinks and beautiful girls," I began to have some qualms, especially after he asked me whether I carried any credit cards. I did not at the time, relying on traveler's checks instead. (Besides, with my meager assistant professor salary, I probably stood no chance of qualifying for one in those more stringent times.) When I told him that I had no credit cards, he looked me over and disdainfully uttered, "*Professore!*" ("Some professor you are!"). In retrospect, I suppose the man was part of a racket. He probably lured gullible single male tourists into the restaurant, where the intended victim was slipped a mickey, stripped of all his money and valuables, and ditched. For many years now, when Mother wants to tease me, she will exclaim with disdain and derision in her voice, "*Professore!*"

By the end of my Italian journey, I began to think that the job perhaps had gone to another candidate. After Italy, I went to Jerusalem to visit my family. Upon my arrival, my parents pleasantly surprised me by handing me at once a letter from Cornell that contained the job offer. I interpreted these three occurrences—the IVY license plate, the "are you hungry" question on the plane, and receipt of the blithesome tidings in Jerusalem of all places—as divine signs and recognized that I was destined to come to Ithaca, New York. My mind was made up. I first phoned Bill Kennedy to accept the job and then, right away, contacted the Northern Illinois department chair, Marilyn Skinner, a gifted classicist and Catullus expert, to inform her of my decision. Marilyn graciously congratulated me on my new Cornell position. (A few years later, in 1991, she herself left Northern Illinois for the University of Arizona in Tucson.) Now, after almost thirty years of working at Cornell, as I am writing these lines, I thank the Almighty for sending me His signs and signals and helping me to reach the right decision.

✳ ✳ ✳

Attending my first Cornell Slavic faculty picnic. (From left): George Gibian, Wayles Browne, Leonard Babby, Sara Pintner (the wife of Walter Pintner), and Nancy Pollak. Ithaca, NY, September 1987.

With Luba. Ithaca, 1991

With Tzakhi and Dina. Ithaca, 1991.

In September 1987, shortly after I began teaching at Cornell, Yulian Semenov, the author of trashy detective and spy novels, came to the university to give a talk. While speaking about his life, Semenov coyly remarked that he, like Chekhov, lived in Crimea. I could not bear this insolence, stood up, and said, "How dare you, a Soviet hack and graphomaniac, pronounce your name and that of Chekhov in the same breath?" I also took Semenov to task for promulgating the banalities of Soviet propaganda. The scandal was brewing. Semenov, who spoke no English (he was addressing the audience through an interpreter), challenged me to a debate in Russian. I rejected such a debate outright. I pointed out that since the audience was predominantly English-speaking, elementary civility suggested using the language understood by all. Semenov realized his powerlessness and was visibly irked. Later he reportedly grumbled, "Just as the public began to warm up to me, this CIA agent ruined it all."

An altogether different event was the appearance of Sergei Dovlatov. In April 1988, Dovlatov gave a talk entitled "The Role of the Russian Writer Today." Like everybody else, I came to this talk looking forward to hearing Dovlatov speak and was sitting in my chair perfectly relaxed. All of a sudden,

Dovlatov, six feet five and powerfully built, with a dark-haired crew cut, emerged on stage and in his *basso profondo* asked the audience in Russian, "Who is Gavriel Shapiro here?" For a second, I felt apprehensive. Why was Dovlatov, whom I had never met before, inquiring about me? It turned out that Michael Scammell, department chair at the time, had given my name to Dovlatov, but he neglected to ask me first to serve as the writer's interpreter (Dovlatov's English was rudimentary). Sheepishly, I came up on stage and, to the best of my modest abilities, translated Dovlatov's talk, which sparkled with wit and humor. After the talk, Dovlatov affably presented me with a collection of his stories, which he humorously inscribed: "To Gavriel Shapiro from his co-lecturer" (*Gavrieliu Shapiro ot sodokladchika*). The untimely passing of Dovlatov—he died in 1990 at the age of forty-nine—was a great loss to all those who valued his incomparable literary talent.

In March 1989, I had the privilege and the pleasure of listening to Yehuda Amichai's (1924–2000) poetry reading and of attending a dinner held in his honor that night. I happened to be seated next to this remarkable Israeli poet, with whom I had a most engaging conversation. We spoke about Russian literature, about the role of the humanities in education, and I shared with Amichai my experience of reading his verses furtively in Soviet Russia. Amichai impressed me as a man of great wisdom and of incredible modesty.

Upon my arrival at Cornell, it became apparent to me that I must publish a book-length study to stand a chance of getting tenure. Realistically, given the time constraints, I would have to turn my dissertation into a book. I was perfectly aware that a dissertation differs significantly from a monograph. I was also well aware that my dissertation, mainly in terms of its language and structure, did not merit publication and required a serious overhaul. As it happens, I was also apathetic toward it and did not at all feel like embarking on the tedious task of revamping the whole thing. In addition, I had no confidence in my written English and, in fact, felt quite uneasy at the prospect of reworking my clumsily composed opus. I needed a great deal of help, editorial first and foremost, and had no idea where to get it. At the same time, I was not in the right emotional space while still recovering from the trauma of divorce. To top it off, the preparation for a slew of new courses was taking up a great deal of my time.

At that critical juncture, I was introduced to Dafna Allon (1913–2006). Mrs. Allon grew up in Johannesburg, South Africa, and earned her Ph.D. from the London School of Economics, where she wrote her dissertation on British colonial policies in Africa. She then continued her studies at the Sorbonne. In addition to being a political person (she was a quasi-communist in her youth, but when I met her she impressed me as a proponent of the Likud party), Mrs. Allon had a penchant for the humanities, including literature. She combined these interests by writing political commentary in her elegant English and by doing quite a bit of translating. She also eventually penned an enthralling book of recollections.[75] When I met Mrs. Allon, she was a handsome lady in her mid-seventies and lived alone in downtown Jerusalem after her husband, a career diplomat, had died.

Unlike other editors who habitually work on a manuscript at their convenience, Mrs. Allon adopted a totally different approach with me. While in Israel during my Cornell winter recess in January 1989, I used to come to her Jerusalem apartment on Palmach Street in the morning, and we worked together on the text, discussing various lexical and stylistic possibilities. We would break for lunch, which Mrs. Allon herself would prepare, and then we would continue revising the manuscript until evening hours. Mrs. Allon and I kept to this regimen day after day, except on Saturdays. We worked in this fashion for four weeks or so and succeeded in editing the manuscript. Most important, under Mrs. Allon's able tutelage, I shed my fear of writing in English. Mrs. Allon not only showed me the beauty of English but also instilled in me the confidence and enjoyment of writing in this majestic language. For all this, I owe her an immeasurable debt of gratitude.

Upon giving the manuscript, which I entitled *Nikolai Gogol and the Baroque Cultural Heritage*, a drastic and much needed facelift, I began casting about for a publisher. It was not easy. After all, it was my very first book about a writer who, unlike Dostoevsky, Tolstoy, and Chekhov, was relatively obscure in the West, including the United States. This is despite the fact that Hollywood produced two movies, loosely based on

---

75   Dafna Allon, *Remembering Tylia: A Memoir* (Dornoch, UK: New Fountainhead, 1999).

Gogol's works—*The Inspector General* (1949) and *Taras Bulba* (1962), with Danny Kaye and Yul Brynner in the respective title roles. Furthermore, the subject matter of my book, although academically innovative, was not in the least bit sensational. I approached numerous university presses, usually by phone (a personal computer was still a relative rarity) and, based on my brief description of the project, received a "not interested" response from each and every one of them. One day, my luck changed for the better when I contacted the Pennsylvania State University Press, even though its profile in the Directory of the Association of American University Presses did not include Russian literature. It turned out that in this particular case the directory was outdated. As I found out, shortly before my phone call, the press decided to branch into new fields and, inter alia, to launch the publication of books in Slavic studies—an auspicious timing indeed! Thus, when I telephoned Philip Winsor, its senior acquisitions editor, and told him about my book, there was a moment of silence on the opposite end of the line, which I correctly interpreted as eagerness on his part. To my pleasant surprise, Mr. Winsor asked me to send him the entire manuscript. Publishers rarely do that, all the more so when it is a first book. Typically, they ask for the introduction and a sample chapter or two. Only then, if they find the material worth pursuing, do they wish to see the complete work. Upon jumping this hurdle, the manuscript first undergoes in-house scrutiny, and if deemed of interest to the press and altogether publishable, is sent out for anonymous peer review. If the author is known and has an established publication record, the press might send the text simultaneously to two readers.

In my case, the press, of course, solicited one reader at a time. The first reader's report, which came in rather expeditiously, was most positive. The reader recommended my book for publication practically without reservations or emendations. Thus encouraged, Mr. Winsor solicited a second reader, with whom things did not go as smoothly. The reader procrastinated for six months or more, and when the response finally arrived, it was rather negative. Fortunately, it was merely half a page long and contained feeble arguments, which I had no trouble rebutting. Nevertheless, I began to worry as time was of the essence, and no wonder: this was my so-called tenure book. To be successfully considered for tenure, I needed to have it published, or at least to have a contract in hand before the procedure gets underway. The indefinite tenure, as it is called, with promotion to associate professor, guarantees a permanent position at the university. Otherwise, if the deadline is not met, the failed candidate receives a grace year and upon its expiration is supposed to leave the university. During that time, the hapless instructor is feverishly seeking another academic position, which was quite difficult to come by in the early 1990s. I tensely wondered what Mr. Winsor would decide to do next. Would he terminate the process, in which case I would need to start all over again at another press (if such a press could be found), or would he seek a third reader? Thankfully, Mr. Winsor strongly believed in my book and solicited an additional reader, who wrote a favorable and timely report. As a result, the book was accepted for publication, and I received the contract from Penn State just ahead of my tenure procedure. (Of late, I was delighted to learn that upon his retirement Mr. Winsor began writing fiction and published a novel entitled *Restoration*.)

The tenure procedure lasted the entire academic year. In the summer of 1993, it resulted in my receiving a congratulatory letter from Cornell president Frank Rhodes on my promotion to associate professor with indefinite tenure. Naturally, I was most pleased. Tenure is a crucial point in any academic career because it grants a great deal of security and stability. Friends commented that my posture, my entire demeanor had changed as if a heavy burden had been lifted off my chest.

Upon publishing the book on Gogol and the Baroque, I turned my attention back to the works of Vladimir Nabokov (1899–1977), for which the ambiance of Cornell and of Ithaca, New York, where the writer spent ten years of his life, was most conducive. After having read *The Luzhin Defense* in Moscow and upon familiarizing myself with Nabokov's many other works in Jerusalem, I became deeply enchanted with his oeuvre. Although I had not conducted any research on Nabokov during my studies at the Hebrew University of Jerusalem, I wrote my first term paper for the

Russian émigré literature seminar at the University of Illinois on *Invitation to a Beheading*. Out of that paper grew three articles, which I published while still working on my master's degree. This novel, the first draft of which Nabokov wrote in the fall of 1934 "in one fortnight of wonderful excitement and sustained inspiration," amazed me by its intricacy and multifacetedness.[76] These attributes are all the more astounding since Nabokov composed this dystopia in the midst of working on his last, longest, and most complex Russian novel—*The Gift*. I decided to explore numerous strands of *Invitation to a Beheading* in a monograph. While doing so, I chose not to confine myself to the rigid structure of a reader's companion. Instead, I decided to pick and choose topics of interest, thereby allowing myself ample freedom and flexibility. Once again, as with Gogol, I treated this work by Nabokov as a cultural historian would. The undertaking was rather daunting and presented quite a challenge. Numerous allusions to historical and cultural events, as well as to works of literature, music, and the fine arts, were unsurprisingly surreptitious, well concealed in the novel, set in no specific time and space. As is often the case, I succeeded in some tasks, failed in others, made some mistakes, but overall I was rather pleased with the result. I entitled the book *Delicate Markers* because Nabokov so dubbed the allusions that he deemed important to unravel in the introduction to his second English-language novel, *Bend Sinister*.

I went through a stringent and arduous search for a publisher. A monograph on one novel, even by a well-recognized writer such as Nabokov, was a tough sell, I was told by editors at various presses, or, in the words of one of them, "not a money maker." Auspiciously, I managed to publish the study against all odds. Thomas R. Beyer Jr., the editor of the Middlebury Studies in Russian Language and Literature series, liked the manuscript and so evidently did the anonymous readers. The book was printed by Peter Lang, a respectable academic press.

As time went by, I became more and more fascinated with Nabokov's works. In my next book, I decided to explore Nabokov's predilection for the visual and the pictorial. By his own admission, Nabokov aspired to become a landscape painter in his boyhood and

---

76 Vladimir Nabokov, *Strong Opinions* (New York: Vintage International, 1990), 68.

early youth. In 1912–14, the young Nabokov's drawing master was Mstislav Dobuzhinsky (1875–1957), who left an indelible mark on him. Dobuzhinsky was a remarkable painter and one of the chief representatives of the *World of Art*, first a periodical and then an artistic association so named. Evidently, it is Dobuzhinsky to whom we are all greatly indebted, at least in part, for Nabokov's becoming a writer. Upon watching the young Nabokov's progress in painting and upon familiarizing himself with his charge's early poems, Dobuzhinsky concluded that Nabokov had a great creative capability—but he should write. In other words, while recognizing his student's enormous talent, the expert painter and astute pedagogue realized that his pupil was incapable of mastering the brush and canvas in such a way as to do the medium justice and suggested he channel his gift into words. As a result, the incomparable verbal artist was born! This was the main thesis of my new book, on which I had worked for about eight years.

In late October 2001, the Almighty sent my way a woman with an unusual name—Tatiela. I just returned to Ithaca from a month-long visit to Berlin, where I conducted research for the book. I met Tatiela in the local Aldi's store, where I frequently shopped, about a mile from my residence in downtown Ithaca. I was waiting in the checkout line after placing my few items on the conveyor belt, when all of a sudden the woman who stood in front turned around and offered for me to go ahead. I thanked her for the offer but politely declined: I found her very attractive and much enjoyed looking at her gorgeous neck. Tatiela promised not to be too long, but in her haste she opened her wallet with such force that its contents flew out and spilled onto the counter. The poor woman became flustered, and with profuse apologies to the customers and the cashier, gathered up the contents with great speed, paid for the groceries, and briskly walked out of the store. I very much wanted to ask her out on a date. So I quickly made my purchase and caught up with her as she was walking away from the cart caddy. I approached her and after a couple of pleasantries suggested we meet for a cup of tea. She blushed profusely, did not proffer her phone or e-mail, and asked instead for mine. I gave her my business card but remarked that the prospect of our seeing each other again did not look too promising. "Not necessarily," was her response. I was very excited about meeting Tatiela and about the possibility of seeing her again, but more than five weeks went by with no word from her. Then one day, out of the blue, she e-mailed me an invitation for a cup of tea. We met at the Ithaca Bakery in early December. As it happens, Tatiela and I have kindred tastes in literature, painting, music, and cinema, and even a compatible sense of humor. We are also of like mind when it comes to many political, social, and environmental issues. Several days later, I invited Tatiela to a matinee concert of classical music followed by dinner. She accepted, and we had a great time. We continued dating and quickly fell in love. In retrospect, it was sheer coincidence that we met at all. Curiously, before that day Tatiela had never been to an Aldi's. Furthermore, at the time of our meeting she happened to live in a different part of the country. But as the popular saying goes, "Coincidence is when God chooses to remain anonymous."

Tatiela with Kari. Courtesy of Tatiela Laake.

Tatiela possesses numerous gifts. She is a fabulous cook and a remarkable handywoman, capable of building a fence, fixing a roof, and putting together bookshelves. Her automotive knowledge is vast, and no mechanic can pull the wool over her eyes. If this were not enough, Tatiela has an impressive vocabulary, writes beautifully, and is a top-notch editor. She also has a great knack for languages, with an attentive ear to accents, be it the Queen's English, the Irish brogue, or the Scottish burr.

Tatiela has always had a strong loving bond with animals of all kinds. Until I met Tatiela, I hardly had any experience with them. Nevertheless, I quickly befriended her pack, first and foremost the kuvaszok, Uta and Kari. For hundreds of years, kuvaszok—canines of Hungarian origin—were bred to guard, from kings to livestock. As guardians, they are aloof to strangers but are extremely devoted to and fiercely protective of their family. Tatiela's pack was no exception. Yet on our very first meeting, when I apprehensively sat down in the passenger seat of Tatiela's SUV, Uta, who stayed in the rear of the car, did not growl at me. Instead, she gently sniffed my ear, rested her head on my shoulder, and kissed me on the cheek. Already as a puppy, Uta's daughter, Kari, demonstrated an impressive academic promise. While staying overnight in her portable den, which was placed in my home library, Kari must have desired some bedtime reading. This presented a challenge because her den was some three feet away from the bookshelves. This hindrance did not stop Kari from diligently working her way to one of the books. To accomplish this feat, she must have been lying down on her side, stretching her front leg through the bars, and using her toes to inch the book toward her. She literally got to the bottom of it and in the process succeeded not only in dog-earing pages but also in tooth-marking numerous footnotes. This way, Kari proved herself not only a voracious reader but also a veritable researcher. Anyway, only a true scholar attends to footnotes first. Kari's studious penchant found further expression in that she loves to lie on the carpet in my office, feeling most comfortable among my many books and watching me write. Perhaps she is waiting for me to hand her the proofs so that she will be able to wooffer some valuable suggestions.

Preparing a manuscript for publication occasionally produces some hilarious moments, and my book on Nabokov and painting was no exception. As I was taking a stroll in downtown Ithaca on a summery Sunday afternoon and discussing the manuscript with Tatiela, I matter-of-factly remarked, "I still need to get back to those three prostitutes. I've been ignoring them." To which Tatiela inquired: "You mean the ones you showed me the other day?" It is no wonder that people within earshot were taken aback by our verbal exchange. We heard a young woman behind us gasp; a middle-aged couple walking toward us stopped abruptly and veered to the right; and a young man, looking like a goody two-shoes, who was approaching us at the crossroad, averted his eyes in discomfiture and quickly walked around us. I suppose they all were flabbergasted by my casual statement and by my partner's nonchalant attitude. Their jaw-dropping reaction to our conversation was entirely understandable. Little did they know that I was not referring to lascivious associations with members of the oldest profession. Instead, I was talking about some challenges I had in describing Otto Dix's painting *Three Prostitutes on the Street*, a reproduction of which I intended to include in my monograph.

On a more serious note, scholarly pursuits may sometimes benefit from lucky circumstances. Thus, my research led me one day to Badalucco, a tiny town with population of approximately 1,200 people in the Liguria region of Italy. While Tatiela and I were riding a bus to Badalucco, we shared with each other our concerns about interactions with the local residents who, so we were told, generally did not speak English. After all, my Italian was rudimentary at best, Tatiela's practically nonexistent. All of a sudden, a woman across the aisle from us, who apparently overheard our exchange, addressed us in perfect English with a slight Irish accent. All three of us struck up a most pleasant conversation. It turned out that the woman, named Deidre, was born and grew up in Dublin but had lived in the area for the past thirty years. This encounter turned out to be most auspicious: Deidre graciously volunteered to be an interpreter in our contacts with townsfolk and municipal officials. She also kindly offered to serve as our cicerone, showing us some of Badalucco's most attractive sites of interest, such as the church of Santa Maria Assunta e San Giorgio, with its ornate Baroque façade and Old Master paintings and sculptures, and walked us through the labyrinth of the town's quaint narrow streets. Come to think of it, we were fortunate to meet her. This was because Deidre, who lived in a cabin on the top of the mountain about five or six miles above the town, would descend to it only twice a month to buy groceries. Tatiela and I learned about it when we invited Deidre to have lunch with us, which she politely declined as she had to climb back up to her cabin before dark. Deidre agreed, however, to have coffee and pastry with us. It turned out that she was a writer and came to the area after being inspired by the works of a local man of letters. Deidre developed a close friendship with the man who eventually bequeathed the cabin to her.

Upon completing the manuscript around 2006, I once again began looking for a publisher and was routinely rejected by countless university presses. Finally, after a long and grueling process of press hunting, I came across Northwestern University Press whose acquisitions editor became truly fascinated by the proposal. The book came out in 2009 under the title *The Sublime Artist's Studio: Nabokov and Painting*. When devising the title, I borrowed the epithet "sublime" from Nabokov's translation of Pushkin's poem "To Dawe, Esqr." (1828) to characterize the writer's own literary legacy. In this poem, Pushkin praises the "pencil," that is, the artistry, of the English portrait painter George Dawe (1781–1829).[77] The rest of the title alludes to the *ut pictura poesis* simile that Nabokov tellingly applies when speaking about his writing process: "I think that what I would welcome at the close of a book of mine is a sensation of its world receding in the distance and stopping somewhere there, suspended afar like a picture in a picture: *The Artist's Studio* by Van Bock."[78]

After its release, I decided to write yet another book on Nabokov. For years, I had been fascinated by the personality of his outstanding father, Vladimir Dmitrievich (1870–1922), a distinguished jurist and statesman at the turn of the twentieth century. Additionally, the senior Nabokov was a great connoisseur of literature, painting, theater, and music as well as a passionate lepidopterist, enthusiastic chess player, and avid athlete. Especially outstanding was the unique nature of their father–son bond. In

---

77 In the original, Pushkin calls Dawe's pencil *divnyi*, that is, "marvelous." Nabokov, of course, knew that the 1812 War Gallery in the Winter Palace (St. Petersburg) contains Dawe's portrait of Major General Ivan Alexandrovich Nabokov (1787–1852), a hero of the Napoleonic Wars. By translating and discussing this Pushkin's poem about Dawe, who portrayed his ancestor, Nabokov subtly linked himself to his most revered poet.

78 Nabokov, *Strong Opinions*, 72–73.

his autobiography, Nabokov lovingly characterized this bond as "the tender friendship" and "the charm of our perfect accord," the formulations I used in the book's title—*The Tender Friendship and the Charm of Perfect Accord: Nabokov and His Father*.[79] In light of this, I found it necessary to examine the importance of V. D. Nabokov as the most influential role model for shaping his celebrated son's world perception. The book was designed to explore the many-sided impact of Vladimir Dmitrievich on his firstborn. Furthermore, on a deeply personal level, I empathized with Nabokov's feelings of losing his father to a senseless sudden, untimely death at the hands of fanatics as had happened to my own father.

The publisher-hunting saga followed the by now well-established scenario. I electronically sent a book proposal out to numerous university presses, only to receive rejections from all of them but one—the University of Michigan Press. The book was accepted for publication and came out in the spring of 2014.

People both inside and outside my discipline tell me that they do not understand why I keep writing about Nabokov. "Isn't it time to write about someone else?" they ask. This question strikes me as odd. First, it is not uncommon among literary scholars to focus throughout their entire career on one great writer: Dante, Shakespeare, Pushkin ... Second, and most important, when I dwell in Nabokov's world, I feel like I am breathing a pure, rarified air of mountain meadows and, to quote Nabokov, am eating "fresh bread with country butter and Alpine honey."[80] Why would I want, to pursue this metaphor further, to descend from the mountain, with its pristine atmosphere and divine delectable nourishment?

Throughout the 1980s, I corresponded with Nabokov's dear ones, Véra (the writer's wife) and Dmitri (their son), and they always responded to my queries most courteously and expeditiously. Véra Nabokov passed away in 1991, and regrettably, I never had the privilege and the pleasure of meeting her in person. I was introduced to Dmitri only years later, in 1996, on his birthday—May 10. On that auspicious day, Michael Scammell, who had translated two of Nabokov's novels, courteously invited me to meet Dmitri, with whom he was well acquainted. The get-together took

---

79 Vladimir Nabokov, *Speak, Memory: An Autobiography Revisited* (New York: Vintage International, 1989), 191.
80 Nabokov, *Strong Opinions*, 152.

place at New York's Hotel Pierre, where Dmitri, like his parents before him, used to stay on his travels to the city. Dmitri invited us to tea in the hotel's ornate lounge and was most charming and hospitable. He kept the appointment in spite of being unwell that day: he ran a fever, had a sore throat, and his voice sounded husky. At that first meeting, I was struck by his imposing six-foot-five-and-a-half-inch frame, by his unusual eyes, colored robin's-egg blue, and by his remarkable resemblance to his father.

Over the years, I had numerous communications with Dmitri by e-mail, by phone, and in person. His conduct was always most amiable, his kindness and generosity endless. How many superb translations of his father's poems did he render upon my request amid his busy schedule! How invaluable was his eagle-eyed editorship of my far-from-perfect articles! How much I benefited from his incomparable knowledge of Italy, its language and culture, when I was writing an article on *Invitation to a Beheading* and Silvio Pellico's *My Prisons*! What a goldmine of information he was about his parents, for whom he had infinite reverence and adoration!

Dmitri was a most stalwart friend, always ready to come to the rescue. When in 1997 the Department of Russian at Cornell was under the threat of imminent annihilation, Dmitri almost single-handedly saved it by writing, in the tradition of his father, an open letter to the university student paper, *Cornell Daily Sun*. In this letter, he protested the department's shutdown and called attention to his father's giving "rebirth and fame to the century-old study of Russian Literature at Cornell."[81] The department, alas, is no more, but Dmitri's miraculous intervention had given several generations of students "the sheer bliss of proper study, within a dedicated department, of one of the world's foremost literatures."[82]

Dmitri was a rare breed. In the tradition of his family, his parents and grandparents, he was a Renaissance man. He was always fascinated, in the parlance of his father, by "merging the precision of poetry and the intuition of science," including modern technology.[83] Thus, one day, he told me over the phone that he was building a computer to his own specifications.

---

81 Dmitri Nabokov, "Nabokov's Son Writes on the Fate of Department," *Cornell Daily Sun*, March 31, 1997, 4.
82 Ibid.
83 Vladimir Nabokov, *Lectures on Literature* (New York: Harcourt Brace Jovanovich, 1980), 6.

Dmitri possessed an enormous linguistic aptitude and literary talent. Here is a case in point. On one of my visits to Montreux, Switzerland, as Dmitri and I were having lunch at his residence, a package arrived. It contained an English translation of "Easter Rain" ("Paskhal′nyi dozhd′"), one of his father's earlier Russian stories. Dmitri found this rendition adequate, but it was clearly not up to his standards. He then suggested that "we" go over the translation "together." Of course, I was merely an apprentice in his master class. And what a master class it was! It was astonishing to be privy to Dmitri's creative lab: his enormous vocabulary in both languages, the dazzling array of synonyms that he tried one by one until finding the most suitable locution. In the end, he magically turned the tolerable translation into a genuine *chef d'oeuvre*. It is a great pity he did not complete his novel and his memoir; it is my sincere hope that someday they may become available in fragments.

Visiting Dmitri Nabokov. West Palm Beach, Florida, October 2007. Courtesy of Ariane Csonka.

It is well known that Dmitri was an accomplished professional opera singer. It is less known that he also had an exquisite taste and supreme erudition in the fine arts. On my visit to West Palm Beach, Florida, I brought him the catalogue of a Metropolitan Museum of Art exhibit that he wanted but was unable to attend. While leafing through the catalogue, Dmitri made profound observations that would have made any art historian green with envy.

In his younger years, in the tradition of his father and grandfather, Dmitri was a remarkable athlete: boxer, tennis player, mountain climber, prize-winning car and boat racer, and helicopter pilot. One day, I got an inkling of just how good Dmitri was in these sports, all of which require dexterity and presence of mind. When Dmitri tore his Achilles tendon, I took him to the hospital. It was he who, despite suffering from an excruciating pain, not only navigated, but in fact helped me operate the SUV through the serpentine streets of Montreux by having a hold on the steering wheel. In this way, Dmitri gave me an unforgettable and, I might add, quite necessary driving lesson.

On that occasion, I had the honor and the delight of meeting Nabokov's sister, Elena Vladimirovna Sikorski (1906–2000). One day, when I was visiting Dmitri in the hospital, a call came in, and he asked me to answer the phone. As I did so, I immediately realized that it was Elena Vladimirovna on the line. I passed the receiver to Dmitri, and he made mention of me in the conversation with his aunt. Consequently, Elena Vladimirovna graciously invited me for a visit at her Geneva residence.

I went to see Elena Vladimirovna on May 3, 1999. I was perfectly aware of her advanced age and planned to stay no more than half an hour. I brought a chocolate torte and a pot of campanulas, better known as bellflowers, which matched her bright blue eyes. As we were drinking coffee, which Elena Vladimirovna herself expertly made, she was telling me about her life during the interwar years in Prague. As not to tire her out, I made a few attempts to leave, but each time I broached the subject Elena Vladimirovna urged me to stay longer. All in all, we talked for three hours. Among other things, Elena Vladimirovna told me about her trip in the early 1970s to St. Petersburg (then called Leningrad). She recounted, with tears in her eyes, how she attempted to visit the family mansion, her birthplace, which Bolsheviks unceremoniously expropriated. When Elena Vladimirovna explained to a concierge that she wanted to go into the building because she was born there, this insolent doorkeeper barked at her, accused her of lying, and barred her from entering the house.

Elena Vladimirovna spoke with great pride about her newly discovered Jewish roots on the maternal side of the family. Physical limitations notwithstanding—Elena Vladimirovna was confined to her apartment and could move around only with the assistance of a walker—she remained cheerful, energetic, and alert. I felt great admiration for this remarkable woman who maintained numerous interests in a wide variety of subjects, from history to current politics, from poetry to science. Elena Vladimirovna's knowledge and understanding of her brother's works were superb. She died in the spring of 2000 at the age of ninety-four.

I talked to Dmitri for the last time in mid-December 2011. I phoned to congratulate him on winning an international literary prize for translating his father's novella *The Enchanter* into Italian (*L'Incantatore*). His sonorous voice as usual was brimming with energy. Dmitri was very pleased when I suggested a visit with him in July. I intended to surprise him by taking him out to celebrate his grandfather's birthday (July 20) in a local restaurant of his choosing. By that time, I expected to complete my book about his grandfather's impact on his father's worldview and writings. I found it most heartening that Dmitri was eagerly looking forward to the book's publication. Dmitri's last words in reference to my anticipated visit, "I shall be waiting!" (*Budu zhdat'!*), I have regarded ever since as otherworldly.

When on February 23, 2012, I received the news of Dmitri's passing, my first reaction was shock and disbelief: "It can't be! There is some mistake here!" I was shaken to the core and physically felt a great void: "Dmitri is no more." As time went by, I began to realize that although his body is not here, his spirit is ever-present. Now since I cannot e-mail, phone, or visit him in West Palm Beach or Montreux, I frequently talk to him in my mind and do not feel the loss as acutely as at that first moment. Thinking about Dmitri brings to mind Ivan Bunin's magnificent "Light Breathing" ("Legkoe dykhanie," 1916), which Dmitri, like his father, held in high esteem. To paraphrase slightly the story's closing lines: "Dmitri's gracious breathing dissipated into the world, in these cloudy skies, in this cold spring wind." Dmitri continues to ennoble our lives and to suffuse them with beneficence and spirituality.

On May 10, 2012, Dmitri's birthday, many people who knew and loved him arrived in Montreux to celebrate his life. We first gathered at the Clarens cemetery chapel for the memorial service, at which Ivan Nabokov, Dmitri's second cousin, delivered a moving eulogy in French, English, and Russian. We then walked to the burial place of Vladimir and Véra Nabokov—Dmitri wished the urn with his ashes to be laid in with those of his parents. We all bade farewell to Dmitri's remains and each placed a white rose on the grave. The reception followed at the outside terrace of the Palace Hotel, where Dmitri's parents had lived for sixteen years (1961–77) and where Véra Nabokov had continued to reside until 1990. Many participants, myself included, shared their reminiscences of Dmitri—his versatility, dedication to his parents, devotion to his father's literary legacy. I stayed in Montreux for several additional days, wishing to visit the gravesite on my own and to reflect upon Dmitri and his life. I was gloriously rewarded for my decision when for a split second I discerned Dmitri's initials, "DN," in a cloud formation over Lake Geneva, which he loved so much.

Now I would like to turn back the clock and to describe my Cornell colleagues, primarily in the Department of Russian Literature. The Prague-born George Gibian had joined Cornell in 1961, and by the time I arrived was in his early sixties. Gibian was Jewish on his father's side and had relatives in Israel, some of whom I once met in Ithaca when they toured the United States with the Kibbutz Combined Choir. Gibian escaped to England in 1939 and then came to the United States, where he obtained his B.A. from the University of Pittsburgh in 1943. George mentioned a couple of times in passing that he had served in the U.S. Army during World War II. Only after his death did I learn from his obituary that he had landed in Normandy in 1944. Several months later, he fought in the famous Battle of the Bulge as part of the Third Army under General Patton and received the Bronze Star with oak leaf cluster and "V" device for his valor. Upon returning to the United States, George earned his M.A. from Johns Hopkins University in 1947 and a Ph.D. in comparative literature from Harvard University in 1951. Before coming to Cornell, he had taught at Smith College and the University of California at Berkeley.

In the beginning, George was rather cool toward me, but gradually he and I developed a nice rapport. We customarily had lunches at the Collegetown Indian restaurant "Sangam," and every now and then, he invited me to play tennis with him at the Cascadilla clay courts. George regularly held parties and receptions at his home in Ithaca and Fourth of July celebrations at his summer retreat on Cayuga Lake—he was always a gracious and magnanimous host. He taught full-time until the age of seventy-five and looked forward to five more years of phased retirement, teaching one semester per year. In the late summer of 1999, I was about to leave for the German capital after having been awarded the Prize Fellowship by the American Academy in Berlin. I shared with George my ideas for the new book on Nabokov and painting, on which I intended to work during my fellowship term, whereas he told me about his research and travel plans. When we had our regular lunch that day, I had no idea that it would be our last. I was astounded and greatly saddened by the news of George's passing. Upon my return to Ithaca, colleagues told me that sometime in October, George started feeling sick but thought it was just a minor case of the flu. He did not bother to get checked out by a doctor, hoping to be able to overcome the illness on the go. It turned out that it was a slowly unfolding heart attack. One day, when George was sitting in an armchair in his home and reading, he was stricken with a convulsive seizure and died instantly.

Another longtime colleague of mine was Patricia Carden. Although Pat's own scholarship had been slim—she authored merely one book on Isaac Babel throughout her forty-year academic career—she was prolific in reviewing the work of other Slavists. In addition, Pat was well versed in the intricacies of administrative affairs and was indispensable as departmental director of undergraduate studies and in drafting all kinds of memoranda pertaining to pedagogical matters. She skillfully helped to navigate the department through the turbulent years of its final existence.

A North Carolina native, Pat spoke with a noticeable Southern drawl, even though she has lived most of her adult life in New York, first studying at Columbia and then teaching at Cornell. When I arrived at the department, Pat and George had not been on speaking terms for quite some time. I did not try to find out the reasons for their quarrel and maintained amicable relations with both of them. Pat proved to be an open-minded, reliable, and trustworthy colleague, a person of good-natured disposition and sound judgment.

Another member of the department, albeit relatively transient (1986–94), was the British-born Michael Scammell. Michael made a name for himself as a translator of Russian literature, from the classics, such as Dostoevsky, Tolstoy, and Nabokov, to mainstream Soviet writers, such as Konstantin Fedin, and even hacks like Yulian Semenov. Aside from his translations, he was known as a journalist: his articles appeared in such periodicals as the *Times Literary Supplement*, *New York Review of Books*, and the *New York Times Book Review*. Michael also wrote two biographies, one on Alexander Solzhenitsyn (1984) and the other on Arthur Koestler (2009). The former was the subject of his doctoral dissertation, which he defended at Columbia in 1985. The following year, he was appointed a visiting professor at Cornell. Shortly after I arrived in 1987, Michael was promoted to full professor and made chair of the department. Coincidentally, at that time the university had a British-born president, a British-born dean of Arts and Sciences, and now a British-born chair of the Department of Russian, which prompted some to joke about a return to colonial times. When his second wife, a Cornell graduate student, earned her Ph.D. and was offered an assistant professorship at Rutgers, Michael left Cornell for his alma mater, Columbia, where he taught nonfiction writing and translation until his retirement in 2011.

Nancy Pollak was yet another member of the department who joined it in 1987, the same year I did. Nancy was born and reared in New Haven, Connecticut, home to Yale University, where her father, Louis H. Pollak, was a law professor and dean of the law school. Among his most notable students were Bill Clinton and Hillary Rodham. Herself a Yale graduate and a student of Omry Ronen, an outstanding Mandel´shtam scholar, Nancy produced a valuable volume on the writings of the poet. Most recently, she has turned her attention to classical references in Mandel´shtam's late poetry. In addition, she has worked on the relationship between the poetry of Robert Frost and A. E. Housman. Aside from her research, Nancy has been translating Russian poetry, from Derzhavin to Pushkin, from Lermontov to Akhmatova. She chaired the department for ten years and was always approachable and fair-minded.

In February 1997, the department came under a threat of a shutdown. The administration imparted to us its plan of disbanding the unit by retiring the older faculty and by transferring Nancy and me to the Department of Comparative Literature. The shutdown was averted only after this plan became public. At the time, two people greatly contributed to the survival of the department. Within the Cornell community, it was Danuta Shanzer, a professor of classics. (Several years later Danuta left Cornell for the University of Illinois and is presently on the faculty of the University of Vienna.) In the outside world, as I noted earlier, support came from Dmitri Nabokov.

At a faculty meeting, which was turned into a Q&A session because there was no quorum, Danuta sent shockwaves through the gathering when she asked about the reasons for the department's shutdown. After numerous people both inside and outside Cornell became aware of the plan, they vehemently protested it. As a result, the move was called off. Both the faculty and the students owe those individuals, and especially Danuta and Dmitri, a great debt of gratitude for a reprieve of another thirteen years.

Nevertheless, in 2010 the administration decided to carry out the previously aborted plan of closing down the Department of Russian, which by then consisted of two literature professors (Nancy Pollak and me) and three language instructors. On July 1, all five of us were officially transplanted to the Department of Comparative Literature. Having their arm twisted, the Comparative Literature faculty welcomed us into their midst but without much enthusiasm. They thought, and justifiably so, that their department should not be used as a dumping ground for castaways. At the time, I felt terrible, as though the rug had been pulled out from under my feet. But even this distressing outcome had a silver lining: the Department of Comparative Literature boasts a doctoral program and enjoys an excellent reputation, both at Cornell and in the discipline at large. It consists of about twenty people, many of whom are first-rate scholars, such as Frederick Ahl, Calum Carmichael, Jonathan Culler, and William Kennedy, to name only a few. A recent positive development, a small step in the right direction that instills some promise, is the department's offering a Russian minor. There is a glimmer of hope—stranger things have happened—that the Russian program will be further upgraded and, who knows, perhaps even reinstated in some foreseeable future to its previous Ph.D. level.

Taking part in the reception at the VIIIth World Congress of the International Council for Central and East European Studies. The City Hall, Stockholm, July 28, 2010. Courtesy of Ivan Esaulov.

AFTERWORD

Looking back on my life, I realize that the Creator had many remarkable surprises in store for me. When I was growing up in Soviet Russia, never did I imagine in my wildest dreams that I would be spending most of my adult life outside the Iron Curtain and benefiting from the liberties and freedoms accorded to people in the democratic societies of Israel and of the United States. Furthermore, I would have been flabbergasted had I been told that despite my earning a master's degree in chemistry from Moscow University, I would end up teaching Russian literature. And, if that were not enough, that I would be holding professorship at Cornell University, one of the best and most reputable academic institutions in the world. My surprise would have been even greater had I known, while surreptitiously reading Vladimir Nabokov's *The Luzhin Defense* in the totalitarian Moscow of the early 1970s, that twenty years down the road I would devote most of my professional career to the exploration of this great master's fictional universe.

As I write these lines, I am approaching my seventieth birthday. Barring the unforeseen and health permitting, I plan to begin a phased retirement in a year or so. Luckily, Cornell has such an arrangement available for its faculty: after turning seventy, one can work one semester a year for the next five years. But even after that period, I do not intend to retire. Meeting and corresponding with colleagues and students, lecturing and attending conferences, as well as writing articles and books, will keep me busy for as long as the Almighty allows. Whatever the rest of my journey is like, I am immensely thankful to my Maker for His kindness and generosity.

INDEX

A
Abraham, 45, 215n69
Abramovich, Lenia, 110
Adiv, Ehud, 204
Ahl, Frederick M., 271
Aivazovsky, Ivan, 33
Akhmatova, Anna, 270
Alciato, Andrea, 246
  Emblematum liber, 246
Aliger, Margarita, 100
Alighieri, Dante, 262
Allon, Dafna, 253
Alterman, Natan, 128
Altschuler, Rabbi David ben Aryeh Loeb, 20
Altschuler, Noach, 20
Altschuler, Rabbi Yechiel Hillel ben David, 20
  Fortress of David, 20
  Fortress of Zion, 20
Amalia Evgen´evna, 88, 89
Amichai, Yehuda, 187, 252
Amin, Hafizullah, 145
Anna Karenina (movie), 103
Anna Karlovna, 61
Anti-Semitism (Jew-hatred, Judeophobia), 2, 56, 76, 82, 91, 93, 96, 106, 110, 111, 113, 114n38, 118, 122, 129, 150, 151–52, 169, 191, 225, 235–36
Arafat, Yasser, 242, 243
Arena (movie), 103–4
Argov, Sasha, 50–51
Arkhipov, Abram, 112
Arndt, Walter, 245
Ashbel, Alexandra (née Kuznetsova), 30–31
Ashbel, Aminadav, 38, 43–45, 197, 198, 200

The Israel Land Development Company: Affairs and Enterprises in the Israeli Cities, 44
Sixty Years of the Israel Land Development Company, 44
Ashbel, Boris, 30, 31
Ashbel, Chaia (née Reines), 21, 22, 24, 25, 28–29
Ashbel, Chana (née Lev), 42, 43, 47
Ashbel, Dov, 38, 39, 40–42, 43, 44, 46, 47, 133, 134, 186n61
  "The Rainfall Conditions in Southern Lebanon, Palestine, and Northern Sinai," 39
Ashbel, Eliah, 42
Ashbel, Eliyahu Shmuel, 24, 29–31
Ashbel, Frieda (née Rozenberg), 30
Ashbel, Gennady, 30, 31
Ashbel, Gina, 195
Ashbel, Gleb, 30, 31
Ashbel, Rabbi Iosef, 20, 40
Ashbel, Rabbi Iosef Menachem, 19, 22–23, 24–25, 31, 34, 36, 37, 38, 39, 42, 43, 48, 49, 56, 121, 186n61, 206
Ashbel, Rabbi Issakhar Ber, 19–20, 21
Ashbel, Malka (née Beirakh), 23–24, 25, 30, 31, 36, 37, 38
Ashbel, Margarita, 31
Ashbel, Maritsa, 30
Ashbel, Matl, 24, 30, 31–34
Ashbel, Moshe (great-great grandfather), 21, 22, 24, 25
Ashbel, Moshe (great uncle), 36, 38, 47, 48, 68, 121, 195, 196
Ashbel, Noach Mendel, 21
Ashbel, Perl, 36
Ashbel, Rivka, 38, 45–47, 131, 208, 209
  As Much as We Could Do, 47

From Zion Goeth Forth Torah, 47
Ashbel, Ruchama (née Ram), 37, 38, 39, 43, 48
Ashbel, Sara, 49, 195
Ashbel, Sara (née Halpern), 44
Ashbel, Shlomo, 38
Ashbel, Shula (née Kavitsky), 47, 48–49, 195, 196
Ashbel, Tzfona, 42–43
Ashbel, Tzofnat, 186n61
Ashbel, Valentin, 31
Ashbel, Yossi, 195
Ashbel, Yuri, 31
Avidan, David, 187
Avidar, General Iosef, 112–13

B

Baal Shem Tov, 19, 20
Babel, Isaac, 213, 268
Balandina, Irina, 60
Balfour, Lord Arthur James, 119n39
Balfour Declaration, The, 119n39, 194
Barasch, Moshe, 68
Bartov, David, 199, 200
Bartov, Ester, 200
Barzilai, Yair, 150
Bashashkin, Anatoly, 82
Baumvol´, Rakhil´, 100
Bazhenov, Vasily, 175
Begin, Menachem, 242, 243
Begun, Iosif, 145n45
Beirakh, Ber, 23, 24, 28, 30
Beirakh, Chava, 23, 28–29, 30
Beirakh, Yaakov, 23, 32
Beliaev, Al´bert, 226
Bely, Andrei, 213
Ben Yehuda, Eliezer, 38
Ben Zvi, Shmuel, 210–11
Ber Vul´f, Rabbi, 24
Bernoulli, Jacob, 120
Berzon, Valentina Yur´evna, 75–76
Beshchev, Boris, 143
Beyer, Thomas R., Jr., 256
Bialik, Chaim Nachman, 53, 128
Bielorai, Chanokh, 44
Bielorai, Rachel (née Ashbel), 44
Bondi, Sergei Mikhailovich, 101
Borshchevsky, Rita, 188, 189
Borshchevsky, Vadim, 187–89

Botticelli, Sandro, 66
Brezhnev, Leonid, 97–98, 139
Bristol, Evelyn, 227
Brodetsky, Tina, 132
Brynner, Yul, 254
Buchanan, Sir George, 29
Buchanan, Meriel, 29
Bulgakov, Mikhail, 99, 213, 227
  The Master and Margarita, 99
  The Theatrical Novel, 227
Bunin, Ivan, 266
  "Light Breathing," 266
Burg, Iosef, 154
Burger, Robert, 221
Bus 405 Terrorist Attack, The, 59
Butyrskaia Prison, 174, 180

C

Carden, Patricia J., 268–69
Carmichael, Calum M., 271
Castro, Fidel, 8–9
Catherine II (the Great), 159, 175, 176
Chabad, 20n12, 189
Chagall, Bella (née Rosenfeld), 25
Chagall, Marc, 25
Chasidism, 19, 20
Chekhov, Anton, 85, 105, 140, 251, 253
  "The Man in a Case," 140n43
  Uncle Vanya, 105n36
Chkalov, Valery, 50
Choldin, Marianna Tax, 221
Chugryshin, Vit´ka, 117, 118
Churikova, Inna, 90
Clinton, Hillary (née Rodham), 269
Clinton, William J., 269
Cohen-Mintz, Tanchum, 122
Conaway, Jeff, 95
Conquest, Robert, 180
Culler, Jonathan D., 271

D

Dąbrowski, Jarosław, 156
Dal´, Vladimir, 72
Dawe, George, 261
Dawson, Clayton L., 223, 224
Delaunay, Vadim, 170
Delicate Markers: Subtexts in Vladimir Nabokov's "Invitation to a Beheading," 256

Derzhavin, Gavrila, 270
DeVito, Danny, 95
Dix, Otto, 260
  Three Prostitutes on the Street, 260
Dmitri Petrovich, 87
Dobuzhinsky, Mstislav Valerianovich, 257
Doctors' Plot, The, 111, 112
Dolinsky, Volodia, 83
Dombrovsky, Yuri, 156
  The Keeper of Antiquities, 156
Dostoevsky, Fedor, 253, 269
Dovlatov, Sergei, 251–52
Drozhzhina, Anna Ivanovna, 81–82
Dubnov, Chaia, 18
Dubnov, Shimon, 18
Dukel´sky, Boris, 10
Dukel´sky, Sofia (née Zil´bershmidt), 10, 15, 16, 95
Dukel´sky-Dikler, Benedikt, 10n6
  Sonnets, 10n6
Dukel´sky-Dikler, Chaim, 10
Dunatov, Rasio, 223, 225
Dvorkin, Colonel, 105

E

Elef Milim, 127, 145
Eliashiv, Shmuel, 180
Elinson, Aaron Isaakovich, 182–83
Elyashev, Israel, 180
Eppel, Asar, 100
Erofeev, Venedikt, 211
  Moscow—Petushki, 211
Eshed, Ofer, 122
Eshel, Tamar, 36
Eviatar, Dafna (née Ashbel), 42
Evtushenko, Evgeny, 99–100, 181
  "The White Snows Are Falling," 99
  Walk on the Ledge, 100
Ezersky, Lev Konstantinovich, 129–30

F

Fadeev, Alexander, 88
Faina Borisovna, 66
Fal´k, Robert, 103
Fedin, Konstantin, 269
Feigina, Liubov´ Yakovlevna, 88–89
Filippov, Ivan, 84–85
Fischer, Louis, 222
Fisher, Ralph T., Jr., 221, 222–23, 226, 229

Fisher, Ruth, 222, 223
Flavius Josephus, 211
  The Jewish War, 211
Frankel, Edith, 213, 218
Frankel, Jonathan, 213
Freedman, Luba (née Shapiro), 13, 47, 48, 56, 59, 63, 64–69, 72, 75, 78, 113, 121, 122, 133, 155, 169, 179, 193, 195, 198, 206, 208, 212
Freedman, Tzakhi, 129
French, Sir John Denton Pinkstone, 202
Frenkel, Sarah, 200
Friedberg, Barbara, 227
Friedberg, Maurice, 218, 224, 225–27, 234
Friedgut, Theodore H., 244
Friedmann, Yochanan, 244
Fromer, Vladimir, 211
Frost, Robert, 100, 270

G

Galich, Alexander, 159
  Matrosskaia Tishina, 159
Gebhart, Émile, 66
Gel´fond, Meir, 185–86
Gibian, George, 267–68
Giliarovsky, Vladimir, 84
  Moscow and Muscovites, 84
Ginzburg, Ania, 76
Ginzburg, Dora Samoilovna, 76
Ginzburg, Mikhail Zinov´evich, 76–77
Gladney, Frank Y., 223, 224–25
Gogol, Nikolai, 224, 229, 230, 234, 237, 242, 246, 253–54, 255, 256
  The Inspector General, 254
  Taras Bulba, 254
Goikhman, Sasha, 82, 110
Goldberg, Leah, 128, 213
Gol´dshtein, Pavel, 144, 186–87
Golonka, Arlene, 95
Gorbanevskaya, Natalia, 170
Gorbunov, Yuri, 161, 162
Gorelik, Chana Aaronovna (née Elinson), 183
Gorelik, Saul Moiseevich, 182–83
Gorky, Maxim, 55
Gottlieb, Fima, 106
Grandmaster, The (movie), 104–5
Grauze, Yuri, 210
Grigorenko, General Petr, 170

Index

Grinberg, Savely, 187
Guber, Mordekhai, 54
Gurvitz, Shmuel, 167
Gutsche, George J., 237, 240
Gvirts, Alik, 110

H
Hadassah Medical Convoy Massacre, The, 43
Hameiri, Tzvi, 150
Hauff, Wilhelm, 80
    The Dwarf Nose, 80
Hechalutz, 183
Herzl, Theodor, 182
Hill, Steven P., 223–24
Hippius, Zinaida, 228
Hoffman, Avraham, 122
Holocaust, The, 2, 12, 63, 137, 150, 235
Housman, A. E., 270
Hughes, Langston, 100
Hussein, King of Jordan, 238

I
Ibn Gabirol, 187
Idan, Eldad, 47
Iezuitova, 98–99
Inspector General, The (movie), 253–54
Iofan, Adol´f L´vovich, 135
Iofan, Boris, 135
Ioffe, Leonid, 127
Ionesco, Eugène, 103
    Rhinoceros, 103
Iosef, Rabbi, Maggid of Lubavitch, 19
Ithream, 5, 6
Ivanov, Al´bert, 144–45
Ivanov, Yuri, 125
    Beware: Zionism!, 125

J
Jabotinsky, Zeev, 181–82
    Feuilletons, 182
Jackson, Robert Louis, 242
Jew-hatred, Judeophobia. See Anti-Semitism
Jonas, Eliyahu, 209
Joyce, James, 240

K
Kagan, Alla (née Liak), 10
Kalis, Emmanuel, 37–38
Kallistratova, Sofia Vasil´evna, 166, 170, 171
Kaminsky, David, 122, 123
Kaner, Dan, 59
Karajan, Herbert von, 102
Kari, 259
Karlinsky, Simon, 219
Karpov, 146
Kartashov, Ivan, 96
Katz, Menachem, 47–48
Katz, Shaul, 48
Katz, Shifra, 48, 113
Katz, Tzivia (née Ashbel), 38, 39, 47–48
Kaye, Danny, 254
Kazakov, Matvei, 175
Kennedy, John F., 169
Kennedy, William J., 246, 247–48, 249, 271
Kerensky, Alexander, 32–33
Kerler, Anna, 147, 243
Kerler, Dov-Ber, 147, 168, 196, 243
Kerler, Iosif, 147, 168, 185, 243
Khan, Mr., 236–37
Khavkin, David, 132
Khavkin, Vladimir, 16
Khodorkovsky, Mikhail, 159
Khrushchev, Nikita, 90, 97, 98, 169
Kichko, Trofim, 125
    Judaism Without Embellishments, 125
King David, 5, 40, 196
King Saul, 5
Kirov, Sergei, 8
Kishon, Ephraim, 129
    Bending over Backwards, 129
Klavdia Ivanovna, 79, 80, 82, 116
Kniga, Galina Khristoforovna, 96
Koestler, Arthur, 127, 269
    The Thirteenth Tribe, 127
Kogan, Boris, 142
Kolin, Izia, 142
Kolin, Mr., 141–42
Kontorer, Anisim, 14–15
Kontorer, Iosif, 15
Kontorer, Yaakov, 14, 163, 206
Korchnoi, Viktor, 105
Korniushina, Polia, 53, 64, 71, 72–73, 79, 84, 116
Korovkin, 75–76
Kosygin, Alexei, 139
Kotov, 146

Kovalenko, Mikhail, 140
Kuznetsova, Matrena Ivanovna, 31

L

Laake, Tatiela, 257–59, 260, 261
Layba, Dina (née Freedman), 39, 165
Lazarev, Colonel, 155, 171
Lebedev, Sasha, 88, 113
Lein, Eida, 60
Leizerovsky, Berko, 5, 6–7, 9
Leizerovsky, Ella, 5, 6, 8, 9, 10, 11–12, 15–16, 17, 45, 52, 53, 56, 57, 58–59, 60–64, 67, 69, 70, 71, 72, 73, 74, 75, 76, 77, 78–79, 80, 81, 83, 84, 87, 90, 92, 93, 94, 95, 101, 102, 103, 104, 109, 110, 111, 112, 115–16, 117, 118, 123, 132, 133, 135, 144, 147, 148, 155, 165, 166, 167, 168, 169, 176, 178, 179, 182, 185, 198, 199, 200, 201, 202, 205, 206, 208, 209, 249
Leizerovsky, Evgenia (née Shafran), 7, 9
Leizerovsky, Gavriel, 5, 7, 10–13, 15, 16, 17, 60, 61, 62, 71, 73, 74, 114, 163, 199, 206
Leizerovsky, Il´ia, 7, 9, 60
Leizerovsky, Sara (née Zil´bershmidt), 7–8, 10, 11, 12, 13, 14, 15, 16, 17, 53, 58–59, 60, 62, 64, 65, 73, 74, 77, 79, 82, 84, 116, 198
Lenin, Vladimir, 9n5, 29, 111, 130, 179
Lermontov, Mikhail, 270
Lerner, Alexander Yakovlevich, 148
Lerner, Volodia, 148
Levanon, Nechemiah, 199, 200
Levik, Vil´gel´m, 100
Levin, Chanokh, 197
   Chefetz, 197
   Krum, 197
Levontin, David Zalman, 188
Liak, Bella, 10
Liak, Grigory, 9
Liak, Il´ia, 6, 9–10
Liak, Leonid, 9
Liak, Tat´iana (née Leizerovsky), 7, 9
Lifshitz, Assa, 208–9
Lifshitz, Barukh, 211
Lisichkina, Zinaida, 16–17
Lloyd, Harold, 83

Lobanov, Volodia, 91
Losev, Lev, 245
Lubetzky, Tzvi, 122
Lubin, Boris Samoilovich, 135
Lubinsky, Chaia Chava (née Shapiro), 19, 28, 29, 31, 51, 52, 53, 117, 129, 155
Lubinsky, Grigory, 29
Luria, Rabbi Itzchak ben Shlomo, 183

M

MacFarlane, Seth, 114n38
MacLeish, Archibald, 100
Maiakovsky, Vladimir, 103, 187
   150,000.000, 103
Makushkin, 92
Mandel´shtam, Osip, 99, 181, 269–70
   Voronezh Notebooks, 99, 181
Margolis, Liah Yakovlevna, 107, 108
Markish, Shimon, 100
Matrosskaia Tishina (jail), 159, 160, 166, 167
Mayber, Israel, 34–35, 68
Maze, Rabbi Yaakov, 60
Me-Bar, Ron, 35
Me-Bar, Yoav, 34, 35
Megged, Aharon, 128
   Chedva and I, 128
   The Living on the Dead, 128
Meir, Golda, 68, 131, 199
Meir, Iosef, 186
Menachem Mendel, Rabbi of Vitebsk, 20
Merezhkovsky, Dmitri, 228
Meyerhold, Vsevolod, 186
Miagkov, Andrei, 104
Michal, 5
Mikhalkov, Sergei, 168
Milevsky, Anton, 75
Milevsky, Ira, 75
Milevsky, Revekka, 75
Milevsky, Yadviga Frantsevna, 75
Milevsky, Zhenia, 75
Milky Way, The (movie), 83
Miller, Laurence, 221
Miłosz, Czesław, 219
Molotov, Viacheslav, 102
Morsztyn, Jan Andrzej, 224
Morsztyn, Zbigniew, 224
Moses, 242–43
Mosfilm Studio, The, 103
Mstislavl´ Riot, The, 17

Index

Mukharinov, Captain, 155, 171
Mukhin, Israel, 110
Mukhin, Zhenia, 110

N

Nabokov, Dmitri, 262–65, 266–67, 270
Nabokov, Elena Ivanovna (née Rukavishnikov), 263
Nabokov, Ivan, 267
Nabokov, Major-General Ivan Alexandrovich, 261n77
Nabokov, Véra (née Slonim), 262, 263, 267
Nabokov, Vladimir Dmitrievich, 261–62, 263
Nabokov, Vladimir, 10n6, 100, 162, 186–87, 191–92, 226, 242, 255–57, 259, 261, 262, 263, 264, 265, 266, 267, 268, 269, 272
    Bend Sinister, 256
    The Enchanter, 266
    The Gift, 192, 256
    Invitation to a Beheading, 162, 256, 263
    The Luzhin Defense, 186, 187, 255, 272
    "The Visit to the Museum," 192
Nagibin, Yuri, 74
    Clean Ponds, 74
Nama, 129, 130
Nasser, Gamal Abdel, 168
Nemirovich-Danchenko, Vladimir, 227
Nicholas I, 17–18
Nikolai Gogol and the Baroque Cultural Heritage, 253–55
Nixon, Richard M., 67, 153, 155
Nudel´, Ida, 145n45

O

Okudzhava, Bulat, 99
Olesha, Yuri, 213
Olivier, Louis, 233, 237, 238
Orlov, Boris, 144

P

Pachmuss, Temira Andreevna, 227, 228–29
Palchan, Izrail´, 190
Palchan, Moshe, 189–90
Pasternak, Boris, 99, 181
    Doctor Zhivago, 99
    "Hamlet," 181
Patton, General George S., 267
Paul I, 6
Pelageia Petrovna, 71, 76
Pellico, Silvio, 263
    My Prisons, 263
Peter I (the Great), 159
Petliura, Simon, 33
Pevzner, Sema, 110
Pigarev, Kirill Vasil´evich, 86
Pigarev, Mitia, 86
Pigarev, Nikolai Vasil´evich, 86
Pinsker, Yehuda Leib, 182
    Auto-Emancipation, 182
Podgornyi, Nikolai, 154
Poe, Edgar Allan, 88
Poliakov, Chaim, 32, 33
Poliakov, Mina, 32, 33
Poljakoff-Mayber, Alexandra, 33, 34, 35–36, 68, 121, 129, 133, 134, 149, 154, 200
Pollak, Louis H., 269
Pollak, Nancy, 269–70
Pol´sky, Viktor, 144
Potak, Dina (née Zil´bershmidt), 15, 16
Potak, Yaakov, 78–79, 94
Preigerzon, Tzvi, 200
Prisoners of Zion, 145, 199
Proffer, Carl R., 242
Protocols of the Elders of Zion, The, 125
Pushkin, Alexander, 85, 101, 129, 181, 222, 237, 261, 262, 270
    Boris Godunov, 85
    Eugene Onegin, 222, 226
    "Exegi monumentum," 181
    Ezersky, 129n41
    "To Dawe, Esqr.," 261

R

Rabinkov, Alexander Anisimovich, 76
Raevsky Hughes, Olga, 219
Rakovsky, Rabbi Yaakov, 198
Ram, Nachman, 37
Ran, 129, 130
Rashi, 20
Refusenik, 141, 142, 143, 145, 149, 172, 199, 200
Reines, Rabbi Itzchak Yaakov, 21
    A New Light on Zion, 21
Rhodes, Frank H. T., 255

Ribbentrop-Molotov Pact, The, 102, 199
Rishal´, Vul´f Iosifovich, 183–85
Rivlin, Iosef Ioel, 39
Rivlin, Reuven, 39
Romanov, Grigory, 151
Romanovsky, Vera Vasil´evna, 77
Ronen, Omry, 269
Roosevelt, Franklin D., 153
Rosenberg, Moshe, 63
Rosenfeld, Chana, 25
Rothschild, Baron Lionel Walter, 119n39
Rovinsky, Lena, 77
Rovinsky, Ol´ga Nikolaevna, 77
Rovinsky, Tat´iana, 77
Rovinsky, Viktor, 77
Rozenblium, Vladimir, 144
Rudenko, Roman, 157, 158
Rurik, Prince, 248

S
Sadat, Anwar, 168
Sal´nikov, Sergei, 82
Sazov, Vasily, 76
Sazova, Inna, 76
Sazova, Nadezhda, 76
Sazova, Sofia, 76
Scammell, Michael, 252, 262, 269
Scherr, Barry, 245, 246
Schneerson, Rabbi Menachem Mendel, 20
Schneur Zalman, Rabbi of Liady, 20
Segal, Isaak Lazarevich, 89–90
Sela, Michael, 149
Semenov, Nikolai Nikolaevich, 107
Semenov, Yulian, 251, 269
Serbsky, Vladimir, 163n51
Sereni, Emilio, 47
Sereni, Enrico, 47
Sereni, Enzo, 47
Serman, Il´ia Zakharovich, 234
Sgan-Cohen, Meir, 197
Shakespeare, William, 262
Shaliapin, Fedor, 16
Shanzer, Danuta R., 270
Shapira, Chaim Moshe, 203
Shapiro, Barukh, 17–19, 55
Shapiro, Batsheva (née Mogilevsky), 29
Shapiro, Dov-Ber, 19, 28–29, 51, 61
Shapiro, Felix, 128, 130
Shapiro, German, 28, 29, 94
Shapiro, Hirsch, 18–19, 28, 29, 51, 114
Shapiro, Il´ia, 164
Shapiro, Yaakov, 3, 17, 19, 29, 33, 39, 40, 45, 50–52, 53–60, 61, 62, 63, 64, 67, 68, 69, 70, 73, 74, 75, 77, 78, 79, 80, 81, 84, 90, 93, 94, 102, 103, 104, 111, 112, 114, 116, 118, 120, 121, 122, 127, 128, 132, 133, 134, 135, 143, 147, 155, 162, 164, 166, 172, 176, 178, 179, 182, 183, 199, 200, 201, 202, 206, 208, 222, 239, 249, 262
Shapiro, Zisl (née Ashbel), 23, 24, 25, 28, 29, 30, 31, 33, 39, 50, 51–52, 53, 68, 82, 114, 117, 119, 133, 137, 155
Sharansky, Natan, 145n45
Sharet, Moshe, 16
Sharon, Ariel, 38
Sharon, Lily, 38
Shervinsky, Sergei, 100
Shirokova, Elizaveta Nikolaevna, 85
Shnirman, Georgy L´vovich, 135
Sholokhov, Mikhail, 88
Shostakovich, Dmitri, 181
Shur, Berta Solomonovna, 181
Shur, Solomon Matveevich, 179–82
Shutov, General, 176, 177
Sikorski, Elena Vladimirovna (née Nabokov), 265–66
Sinyakov, Misha, 124, 125
Sipachev, Sasha, 66
Skinner, Marilyn, 249
Skoptsov, 169
Skovoroda, Grigory, 234
Smirnov, Colonel, 144
Solzhenitsyn, Alexander, 82, 99, 269
  The Cancer Ward, 99
  In the First Circle, 99
  The Gulag Archipelago, 99
  "Matrena's Homestead," 82
Sorkina, Roza Markovna, 62
Stalin, Joseph, 8, 52, 98, 102, 109, 110–11, 112, 130, 140, 162, 183, 186, 190, 216
Stampfer, Shaul, 127
Stanislavsky, Konstantin, 85, 227
Starkman, Chaim, 122

Stechkin, Boris Sergeevich, 56
Stein, Gabriel, 208
Stein, Heda, 211
Stein, Mr., 87–88, 89
Steinberg, Ada, 213
Stern, Isaac, 102
Strel´tsov, Eduard, 82
Struve, Gleb, 219
Stuart, Mary, 221
Sublime Artist's Studio: Nabokov and Painting, The, 256–57, 259–60, 261
Surkov, 77
Szymborska, Wisława, 65
 "A Little Girl Tugs at the Tablecloth," 65

T

Tanenbaum, Rabbi Marc H., 173–74
Taras Bulba (movie), 253–54
Tarle, Evgeny, 16
Taxi (sitcom), 95
Tchernichovsky, Shaul, 43
 "Between the Straits," 43
Ted (movie), 114n38
Tekoah, Iosef, 131
Telegin, Captain, 105, 106
Telesin, Julius, 100–1
 One Thousand and One Anecdotes, 101
Telesin, Zinovy, 100
Tender Friendship and the Charm of Perfect Accord: Nabokov and His Father, The, 261–62
Ternovsky, Leonard, 148
Terras, Victor, 242
Tiutchev, Fedor, 86, 181
 "Silentium!," 181
Tolstoy, Leo, 103, 253, 269
 Anna Karenina, 103
Torbin, Serezha, 106
Trakhtman-Palchan, Leah, 190
Travers, Bill, 94
Trumpeldor, Iosef, 112
Tur, Abram, 6–7
Tur, Mania (née Poliakov), 32, 33
Tur, Matil´da (née Levit), 6
Turgenev, Ivan, 85
Twain, Mark, 37, 88, 129
 The Adventures of Tom Sawyer, 88
The Innocents Abroad, 37
Twardowski, Samuel, 224
Tyshler, Alexander, 103
Tzfasman, Iosef Leib, 51, 52, 53–54

U

Ullmann, Lisa, 211–12
ut pictura poesis, 261
Uta, 259

V

Valakh, Yona, 187
Valentina Georgievna, 183
Valette, Francis, 237
Vámbéry, Ármin, 127
Van Gogh, Vincent, 65
Vanunu, Mordekhai, 204
Vasserman, Yuri, 210
Venevitinov, Dmitri, 85
Vered, Dan, 205
Viaz´mensky, Abram, 8, 9
Viaz´mensky, Aizik, 7, 8
Viaz´mensky, Boris, 8, 9
Viaz´mensky, Etta, 8
Viaz´mensky, Maria (née Leizerovsky), 7, 8
Viaz´mensky, Matvei, 8
Vilensky, 179
Vilnay, Zev, 202
Vinnik, Fima, 124–25
Vinogradov, Vladimir Nikitich, 111–12
Vizel´man, Lenia, 110
Voinovich, Vladimir, 136
 The Anti-Soviet Soviet Union, 136
Vol´fson, 93–94
Volodarsky, Ig'al, 122
Vornovitsky, Zhenia, 87–88
Voznesensky, Andrei, 99–94

W

Waldheim, Kurt, 36
Warren, Sir Charles, 37
Wayne, John, 35
Webster, Noah, 72
Wee Geordie (movie), 94
Weiner, Jack, 240
Weizmann, Chaim, 199
Who's Who in Israel, 133, 134

Wiesel, Elie, 235
The Jews of Silence, 235
Winsor, Philip, 254, 255
Restoration, 255
Wittenberg, Chesia, 37
Wittenberg, Moshe, 37, 38
World of Art, The, 257

Y

Yaki, 216, 217, 218
Yehoshua, Avraham B., 128
    "The Continuing Silence of a Poet," 128
Yurasova, Lidia Sergeevna, 86, 87

Z

Zaichik, Mark, 211
Zakrevsky, Count Arseny, 84
Zamiatin, Evgeny, 29
    "The Cave," 29
Zand, Mikhail, 190–91
"Zangen," 51, 53
Zarai, Rika, 129, 130
Zeiger, Ilan, 122
Zelikin, Itzchak, 17
Zhemaletdinov, Gaiar, 87
Zhukov, Yuri, 226
Zil′bershmidt, Enta-Reiza (née Kontorer), 14, 15, 16, 198
Zil′bershmidt, Gersh, 14, 15, 16
Zil′bershmidt, Izrail′, 15, 16–17, 116
Zionism, 21, 125, 128, 158–59, 215
Zionist, 3, 21, 47, 52, 105, 122, 124, 125, 128, 132, 134, 135, 140, 145n45, 146, 160, 168, 180, 182, 183, 185, 189, 190, 199, 200, 215
Zolotukhin, Major, 158
Zoshchenko, Mikhail, 213
Zuta, Rama (née Avidar), 113

www.ingramcontent.com/pod-product-compliance
Lightning Source LLC
Chambersburg PA
CBHW050104170426
43198CB00014B/2449